D0350468

Crossing the Divide

LEADERSHIP FOR THE COMMON GOOD

HARVARD BUSINESS SCHOOL PRESS

CENTER FOR PUBLIC LEADERSHIP
JOHN F. KENNEDY SCHOOL OF GOVERNMENT
HARVARD UNIVERSITY

The Leadership for the Common Good series represents a partnership between Harvard Business School Press and the Center for Public Leadership at Harvard University's Harvard Kennedy School. Books in the series aim to provoke conversations about the role of leaders in business, government, and society, to enrich leadership theory and enhance leadership practice, and to set the agenda for defining effective leadership in the future.

OTHER BOOKS IN THE SERIES

Changing Minds
by Howard Gardner

Predictable Surprises
by Max H. Bazerman and
Michael D. Watkins

Bad Leadership
by Barbara Kellerman

Many Unhappy Returns
by Charles O. Rossotti

Leading through Conflict
by Mark Gerzon

Senior Leadership Teams
by Ruth Wageman,
Debra A. Nunes,
James A. Burruss, and
J. Richard Hackman

Five Minds for the Future
by Howard Gardner

The Leaders We Need
by Michael Maccoby

Through the Labyrinth
by Alice H. Eagly and
Linda L. Carli

*The Power of
Unreasonable People*
by John Elkington and
Pamela Hartigan

Followership
by Barbara Kellerman

Immunity to Change
by Robert Kegan and
Lisa Laskow Lahey

Crossing the Divide

Intergroup Leadership in a World of Difference

Todd L. Pittinsky

Editor

HARVARD BUSINESS PRESS
Boston, Massachusetts

To those who do the work

of bringing groups together,

for all our good.

Library of Congress Cataloging-in-Publication Data
    Crossing the divide: intergroup leadership in a world of difference / Todd Pittinsky, editor.
        p. cm.—(Leadership for the common good)
    ISBN 978-1-4221-1834-4 (hardcover : alk. paper)
    1. Leadership. 2. Leadership—Cross-cultural studies. 3. Intergroup relations.
    4. Intergroup relations—Cross-cultural studies. I. Pittinsky, Todd L.
    HM1261.C758 2009
    303.3'4—dc22

                                                                    2008047705

Contents

PART II

Tools and Pathways

PART III

Cases in Context

Acknowledgments

My gratitude and acknowledgments begin with the "Crossing the Divide" conference on which this book is based and then move forward and backward in time, extending from those who helped put this book into shape to those who set me on my course.

I am very thankful to the Center for Public Leadership at the Harvard Kennedy School, particularly its director, David Gergen, its co-director, Andy Zelleke, and its executive director, Donna Kalikow, for enabling me to assemble the conference and then to assemble this book for those who did not have the opportunity to be there. The center's vision for extending the frontiers of leadership studies provided a platform to take the emerging idea of *intergroup leadership*—leadership that deliberately brings different groups together—to a new level of richness and, I hope, usefulness.

I thank the more than fifty scholars and leaders who took part in the conference. Although not all were working directly on intergroup leadership, they made the effort to bring their own very interesting and important perspectives to bear on it. Then they did just what one hopes for at such a conference: exchanged ideas and pushed each other's thinking further still. I owe an extra debt of gratitude to the twenty-eight individuals who wrote up their ideas for this volume.

But a conference involving only the participants would stand a slim chance of success. Laura Bacon applied her most unusual, and simply wonderful, mix of intellect, passion, and humor to the task of envisioning and planning for the day. Daniel Goodman adroitly managed the logistics of the day, with valuable guidance from Luiza Pellerin and Camiliakumari of Wankaner and joined by talented students from the Allophilia Lab. Loren Gary provided valuable advice at different points of the planning. Heidi Hart-Gorman skillfully managed the financial pieces of the puzzle.

With the conference over, the work of producing this book began. I must first thank Harvard Business School Press. Although they rarely publish edited volumes, they took a chance on this one and backed up their bet with the support and great skill of senior editor Jeff Kehoe and assistant editor Ania Wieckowski and with valuable input from two anonymous reviewers.

Outside the press, Owen Andrews dedicated his keen intellect and steady exertion to making this book a reality; it would not have been possible without him. John Elder lent his sharp eye, insights, and skill at refining ideas to giving the book's profusion of thoughts their richest and strongest forms. Sloan Strike engaged the chapters with fresh eyes, providing feedback to authors at critical junctures, and helped keep the process moving. Sue Hussein Morris paid attention to the details in the chapters, copyediting to make sure they did not get in the way of the ideas.

Having acknowledged at least some of the people who guided me through the conference and beyond, I must thank the colleagues who helped bring me to that point in the first place. J. Richard Hackman, Barbara Kellerman, and Joseph Nye, among others, have given me both intellectual inspiration and helpful advice and feedback with which to pursue the fascinating intersection of intergroup relations and leadership. I am extremely grateful to the Ash Institute for Democratic Governance and Innovation at the Harvard Kennedy School for supporting my ongoing research on allophilia and intergroup leadership.

Finally, there are the people who have always showed me the way and cheered me on in life, teaching me by their love and their actions what is most important about community. I thank my family: Janet and Bernard; Matthew, Julie, Marin, and Luke; Scott; Larry, Jill, Lauren, Marc, and Harris. I thank my dearest friends: Barbara, Mags, Margaret, Michelangelo, Sandy, and Yuquita. And I thank Vladi for being both dearest friend and family and for blessing me with the incitement and companionship of both.

Introduction

Intergroup Leadership

What It Is, Why It Matters,
and How It Is Done

The essays in this book introduce cutting-edge scholarship addressing an age-old problem.

We live in a world of difference. We encounter diversity of nationality, political party, ethnicity, religion, socioeconomic status, generation, and countless other categories in all the communities of which we are a part—work, neighborhood, nation, and the world. And we not only encounter diversity, we often run up against it. Social scientists speak of the *in-group*—the social group to which an individual belongs—and the *out-group*—any group to which that individual does not belong. The very term *out-group* brings to mind a sense of discomfort, if not conflict. In fact, leaders in all sectors—business, government, charitable, and nonprofit—and at all levels are regularly faced with problems rooted in the feeling that *we* aren't like *them* and *they* aren't like *us*. Mayors and neighborhood activists try to cope with gangs in conflict. CEOs nudge their executives to rise above divisional turf battles. Leaders of the 1960s civil rights movement wonder how to pass their legacy to a younger generation so different from their own.[1] Immigrants struggle to become full-fledged citizens of countries uneasy about the impact of new groups and cultures.

And of course, leaders of many countries face the threat, the reality, or the aftermath of sectarian violence, civil war, or war with another country.

For these leaders, bringing groups together—changing in positive ways how members of different groups think and feel about each other and therefore how they treat each other—is a central task of leadership. What does the field of leadership studies offer them? Bringing groups together has been studied extensively as an aspect of intergroup relations but remains dangerously underexamined as an aspect of leadership. It is the ambition of this book to step into that breach and make the case that this is something leaders can and must do.

A Collective of Groups: The Case for Intergroup Leadership

Any high school administrator can tell you that the student body is not only a collection of individual students but also a collection of groups— cliques, teams, ethnic groups, boys and girls, and sometimes gangs—and that these groups matter. Leadership scholars are often concerned with how leaders can define and sustain a collective, without which there would be nothing to lead. But by and large, these scholars have conceptualized this task as the challenge of bringing together individuals, with little thought given to the various subgroups to which those individuals belong.[2] But a leader's followers come with powerful and important allegiances to the groups of which they are already members—ethnic, professional, regional, and so on. Accordingly, students of leadership need to focus on how these groups can be brought together to create and sustain a collective.

Intergroup leadership—the subject of this book—is defined as leadership that brings groups together.[3] Research and theory on intergroup leadership conceptualize the core leadership task of creating a collective for leadership as not only bringing together different individuals but also bringing together the different subgroups to which they belong.

Intergroup leadership can be both an end and a means. Bringing groups together can be a primary goal of leadership. For many institutions dedicated to interfaith dialogue or gang reconciliation, the goal is improved relations among groups. Bringing groups together into a collective can also be a *means*—a step toward achieving other collective goals, such as bringing a new product to market in a joint venture or uniting various ethnic groups into a populace that can achieve economic, military, or social and cultural goals.

How is intergroup leadership accomplished? The contributors to this book pursue the science—and perhaps the art—of intergroup leadership from a number of theoretical and practical angles. As already mentioned, the theoretical need for understanding this neglected topic is great. As for the practical need, it leaps from the pages of any newspaper.

Leading by Dividing

Certainly, leaders have always been advised and expected to develop and maintain group cohesiveness.[4] Research has demonstrated that group cohesiveness is positively related to such important leadership processes as follower trust, follower willingness to sacrifice for the leader, follower satisfaction, and followers' shared belief in their group's collective ability to achieve a goal.[5]

But group cohesion can exact a price. Classic research by sociologists and psychologists has identified a general tension between internal cohesion (the extent to which members of a group feel bound together) and external conflict.[6] The more intensely a group feels its own solidarity, the more "other" everyone else may seem and the easier it can be to end up in competition or conflict with them.[7]

For leaders, this trade-off between internal cohesion and external conflict, which I refer to as the *in-group/out-group trade-off*, can be either a boon or a trap.[8] A shortsighted or unwise leader may not even recognize the problem.[9] Leaders whose positions are threatened are often happy to exploit—or in some cases even create—intergroup hostilities in order to secure their hold on power.[10] Embattled leaders know that a common enemy, whether real or invented, can help them establish their credibility, define their constituencies, and motivate their followers. How much team spirit has been stoked up by getting everyone to hate the New York Yankees or Microsoft? But history shows that such a strategy can be all too effective when leaders scapegoat or demonize other ethnic groups or nations. Leaders played a major role in creating violence in a previously peaceful Yugoslavia. Serbian political and social elites demonized and dehumanized other ethnic groups to create a crisis atmosphere in which they could mobilize a followership.[11] In Iraq, Saddam Hussein pitted one religious group against another, in part to strengthen his own position. The consequences of that strategy are still clearly seen in the difficulty Iraqis confront in establishing a representative government.[12]

An image of the out-group as an enemy can be self-reinforcing.[13]

Emotional responses (such as fear and anger) and their associated actions (such as retreating and attacking) can lead followers to support a leader's unfriendly or hostile behavior and policies toward the enemy group.[14] And in fact, an action taken by someone already perceived to be an enemy is perceived as more harmful than the very same action taken by someone perceived as an ally.[15]

To make matters trickier still, one group's cohesion can make it seem more threatening to other groups. Actions taken by an out-group will be perceived as more harmful to the extent that the out-group is perceived as being cohesive.[16] Such findings suggest that leaders do not even need to use explicitly demonizing language to evoke the perception that an out-group is threatening. Language implying that it is cohesive—expressions such as "Russia feels entitled" or "Beijing is angry"—may be sufficient to increase the perception of threat and contribute to intergroup conflict.[17]

But if leaders can create intergroup conflict, have they not also the power to create intergroup harmony—in effect, to practice intergroup leadership? The answer offered in this book is yes, but it will not be easy. Leaders must reassess or eschew some successful tactics for consolidating power through building group cohesion. A leader must think very carefully about rallying the troops. After all, what are troops for except to fight?

Leading by Uniting:
A Growing Imperative

Intergroup leadership is an alternative model that resolves the in-group/out-group trade-off in a different way. It seeks to bring different groups together by lessening the ill will between them *and* by creating good will—two separate tasks, as you will see shortly. Around the world, calls for such leadership are already strong and likely to grow stronger.[18] Within many countries, it is less and less the case that any single racial or ethnic group can forcefully claim a numeric majority.[19] By 2050, that will likely be the case in the United States as well.[20] Leaders of countries without natural majorities will need to bring racial and ethnic groups together in order to lead effectively.

The need is just as great—and painfully obvious—in countries where there is both a clear majority and minorities who are vulnerable to its power. And as terrorist groups have shown, minority groups can wield great power against majority groups, too. On a larger scale, political leaders in geographic regions such as Europe, Southeast Asia, and the Pacific Rim seek to bring together historically suspicious and sometimes even hostile countries to achieve joint economic competitiveness and progress.[21] Within business organizations, leaders struggle to bring together disparate work groups, divisions, and acquisitions.

Intergroup leadership becomes increasingly important as leaders are forced to tackle questions of the common good that extend far outside their formal authorities and responsibilities.[22] Perhaps the most obvious example today is the problem of global warming and other environmental changes potentially harmful to human life. We desperately need American leaders who will consider the welfare of foreigners as seriously as they consider the welfare of Americans, Chinese leaders who will consider the welfare of foreigners as seriously as they consider the welfare of the Chinese, and so on. Even a relatively small country can do disproportionate harm to the world by allowing shipping practices that result in huge oil spills or by failing to control the dumping of toxic waste.

The argument, of course, is not that leaders must privilege other groups' good as highly as that of their own. Although a few leaders adopt that path, it may not always be practical or desirable. But we do need and will benefit from leaders who are more determined to bring groups together than to profit by splitting them apart.

Happily, the prospects of moving beyond the in-group/out-group trade-off have been boosted by an interesting trend in the social sciences. Until recently, it had been widely argued that an in-group "derives its identity from the fact of its opposition to the other."[23] But researchers are increasingly reporting that strong in-group affiliations do not have to lead to negative relations with out-groups.[24] Instead, they argue that the two types of relationship are more independent.[25] For example, research in South Africa found that identification with one's own ethnic group was not a very good predictor of intolerance; neither black nor white identification was associated with much intolerance of the other group.[26]

South Africa, of course, was the scene of Nelson Mandela's inspired intergroup leadership. How often can such success be repeated without such a leader? With the advance of the scholarly study of intergroup leadership, we may be able to depend less on the wisdom of the occasional inspired intergroup leader, such as Mandela or Martin Luther King, Jr., and more on a tested and accepted body of practice, so that more leaders can succeed in bringing groups together.

The Trap of the Leader's Own Group Affiliations

In various parts of the world, one can find images of Jesus the white man, Jesus the black man, Jesus the Chinese man, and so on. Putting aside the question of the ethnicity of the historical Jesus, these racially diverse artistic portrayals show that many Christians want their religious leader to be directly affiliated with their own group. This is a tension experienced by all aspiring intergroup leaders in any context: however fervently they promote the transcendence of subgroup identities, they inevitably have one (or more) subgroup identities themselves. A president in a multiparty system remains a member of his or her own political party, an interfaith leader retains his or her own religion, a neighborhood organizer still lives in one part of town and not the others. So it can be hard for a leader to rise above his or her own natural affiliations.

This goes beyond the familiar failing of favoritism. Even basic leadership processes, such as establishing credibility and mobilizing followers, have been found to be more difficult with followers from a different group.[27] For example, social attraction processes make followers more likely to agree and comply with a prototypical leader—one who they feel is "like them."[28] But of course, the more prototypical a leader is of one group, the less prototypical she or he will be of other groups.

Such tensions cannot be eliminated, but they can be managed. One way, which I have been researching, is to foster positive attitudes about the "others" in their very otherness. (Such attitudes, termed *allophilia*, are touched on later.) When positive attitudes toward others develop, the leaders' otherness, while not disappearing, becomes less of a liability. The chapters in this volume show a number of other ways in which leaders can more effectively lead followers from other groups.

Together but Not the Same

The very phrase *intergroup leadership* embodies a tension between the separateness of distinct groups (*intergroup*) and their integration (requisite for successful *leadership*). Intergroup leadership honors that tension; it is concerned with bringing subgroups together without trying to eliminate their differences—or even wanting to do so.

A variety of research indicates that weakening or eliminating subgroup identities in order to improve intergroup relations is neither necessary nor sufficient. Subgroup identities are not necessarily the obstacles to unity that they have often been assumed to be.[29] Research on dual identities sees superordinate identities and subgroup identities as natural companions. For example, citizens of countries in the European Union are encouraged to think of themselves both as "European" (a shared identity) and as British, French, Romanian, Spanish, and so on. Many American immigrants and children of immigrants feel very strongly that they are equally and simultaneously American and Puerto Rican, Japanese, Italian, Cameroonian, and so on.

It is true that research has shown the benefits of emphasizing "we" in cases of "us and them," but ignoring subgroup identities in the name of unity is often neither possible nor desirable.[30] For example, it is easy to show that Christians, Jews, and Muslims have a common heritage in the family of Abrahamic faiths, but it has proven difficult to make very many Christians, Jews, and Muslims actually feel this way about each other. In the U.S. political system, Republicans and Democrats share an identity as American citizens, but that identity is typically overshadowed by their critically important party identities.

Even when a superordinate identity is strong enough to overtake subgroup identities, its relative salience and influence can ebb and flow.[31] Superordinate identities may be more effective when groups cooperate to confront a mutual threat than in the absence of that threat. Intergroup hostilities often reemerge even after they seem to have disappeared.[32] In both the former Yugoslavia and Rwanda, after years of intermarriage among the ethnic subgroups, ethnic identities were revived as means of dividing and killing. A more enduring alternative to dissolving subgroup identities into a superordinate identity might be to promote positive attitudes and relations among the subgroups—getting the subgroups to appreciate and like each other's differences rather than merely tolerating or discounting them when the circumstances call for it.

Even if it were possible to completely dissolve subgroup identities into a superordinate identity, it would not necessarily be a good idea to do so. Evidence suggests that social diversity—although "as full of quarrels as an egg is full of meat"—also has benefits. By contrast, an emphasis on a common identity may reduce access to those benefits by encouraging adherence to a single set of norms, limiting the collective's range of thought and action, and undermining group creativity and collective effectiveness.[33] Intergroup leadership, on the other hand, seeks to create a collective that can tap the benefits of its own diversity.[34]

Although some leadership models might promote dual identities for normative reasons (i.e., considering diversity as desirable for its own sake), the intergroup leadership model does so for a pragmatic reason. Encouraging individuals to completely forget about themselves as members of certain groups in favor of their membership in still larger groups simply does not seem viable. The insufficiency of such attempts is recognized, implicitly if not explicitly, in many of the chapters of this book.

Two Dimensions of Intergroup Leadership

Much research explores negative sentiment among groups (i.e., prejudice and discrimination), but surprisingly little research considers forms of liking, and still less considers forms of liking that are not shaded by sympathy or pity. This realm is precisely the one staked out by research on *allophilia*, a term for positive feelings of kinship, comfort, affection, engagement, and enthusiasm concerning members of a group different from one's own. My own research indicates that the opportunity for leaders to create positive relations among distinct subgroups is rooted, in part, in the independence of positive and negative intergroup attitudes. That is, allophilia and prejudice both exist and are two distinct dimensions of intergroup relations, each with distinct causes and distinct consequences.[35] For example, allophilia research has demonstrated that the presence of positive intergroup attitudes is an important antecedent of willingness to act on behalf of other groups and is a stronger predictor of such behavior than the presence or absence of negative prejudice.[36]

This makes positive intergroup attitudes a key to moving intergroup relations past mere tolerance to willing, active coexistence and cooperation. But note that this promise depends on the recognition that positive and negative intergroup attitudes are two distinct dimensions, more independent of each other than is commonly recognized. Liking a group different from one's own is therefore not simply a case of not disliking it. If positive intergroup feelings are to be achieved, they must be deliberately and specifically promoted. Simply not promoting hate, or seeking tolerance, will not do.

Leaders often do understand the need to create positive relations among subgroups, but then they frame their responses largely as reducing negative relations—eliminating conflict, fighting prejudice, and so on. In doing so, they assume that to reduce the negative is to increase the positive and that an absence of hate is a sufficient condition for positive inter-group relations. But the independence (or bidimensionality) of positive and negative intergroup attitudes means that leaders who seek to create a collective from diverse (and possibly hostile or mutually indifferent) sub-groups must take separate measures to reduce negative intergroup atti-tudes *and* increase positive ones.[37]

As you read the chapters in this volume, take time to consider whether the described effects of intergroup leadership are being achieved by re-ducing negative relations, increasing positive relations, or both.

The Goals of This Book

The essays in this volume bring to mind a remark made by Kurt Lewin, one of the modern pioneers of social, organizational, and applied psychol-ogy. Lewin famously observed that "there is nothing so practical as a good theory" and in doing so called into question the commonly assumed di-chotomy of theoretical and applied work.[38] The study of intergroup lead-ership is intellectually compelling; equally compelling are the possibilities for making it work for the people who suffer every day for lack of it. In as-sembling this book, I therefore had both scholarly and practical audiences in mind. Although each chapter of the book stands alone, together they chart a trajectory from theoretical understanding to practical application in diverse contexts.

From a scholarly point of view, the essays in this book explore the in-tersection of two powerful research streams: intergroup relations and leadership. Students of either field will find much of interest. Many disci-plines (including psychology, sociology, political science, and history) and cross-disciplinary fields (including public policy, organizational behavior, diplomacy, conflict resolution, interreligious dialogue, and ethnic and race relations) have turned their attention to the quality of intergroup re-lations. I sought to reflect that diversity of approaches in this volume. With it comes an exciting range of levels of analysis, from the traits and skills of individual leaders to the social and structural requisites for inter-group leadership. Individuals matter, as you will see, and so do social structures.

Several of the authors look for inspiration to classic research on inter-group relations, such as Allport's and Pettigrew's examinations of contact between groups and the circumstances in which it can improve intergroup relations, and Sherif's work on common goals and the circumstances in which they encourage groups to trust each other.[39] Perhaps the most common points of departure are Tajfel's and Turner's theories of social identification and social categorization as drivers of intergroup relations and thus of intergroup leadership. Research on leadership from the social identity and social categorization perspectives is a particularly fruitful approach to understanding the challenges of intergroup leadership, with the potential to address intergroup dynamics in organizational, national, and multinational settings.[40] Several of the authors take off from more recent social identity work on the role of a common and overarching identity in improving intergroup relations, and from still more recent work on dual identities, which recommends a balance between a common identity and the subgroup identities that people already cherish.[41]

But I have no wish to reach only those who analyze. The many approaches to understanding intergroup leadership show tremendous potential for promoting positive relations in real life. In a variety of ways, all the essays in this book address those who act—who seek to do the work of leading by uniting, rather than by dividing—and many of the chapters adopt this as their central concern. In the twenty-first century, intergroup leaders must take center stage at every level.

For two reasons, this book is not for those who seek a quick "One Minute Manager" approach to leadership. First, the study of intergroup leadership is new. It will develop only as leaders put it into practice and as theories and models are refined. History gives us countless examples of in-group leadership but few cases of intergroup leadership; we therefore need to get to work creating new history with new examples from which to learn. Second, the work of intergroup leadership is intrinsically one-size-fits-one—a delicate balance of in-group and out-group relations, unique to each situation, with the leader in the precarious position of central node. Although we cannot give you a recipe, we can give you the key ingredients.

Nor is this book for those who seek the easiest leadership path. Leading by dividing is easy, and, as history teaches, it works very well. But its successes are won at considerable cost. To secure in-group leadership, leaders sacrifice intergroup relations, alienating—and often oppressing—one or more out-groups. Intergroup leadership inherently seeks the greater good for all, but with its focus on immediate in-group gains and benefits, it poses far greater challenges than in-group leadership. This book is for leaders and aspiring leaders who have a high tolerance for challenge, tension, and scrutiny.

The Road Ahead

This book has three parts. Part I, Insights and Concepts, can be read as a primer on the core concepts with which to think about intergroup leadership, whether observed in the present or envisioned in the future. The chapters by Michael Hogg and by the team of Michael Platow, Stephen D. Reicher, and S. Alexander Haslam introduce essential concepts of social identity (the sense of belonging to a group that powerfully defines individual and collective behavior) and self-categorization (how one does or does not subjectively locate oneself in different groups). In other chapters, the team of John Dovidio, Sam Gaertner, and Marika Lamoreaux and the team of Margarita Krochik and Tom Tyler explore the topics of common or superordinate identity (an overarching identity that can be shared by members of different groups), subgroup identity (the idea that our group memberships are nested; although we belong to groups, within those groups we belong to still other, smaller groups), leader prototypicality (the degree to which a leader is representative of the members of a group she or he aspires to lead), and dual identity (the notion of maintaining both a subgroup identity and a superordinate group identity). Jolanda Jetten and Frank Mols guide us in understanding leadership in the context of marginalized groups and in terms of minority and majority status (the consideration that individuals belong not only to different groups but also to groups that differ in size, status, and power).

These chapters may seem unnecessary to those eager for practical applications of intergroup leadership concepts, but they will reward a patient reader. The comprehensive, systems-level concepts presented in Part I will allow readers to recognize the intergroup opportunities and challenges in specific, real-world leadership situations. What's more, they will resurface frequently in the subsequent chapters.

In Part II, Tools and Pathways, our contributors connect those basic ideas to each other and to the real-world challenges and opportunities of intergroup leadership. Here, the authors adopt the perspective that intergroup leadership needs both to be understood and practiced, sometimes by individuals and sometimes by groups or institutions. You may notice even more use of action verbs in these chapters: *creating* superordinate identities, *building* trust between in-groups and out-groups, *negotiating* group boundaries, *bridging* groups, and *linking* group and superordinate interests. Rosabeth Moss Kanter explores how groups can reach common ground. Chris Ernst and Jeff Yip examine how intergroup leaders can span group boundaries. Roderick Kramer develops perspectives on how trust can emerge in intergroup negotiations. In a similar vein, Heather Caruso, Todd Rogers, and Max Bazerman consider how to foster collaboration among organizational subgroups. Ronald Heifetz probes the risks and challenges of leading adaptive change—change that enables groups to respond to and survive a dire challenge or threat—across subgroups.

Part III, Cases in Context, explores the complexities of a wide range of situations in which intergroup leadership is needed. Some readers will encounter situations in these chapters that they know well and that stir their passion for leadership across divides. Other readers will be eager to learn about unfamiliar contexts that call for intergroup leadership. Candi Castleberry-Singleton explores the challenge of managing diversity and bringing marginalized groups into the centers of power in corporate America. Mark Gerzon examines the challenging barriers of group affiliation and mistrust that make it hard for Democrats and Republicans to work together in the U.S. Congress. Eboo Patel, April Kunze, and Noah Silverman survey the challenges interfaith leaders face and the practices that can help them work across religious boundaries. Several chapters are devoted to intergroup leadership in national and geographic contexts: May Al-Dabbagh on successful intergroup cooperation among politically marginalized Saudi women; Irit Keynan and Alan Slifka (in separate chapters) on the challenges and risks of building political and social bridges among divided groups in Israel; and Robert Rotberg on the many examples in postcolonial Africa of the failed politics of in-group leadership—and the rare successes and emerging promise of intergroup leadership there. All told, readers will see that, whatever the situation in which one seeks to understand or advance intergroup leadership, one joins a diverse community that is trying to influence the course of organizational life in new ways through leadership.

No matter how many points of view the contributing authors bring to a book, it will still reflect some aspect of the editor's point of view. Such is the case with this book. For me, intergroup leadership is where science meets practice in the service of society. Both theoretically and practically, the potential payoffs of intergroup leadership research are great. It invites us not only to better understand an important but poorly understood phenomenon, always a worthwhile scientific goal, but also to better imagine a world in which different groups are neither in conflict with each other nor simply tolerating each other but instead are actively and happily engaged with each other for the common good, in part through the efforts of leaders who know what intergroup leadership is, why it matters, and how it is done.

Todd L. Pittinsky
todd@pittinsky.com

Notes

1. Ronald Smothers, "Living and Shaping Legacy of Civil Rights Leader," *New York Times*, November 26, 1994, http://query.nytimes.com/gst/fullpage.html?res=940DE4DD 1530F935A15752C1A962958260.

2. For example, transformational leadership examines the motivational processes whereby followers are prompted to transcend their own self-interest and embrace collective goals and values; Bernard M. Bass, "Leadership: Good, Better, Best," *Organizational Dynamics* 13 (1985): 26–40. The leader-member exchange (LMX) theory of leadership examines the quality of relations between leaders and followers, ignoring those between groups of followers; George B. Graen and Mary Uhl-Bien, "Relationship-Based Approach to Leadership: Development of Leader-Member Exchange (LMX) Theory of Leadership over 25 Years: Applying a Multi-level Multi-domain Perspective," *Leadership Quarterly* 6 (1995): 219–247.

3. Todd L. Pittinsky and Stefanie Simon, "Intergroup Leadership," *Leadership Quarterly* 18 (2007): 586–605; Todd L. Pittinsky, "A Two-Dimensional Theory of Intergroup Leadership: The Case of National Diversity "(unpublished manuscript, 2008).

4. Gregory H. Dobbins and Stephen J. Zaccaro, "The Effects of Group Cohesion and Leader Behavior on Subordinate Satisfaction," *Group & Organization Studies* 11 (1986): 216; and Robert Weinberg and Matthew McDermott, "A Comparative Analysis of Sport and Business Organizations: Factors Perceived Critical for Organizational Success," *Journal of Applied Sport Psychology* 14 (2002): 282–298. Cohesiveness is described as the goal of transformational and of charismatic leadership in Dong I. Jung and John J. Sosik, "Transformational Leadership in Work Groups: The Role of Empowerment, Cohesiveness, and Collective Efficacy on Perceived Group Performance," *Small Group Research* 33 (2002): 313–336, and in Jaepil Choi, "A Motivational Theory of Charismatic Leadership: Envisioning, Empathy, and Empowerment," *Journal of Leadership and Organizational Studies* 13 (2006): 24–37.

5. Regarding follower trust and willingness to sacrifice for the leader, see Boas Shamir, Eliav Zakay, Esther Breinin, and Micha Popper, "Correlates of Charismatic Leader Behavior in Military Units: Subordinates' Attitudes, Unit Characteristics, and Superiors' Appraisals of Leader Performance," *Academy of Management Journal* 41 (1998): 387–409. For follower satisfaction, see Dobbins and Zaccaro, "The Effects of Group Cohesion," 203–219. For followers' shared belief in their group's collective ability to achieve a goal, see Albert Bandura, *Self-Efficacy: The Exercise of Control* (New York: W. H. Freeman, 1997); and David M. Paskevich, Lawrence R. Brawley, Kim D. Dorsch, and W. Neil Widmeyer, "Relationship Between

Collective Efficacy and Team Cohesion: Conceptual and Measurement Issues," *Group Dynamics: Theory, Research, and Practice* 3 (1999): 210–222.

6. Kyriacos C. Markides and Steven F. Cohn, "External Conflict/Internal Cohesion: A Reevaluation of an Old Theory," *American Sociological Review* 47 (1982): 88–98; Todd L. Pittinsky, "Allophilia: A Framework for Intergroup Leadership," in *Building Leadership Bridges: Emergent Models of Global Leadership*, ed. Nancy S. Huber and Mark C. Walker (College Park, MD: International Leadership Association, 2005), 34–49.

7. K. L. Dion, "Cohesiveness as a Determinant of Ingroup-Outgroup Bias," *Journal of Personality and Social Psychology* 28 (1973): 163–171; B. A. Bettencourt, K. Charlton, and C. Kernahan, "Numerical Representation of Groups in Cooperative Settings: Social Orientation Effects on Ingroup Bias," *Journal of Experimental Social Psychology* 33 (1997): 630–659 (Study 2); J. W. Jackson and E. R. Smith, "Conceptualizing Social Identity: A New Framework and Evidence for the Impact of Different Dimensions," *Personality and Social Psychology Bulletin* 25 (1999): 120–135; M. Karasawa, "Effects of Cohesiveness and Inferiority upon Ingroup Favoritism," *Japanese Psychological Research* 30 (1988): 49–59; and L. Petersen, J. Dietz, and D. Frey, "The Effects of Intragroup Interaction and Cohesion on Intergroup Bias," *Group Processes & Intergroup Relations* 7 (2004): 107–118.

8. Pittinsky and Simon, "Intergroup Leadership," 586–605.

9. Robert J. Sternberg, "A Systems Model of Leadership: WICS," *American Psychologist* 62 (2007): 34–42.

10. Frits Bekkers, "Threatened Leadership and Intergroup Conflicts," *Journal of Peace Research* 14 (1977): 223–247; Jacob M. Rabbie and Frits Bekkers, "Threatened Leadership and Intergroup Competition," *European Journal of Social Psychology* 8 (1978): 9–20; and Margaret G. Hermann and Charles W. Kegley, Jr., "Ballots, a Barrier against the Use of Bullets and Bombs," *Journal of Conflict Resolution* 40, (1996): 436–459.

11. Anthony Oberschall, "The Manipulation of Ethnicity: From Ethnic Cooperation to Violence and War in Yugoslavia," *Ethnic & Racial Studies* 23 (2000): 982–1001.

12. Khalilzad Zalmay, "U.S. Envoy Outlines Political Blueprint for Iraq," *Los Angeles Times*, February 12, 2008, M.5.

13. Cohesiveness in groups can foster competition with out-groups; Ronald J. Fisher, "Intergroup Conflict," in *The Handbook of Conflict Resolution: Theory and Practice*, ed. Morton Deutsch and Peter Coleman (San Francisco: Jossey-Bass, 2000), 166–184. Cohesion predicts both behavioral and attitudinal intergroup bias; Lowell Gaertner and John Schopler, "Perceived Ingroup Entitativity and Intergroup Bias: An Interconnection of Self and Others," *European Journal of Social Psychology* 28 (1998): 963–980. Forms of militant leadership characterized by high group cohesiveness support both aggressive objectives and contentious tactics; Fisher, "Intergroup Conflict," 166–184. There can even be a self-reinforcing cycle in which intergroup conflict begets group cohesion; Lewis A. Coser, *The Functions of Social Conflict* (New York: Free Press, 1956); and Muzafer Sherif, *The Psychology of Social Norms* (Oxford, UK: Harper Torchbooks, 1966).

14. Marilynn B. Brewer and Michele G. Alexander, "Intergroup Emotions and Images," in *From Prejudice to Intergroup Emotions*, ed. D. Mackie and E. Smith (New York: Psychology Press, 2002), 209–225.

15. Richard K. Herrmann, James F. Voss, Tonya Y. E. Schooler, and Joseph Ciarrochi, "Images in International Relations: An Experimental Test of Cognitive Schemata," *International Studies Quarterly* 41 (1997): 403–433.

16. Emanuele Castano, Simona Sacchi, and Peter Hays Gries, "The Perception of the Other in International Relations: Evidence for the Polarizing Effect of Entitativity," *Political Psychology* 24 (2003): 449–468.

17. Ibid., 465.

18. John M. Bryson and Barbara C. Crosby, "Leadership for the Common Good," in *Creating a Culture of Collaboration: The International Association of Facilitators Handbook*, ed. Sandy Schuman (San Francisco: Jossey-Bass, 2006), 367–396; Gill R. Hickman, "Organizations of Hope: Leading the Way to Transformation, Social Action, and Profitability," in *Im-*

proving Leadership in Nonprofit Organizations, ed. Ronald E. Riggio and Sarah S. Orr (San Francisco: Jossey-Bass, 2004), 151–162; Joseph C. Rost, *Leadership for the Twenty-First Century* (New York: Praeger, 1991); and J. Sternberg, "A Systems Model of Leadership."

19. For example, see Ron Johnston, Michael Poulsen, and James Forrest, "Ethnic and Racial Segregation in U.S. Metropolitan Areas, 1980–2000," *Urban Affairs Review* 42 (2007): 479–504.

20. Jeffrey S. Passel and D'Vera Cohn, "U.S. Population Projections: 2005–2050," Pew Research Center, Social and Democratic Trends, http://pewsocialtrends.org/pubs/703/population-projections-united-states.

21. Joseph. S. Nye, "East African Economic Integration," *Journal of Modern African Studies* 1 (1963): 475–502; and Joseph S. Nye, *Pan-Africanism and East African Integration* (Cambridge, MA: Harvard University Press, 1967).

22. Bryson and Crosby, "Leadership for the Common Good," 367–396; Hickman, "Organizations of Hope," 151–162; Rost, *Leadership for the Twenty-First Century*; and Sternberg, "A Systems Model of Leadership," 34–42.

23. Fisher, "Intergroup Conflict," 182.

24. For examples, see Marilynn Brewer, "The Psychology of Prejudice: Ingroup Love or Outgroup Hate?" *Journal of Social Issues* 55 (1999): 429–444; Steve Hinkle and Rupert Brown, "Intergroup Comparisons and Social Identity: Some Links and Lacunae," in *Social Identity Theory: Construction and Critical Advances*, ed. D. Abrams and Michael Hogg (London: Harvester Wheatsheaf, 1990), 48–70; Rick Kosterman and Seymour Feshbach, "Toward a Measure of Patriotic and Nationalistic Attitudes," *Political Psychology* 10 (1989): 257–274; and Bernadette Park and Charles M. Judd, "Rethinking the Link Between Categorization and Prejudice Within the Social Cognition Perspective," *Personality and Social Psychology Review* 9 (2005): 108–130.

25. This has been shown in the laboratory and in field settings. For lab studies, see Marilyn B. Brewer and Linnda R. Caporael, "An Evolutionary Perspective on Social Identity: Revisiting Groups," in *Evolution and Social Psychology*, ed. Mark Schaller, Jeffrey A. Simpson, and Douglas T. Kenrick (Madison, CT: Psychosocial Press, 2006), 143–161; and R. M. Montoya and T. L. Pittinsky, "Group Identification and Intergroup Bias in Competitive and Cooperative Contexts" (unpublished manuscript, 2008). For field studies, see James L. Gibson, "Do Strong Group Identities Fuel Intolerance? Evidence from the South African Case," *Political Psychology* 27 (2006): 665–705.

26. Gibson, "Do Strong Group Identities Fuel Intolerance?"

27. When followers belong to a different subgroup than that of their leader, it results in decreased follower satisfaction; Julie M. Duck and Kelly S. Fielding, "Leaders and Subgroups: One of Us or One of Them?" *Group Processes & Intergroup Relations* 2 (1999): 203–230. Followers' membership in a different subgroup than that of their leader also decreased their identification with the organization, support of and trust in their leaders, perception of their leaders' fairness, and concern for the group; Julie M. Duck and Kelly S. Fielding, "Leaders and Their Treatment of Subgroups: Implications for Evaluations of the Leader and the Superordinate Group," *European Journal of Social Psychology* 33 (2003): 387–401.

28. Prototypicality is a linchpin of Hogg's social identity theory of leadership, which argues that leadership can be understood as a group process arising from social categorization and depersonalization processes linked with social identity; Michael A. Hogg, "A Social Identity Theory of Leadership," *Personality and Social Psychology Review* 5 (2001): 184–200. See also Stephan D. Reicher, S. Alexander Haslam, and Michael J. Platow, "The New Psychology of Leadership," *Scientific American Mind* 8 (2007): 22–29.

29. In fact, there are other ways to improve intergroup relations aside from forming a common "we" identity; Bernadette Park and Charles M. Judd, "Rethinking the Link Between Categorization and Prejudice Within the Social Cognition Perspective," *Personality and Social Psychology Review* 9 (2005): 108–130.

30. See Norman Miller and Marilynn B. Brewer, "Categorization Effects on Ingroup and Outgroup Perception," in *Prejudice, Discrimination, and Racism*, ed. John F. Dovidio and

Samuel L. Gaertner (San Diego: Academic Press, 1986), 209–230; Samuel. L. Gaertner, John F. Dovidio, Phyllis A. Anastasio, Betty A. Bachman, and Mary C. Rust, "The Common Ingroup Identity Model: Recategorization and the Reduction of Intergroup Bias," in *European Review of Social Psychology*, ed. Wolfgang Stroebe and Miles Hewstone (London: Wiley, 1993), 1–26.

31. For examples, see research on various models and theories including (a) the alternation model: Teresa D. LaFromboise and Wayne Rowe, "Skills Training for Bicultural Competence: Rationale and Application," *Journal of Counseling Psychology* 30 (1983): 589–595; (b) code-switching theories: Murial Saville-Troike, "The Development of Bilingual and Bicultural Competence in Young Children" (ERIC Document Reproduction Service No. ED 206 376) (Urbana, IL: Clearinghouse on Elementary and Early Childhood Education, 1981); and (c) identity adaptiveness: Todd L. Pittinsky, Margaret Shih, and Nalini Ambady, "Identity Adaptiveness: Affect Across Multiple Identities," *Journal of Social Issues* 55 (1999): 503–518.

32. Pittinsky and Simon, "Intergroup Leadership," 586–605.

33. The "egg" quotation is from William Shakespeare, *Romeo and Juliet*, ed. John Seely (Oxford: Heinemann, 1993), 3.1.23. For the benefits of social diversity, see Donald M. Taylor and Wallace E. Lambert, "The Meaning of Multiculturalism in a Culturally Diverse Urban American Area," *Journal of Social Psychology* 136 (1996): 727–740. On the reduction of the accessibility of those benefits, see John W. Berry, Rudolf Kalin, and Donald M. Taylor, *Multiculturalism and Ethnic Attitudes in Canada* (Ottawa: Minister of Supply and Services, 1977).On subgroups and superordinate groups, see Margarita Krochik and Tom R. Tyler, "United Pluralism: Balancing Subgroup Identification and Superordinate Group Cooperation," chapter 4 in this volume. On creativity, see Anthony L. Antonio, Kenji Hakuta, David A. Kenny, Shana Levin, and Jeffrey F. Milem, "Effects of Racial Diversity on Complex Thinking in College Students," *Psychological Science* 15 (2004): 507–510. On group effectiveness, see Samuel R. Sommers, "On Racial Diversity and Group Decision Making: Identifying Multiple Effects of Racial Composition on Jury Deliberations," *Journal of Personality and Social Psychology* 90 (2006): 597–612.

34. Astrid C. Homan, Daan van Knippenberg, Gerban A. Van Kleef, and Carsten K. W. De Dreu, "Interacting Dimensions of Diversity: Cross-Categorization and the Functioning of Diverse Work Groups," *Group Dynamics: Theory, Research, and Practice* 11 (2007): 79–94.

35. Todd L. Pittinsky, Seth A. Rosenthal, and R. Matthew Montoya, "Liking ≠ Not Disliking: The Functional Separability of Positive and Negative Attitudes Toward Minority Groups" (unpublished manuscript); Todd L. Pittinsky, Seth A. Rosenthal, and R. Matthew Montoya, "Measuring Positive Attitudes Toward Outgroups: Development and Validation of the Allophilia Scale," being prepared for *Beyond Prejudice Reduction: Pathways to Positive Intergroup Relations*, ed. Linda Tropp and Rebecca Mallett (Washington, DC: American Psychological Association).

36. Pittinsky, Rosenthal, and Montoya, "Liking ≠ Not Disliking.

37. Pittinsky and Simon, "Intergroup Leadership," 586–605.

38. Kurt Lewin, *Field Theory in Social Science: Selected Theoretical Papers*, ed. Dorwin Cartwright (Oxford, UK: Harpers, 1951).

39. Gordon W. Allport, *The Nature of Prejudice* (Oxford, UK: Addison-Wesley, 1954); Thomas F. Pettigrew, "Intergroup Contact Theory," *Annual Review of Psychology* 49 (1998): 65–85; and Muzafer Sherif, *Intergroup Conflict and Cooperation: The Robbers Cave Experiment* (Norman, OK: University Book Exchange, 1961).

40. Social identity perspectives on leadership shed valuable light on what may be termed *intragroup leadership*—the dynamics between a single leader and a single group of followers; Michael A. Hogg, "A Social Identity Theory of Leadership," *Personality and Social Psychology Review* 5 (2001): 184–200. For this reason, many of the authors in this volume take a social identity perspective.

41. A common in-group identity has been shown to improve intergroup relations; Samuel L. Gaertner, John F. Dovidio, Brenda S. Banker, Missy Houlette, Kelly M. Johnson, and Elizabeth A. McGlynn, "Reducing Intergroup Conflict: From Superordinate Goals to Decategorization, Recategorization, and Mutual Differentiation," *Group Dynamics: Theory, Research, and Practice* 4 (2000): 98–114. Research suggests that dual identities can minimize some of the risks of focusing exclusively on a superordinate identity; Matthew J. Hornsey and Michael A. Hogg, "Subgroup Relations: A Comparison of Mutual Intergroup Differentiation and Common Ingroup Identity Models of Prejudice Reduction," *Personality and Social Psychology Bulletin* 26 (2000): 242–256. Miles Hewstone and Rupert Brown describe the mutual intergroup differentiation model in *Contact and Conflict in Intergroup Encounters* (Oxford, UK: Blackwell, 1986).

PART I

Insights and Concepts

1

Leadership Across Group Divides

The Challenges and Potential of
Common Group Identity

John F. Dovidio

Yale University

Samuel L. Gaertner

University of Delaware

Marika J. Lamoreaux

Georgia State University

GROUP LIVING represents a fundamental survival strategy, developed across human evolutionary history, that characterizes the human species. For long-term survival, people must be willing to rely on others for information, aid, and shared resources; they must also be willing to offer information, give assistance, and share resources with others. Group membership provides necessary boundaries for mutual aid and cooperation.

Group boundaries, however, also have fundamental intergroup consequences. Whether they are defined by culture, race or ethnicity, or role within an organization, group boundaries distinguish who is "in" from who is "out." Moreover, interactions between groups involve greater greed, fear, and mistrust than interactions between individuals. As a consequence, conflict between groups is a ubiquitous phenomenon. It characterizes all cultures and has been a central theme across all of human history. Yet cooperation and harmony between members of different groups are critical not only within societies and organizations but also for global stability and productivity. How can leaders effectively shepherd members of different groups to work cooperatively rather than competitively and place the collective welfare over their own group's gain?

This chapter focuses on how leaders can bring together different groups, with different perspectives and often mutual mistrust, in stable and productive relations. In this chapter, we examine the importance of social identity, as compared with personal identity, and we illustrate how leaders can redirect and manage the forces of social identity that can divide groups to promote positive relations and to expand the resources available for group functioning and activity.

Group Membership: Social Categorization and Social Identity

Group membership is critical to one's self-esteem, sense of psychological security, and physical well-being. In this section, we consider two fundamental processes involved in the collective experience: social categorization and in-group identity.

> *Social categorization:* Categorization is an essential basis for human perception, cognition, and functioning. *Categorization* is the process by which individuals quickly and effectively sort the many different objects, events, and people they encounter into a smaller number of meaningful units. In this respect, people can be characterized as *cognitive misers* who compromise total accuracy for efficiency when confronted with the often overwhelming complexity of their social world.[1]
>
> When people are categorized into groups (i.e., *social categorization*), something that often occurs spontaneously on the basis of physical similarity, proximity, or shared fate, differences between members of the same category tend to be perceptually minimized, whereas differences between groups tend to be exaggerated and overgeneralized.[2] For example, when people meet someone who would normally be considered a distant acquaintance while traveling abroad, they sponta-

neously feel more close, connected, and similar to the person because of the *salience* of their common group membership in that context.

Moreover, in the process of categorizing people into groups, people classify themselves *into* one of the social categories (and *out of* the others). The distinction between in-group and out-group members as a consequence of social categorization has a profound influence on affect, cognition, and behavior.[3] People spontaneously experience more positive emotion toward other members of the in-group than toward members of the out-group and think about in-group and out-group members in fundamentally different (i.e., biased) ways. Positive behaviors of in-group members are seen as further evidence of in-group virtues, whereas negative actions by in-group members are typically discounted and often overlooked.

In terms of social relations and behavioral outcomes, people are more sensitive to the needs of in-group than of out-group members, more helpful toward in-group than toward out-group members, more trusting of in-group members, more likely to work harder to benefit the in-group, and more likely to be cooperative and exercise more personal restraint when using endangered common resources when these are shared with in-group members than with others.[4]

Social identity: The essentially automatic process of distinguishing the group containing the self (the in-group) from other groups (the out-groups) represents a foundational principle in some of the most prominent contemporary theories of intergroup behavior, such as social identity theory and self-categorization theory.[5]

These perspectives posit that a person defines the self along a dimension from *personal identity*, as a unique individual with distinct characteristics and personal motives, to *collective identity*, as the embodiment of a social collective that reflects shared characteristics and goals. At the individual level, one's personal welfare and goals are most salient and important. When personal identity is more salient, an individual's needs, standards, beliefs, and motives better predict behavior. In contrast, when social identity is more strongly activated, "people come to perceive themselves more as interchangeable exemplars of a social category than as unique personalities defined by their individual differences from others."[6] Under these conditions, collective needs, goals, and standards are primary.

People who more closely identify with their group adhere more strongly to intragroup norms. Thus, whether personal or collective identity is more salient critically shapes how a person perceives, interprets, evaluates, and responds to situations and to others.

Not only do psychological biases produce perceptions of competition and motivate actual competition between groups, but also competition between groups itself acts to increase bias and distrust. When people perceive out-group members as a threat, they tend to derogate them and discriminate against them more directly. Thus, psychological biases and actual competition often reinforce each other to escalate intergroup tension and conflict.

Taken together, these findings paint a bleak picture for intergroup relations. However, helping leaders understand the factors that contribute to intergroup bias and the underlying principles that shape intergroup relations can help leaders develop effective strategies for improving intergroup relations.

Improving Intergroup Relations:
The Common In-Group Identity Model

Because identification with social groups is a basic process that is fundamental to intergroup bias, social psychologists have targeted this process as a starting point for improving intergroup relations. The approach we have employed, the common in-group identity model, builds on the foundation of research on social identity.[7]

This strategy emphasizes the process of *recategorization*, whereby members of different groups are induced to conceive of themselves as a single, more inclusive superordinate group rather than as separate groups. With recategorization, as proposed by the common in-group identity model, the goal is to reorganize the perception of intergroup boundaries, redefining who is conceived of as an in-group member, to reduce bias.[8] If members of different groups are induced to conceive of themselves as a single more inclusive, superordinate group, then attitudes toward former out-group members can become more positive through processes involving pro-in-group bias, thereby reducing intergroup bias.

Leaders can achieve or reinforce a common in-group identity by increasing the salience of existing common superordinate memberships (e.g., a school, a company, a nation) in two ways: by contrasting the in-group with relevant out-groups or by emphasizing the shared fate of group members. Leaders can also create new common connections and identity by introducing opportunities for active cooperation among members within a group or framing intergroup relations as competitive. Even relatively minor interventions—such as increasing the physical similarity among group members using clothing or visible insignias, bringing members into closer physical proximity, or creating positive affect (e.g., with an unexpected gift)—facilitate the development of common identity.

The value of creating a one-group representation for reducing inter-group bias has been consistently supported by research over the past twenty years.[9] Laboratory studies have demonstrated that diverse inter-ventions that produce more-inclusive representations of different groups, such as such as fostering cooperation, enhancing perceptual similarity, and inducing positive affect, systematically reduce intergroup bias. These re-sults have been replicated in field settings involving high schools, banking mergers, and blended families with children and in different cultures.

Moreover, emphasizing group boundaries, thereby increasing the sense of "we-ness," often strengthens the position of leaders, who are subse-quently seen as more prototypical and thus representative of the group.[10] Leaders who more closely reflect the prototypical characteristics of the group receive more popular support, are seen as more charismatic, and are more influential. Thus leaders have a broad range of techniques for rein-forcing or altering the inclusiveness of group boundaries.

Despite the evidence for the benefits of a common group identity on group functioning and relationships, it is critical to recognize that people have multiple group memberships and identities. These can be seen as com-patible or incompatible with a common group identity and thus strengthen or undermine the stability of the group boundary.

Challenges of a Superordinate Identity: Multiple Categorizations and Identities

One implication of people's multiple group memberships is that beyond a laboratory setting it is often difficult to sustain a superordinate group identity in the face of powerful social forces that emphasize different group identi-ties. Thus, when social identities are culturally important, such as race or ethnicity, the impact of interventions that temporarily induce feelings of common identity may quickly fade as the original, different category membership becomes reactivated through everyday experiences.

Moreover, when group identities and their associated cultural values are vital to one's functioning, then demands to abandon these group identities or to adopt a color-blind ideology are likely to arouse tension and conflict. In particular, social identity theory proposes that when the integrity of group identity is threatened, people are motivated to reaffirm their distinctive group identity (an example is the black pride movement of the 1960s).[11] Consequently, even though attempts to emphasize a common group identification may successfully improve intergroup attitudes among people who are weakly identified with their group, these initiatives frequently exacerbate bias among those who are strongly identified with their group and thereby may increase group tensions and conflict.[12]

Another potential effect of attempting to create a single, superordinate identity is that it can limit the potential benefits of diversity for group performance. Although diversity is often associated with social tensions, it offers unique benefits for problem solving and task accomplishment.[13] The presence of minorities in groups, whether defined in terms of racial or ethnic group membership or opinion position, stimulates novel perspectives and creative problem solving.[14]

In addition, groups that are more diverse showed greater integrative complexity in their problem-solving activities. In the context of jury decision making, Sommers demonstrated that racially diverse juries considered the evidence more fully and complexly in developing their consensus judgments than did racially homogeneous (all-white) juries.[15] In contrast, when a single identity is more salient, people show greater adherence to a single set of norms, leading to more uniform and conventional thought and action. Emphasizing only the common connection among group members at the expense of acknowledging diversity can thus limit groups' creativity and certain types of effectiveness.

Creating a single group identity, and an associated set of standards, without explicitly recognizing the value of other identities can adversely affect within-group dynamics in two other ways. First, because people tend to project their values onto the standards of the superordinate group, they perceive members of the group who deviate from these projected values as inferior and thus less worthy of respect and attention.[16] Second, when the situation demands that a group forsake its cultural values, standards, or language to achieve a superordinate identity, members who retain a sense of their subgroup identity may feel like tokens rather than central members of the group. Consequently, they experience feelings of isolation and low levels of group commitment, both of which adversely affect their performance. To the extent that people feel that their membership in another group is not valued, they are also likely to experience a stereotype threat.[17] This threat produces behavior consistent with the negative expectations associated with their group membership. For instance, when a situation draws more attention to their race, black students perform more poorly on achievement tests, confirming negative intellectual stereotypes of blacks even among students who personally reject these stereotypes.

Thus, although there are considerable benefits for leaders in promoting a superordinate identity within homogeneous groups, such efforts can also have important limiting or negative consequences when there are important dimensions of diversity within the group. It is therefore important for practical as well as theoretical reasons to consider more-complex forms of social identity in which more than one identity is salient at a time.

Dual Identity

In the context of the common in-group identity model, the development of a common in-group identity need not require each group to forsake its less inclusive group identity. In particular, the most recent emphasis of our work has focused on a second form of recategorization: the impact of a *dual identity*, in which the superordinate identity is salient but conjoins with a salient subgroup identity (a "different groups working together on the same team" representation). In this respect, the common in-group identity model is aligned with *bidimensional* models of acculturation—in which cultural heritage and mainstream identities are relatively independent—and not with *unidimensional* models, which posit that cultural identity is necessarily relinquished with adoption of mainstream cultural identity. Whereas a one-group representation relates to assimilation from an acculturation perspective, a dual identity corresponds to a pluralistic integration (multiculturalism).

Because individuals frequently belong to several groups simultaneously and possess multiple potential identities, it is possible to activate or introduce a shared identity even while separate group identities are salient. Within an organization, people may see themselves as members of two different units (for example, accounting and marketing) but may also perceive members of each group in terms of a cross-cutting membership (e.g., senior or junior organizational status). The dual-identity approach is a particular form of crossed categorization in which the original group boundaries are maintained, but within a salient superordinate group identity that represents a higher level of inclusiveness. Accountants and marketers may perceive themselves as different groups within a company, but they simultaneously categorize both groups within the superordinate organizational identity relative to employees of a competing company.

Establishing a common superordinate identity while maintaining the salience of and respect for subgroup identities may be effective in reducing tensions and bias between subgroup members, because it permits the benefits of a common in-group identity to operate without arousing countervailing motivations to achieve positive intergroup distinctiveness. Moreover, this type of recategorization may be particularly effective when people have strong allegiances to their original groups. In this respect, the benefits of a dual identity may be especially relevant in interracial and interethnic group contexts.

Consistent with our hypothesis that a dual identity represents a form of recategorization that can facilitate positive relations for minority group members, we found that students who described themselves as *both* an American and as a member of their racial or ethnic group showed less bias toward other groups within their school compared with those who described themselves only in terms of their subgroup identity.[18] In addition, perceptions of a superordinate connection enhance interracial trust and acceptance of authority within an organization even when racial identity is strong for minority group members.[19] Also, minority group members show greater trust, group commitment, and responsiveness to feedback when they feel that their subgroup identity is respected by the leader and other group members within the context of a superordinate group identity.[20] Thus, even when subgroup identity is salient, the simultaneous salience of a common in-group identity promotes greater harmony and cohesiveness.

Although these findings support the value of developing a dual identity as an alternative to a one-group representation for improving the attitudes and commitment of minority group members toward their group, we caution that the effectiveness of a dual identity may be substantially moderated by the complementarity and compatibility of the superordinate and subgroup identities. Brown and Hewstone posit that relations within task-oriented groups containing members with different subgroup identities can be harmonious and productive even when subgroup identities remain strong but are maintained in the context of cooperative interaction.[21] In contrast, when the other identity is perceived or experienced in conflict with the superordinate identity—such as maintaining premerger company identities within a merged organization or separate family identities within a blended family—stronger dual identities are related to greater tension and less-positive relations.

Perceptions of context and the compatibility of dual identities may differ across members of a superordinate group. One systematic influence on these perceptions is whether the person is a member of a high- or low-status—majority or minority—subgroup.

Challenge of a Dual Identity: Minority and Majority Perspectives

The different status and social realities of minority and majority group members influence their perspectives on relations within a group. In general, majority and minority group members have different preferences for recognition within a superordinate entity. Whereas minority group members typically want to retain their cultural subgroup identity (pluralistic integration, multiculturalism), majority group members favor the assimilation of minority groups into one single culture (a traditional "melting pot" orientation)—the dominant culture.[22]

Not only do minority and majority groups have different preferences for representations within a dual identity, but also the two associated cultural ideologies of assimilation (color-blind orientation) and integration (multicultural orientation) have often been considered oppositional. Assimilation requires minority group members to conform to dominant values and ideals, often requiring that they abandon inconsistent racial or ethnic group values, to achieve full citizenship and be accepted in society. Multicultural integration, in contrast, strives to be inclusive by recognizing, and often celebrating, intergroup differences and their contributions to a common society.

In part as a consequence of their oppositional nature, the different preferences of majority groups (for assimilation and a color-blind perspective) and of minority groups (for a dual identity and a multicultural perspective) can have an important, and often underappreciated, impact on intergroup relations. People who endorse one type of orientation typically feel threatened by members of other groups who advocate another orientation.[23] We have found, for example, that white students had more negative impressions of and reactions to black students within the university when blacks presented themselves in ways that deviated from a single, superordinate university identity and emphasized their racial identity. Also, as discussed earlier, imposing a common group identity on people who have strong subgroup identities—as is characteristic of many minority group members—generates identity threat and produces negative reactions. However, when intergroup experiences validate and reinforce one's preferred group representation, greater commitment and investment in the superordinate organization result.[24]

The different orientations of majority and minority group members toward assimilation and integration are also reflected in their responses to others. The different perspectives, preferences, and standards of majority and minority group members thus pose a dilemma for leaders. Emphasizing either a singular common group identity or a dual identity produces a positive response from some group members but a negative response from others.

Resolving the Dilemma of Majority
and Minority Perspectives

As we noted earlier, situations of positive interdependence are among the most effective means for creating a strong sense of common identity among individuals and members of subgroups. Cooperative interdependence is also particularly well suited for addressing the perceptions of both majority and minority group subgroup members within a superordinate group. In particular, cooperative group tasks can be structured so that success requires the joint and distinctive resources of both subgroups, a strategy we term *instrumental cooperation*.[25] Instrumental cooperation involves the recognition that the subgroups are different in important ways, the differences potentially enhance the resources available to the group as a whole, and the differences between groups can be harnessed in a way that can improve the effectiveness and welfare of the larger group and its members in general. Because a critical element in instrumental cooperation is the recognition of differences and their value, leaders can play an important role in appropriately shaping the perceptions of group members.

From the perspective of majority subgroup members, when the conditions of instrumental cooperation are satisfied, then recognition of difference is no longer perceived as dysfunctional; members' efforts support a superordinate goal, and success brings reward and recognition to the superordinate group as a whole. From the perspective of minority group members, when these conditions are satisfied, then their distinctive sub-group identity is recognized rather than threatened, and their unique contribution is necessary and valued. Superordinate and subgroup identities are seen as compatible, complementary, and instrumental to goal achievement, and success reinforces both their identities and their superordinate connection.

This perspective is similar but not identical to the mutual intergroup differentiation model.[26] That model also recognizes that primarily emphasizing the similarities between groups arouses motivations to achieve positive distinctiveness for one's group and thereby exacerbates a sense of difference. Whereas the mutual intergroup differentiation model focuses on the general value of acknowledging group differences within a cooperative relationship, however, the instrumental cooperation position extends these ideas by identifying the conditions that maximize the benefits of contact and interaction.[27] This position proposes that for contact and interaction to be most effective, the contributions of the subgroups must improve the quality of the final product by using each subgroup's specific skills to the whole group's advantage.

Conclusion

In this chapter, we have proposed that effective leadership needs to consider the importance of social identity processes to group dynamics. Creating and reinforcing a common in-group identity often promote cohesiveness and positive relations among group members, facilitate their commitment to the group, and strengthen a leader's position of authority. However, when diversity exists in a group, the challenge for leaders is to reconcile the typical preferences of the majority group for assimilation (a singular one-group identity) and of minority groups for pluralistic (multicultural) integration; leaders also must effectively manage the friction caused by recognition of difference in ways that produce complex and novel approaches to group problem-solving tasks. We propose that instrumental cooperation, in which success requires capitalizing on the unique strengths of each group, can satisfy both the majority group's desire for common identity and the minority group's needs for positive distinctiveness. Thus, to lead across the group divide, leaders need to recognize and appreciate the different perspectives and motivations of the members of the different groups and not only manage the activity of individuals but also shape perceptions in ways that satisfy the unique needs of members of different groups.

Notes

Authors' Note: Preparation of this chapter was supported by NSF Grant # BCS-0613218 awarded to the first two authors.

1. S. T. Fiske and S. E. Taylor, *Social Cognition*, 2nd ed. (New York: McGraw-Hill, 1991).

2. For a review, see J. C. Turner et al., *Rediscovering the Social Group: A Self-Categorization Theory* (Oxford, England: Basil Blackwell, 1987).

3. For a review, see Samuel L. Gaertner and John F. Dovidio, *Reducing Intergroup Bias: The Common Ingroup Identity Model* (Philadelphia: The Psychology Press, 2000).

4. Ibid.

5. For social identity theory, see H. Tajfel and J. C. Turner, "An Integrative Theory of Intergroup Conflict," in *The Social Psychology of Intergroup Relations*, ed. W. G. Austin and S. Worchel (Monterey, CA: Brooks/Cole, 1979), 33–48. For self-categorization theory, see Turner et al., *Rediscovering the Social Group.*

6. Turner et al., *Rediscovering the Social Group*, 50.

7. Gaertner and Dovidio, *Reducing Intergroup Bias.*

8. Ibid.

9. For reviews, see Gaertner and Dovidio, *Reducing Intergroup Bias*; and Samuel L. Gaertner and John F. Dovidio, "Addressing Contemporary Racism: The Common Ingroup Identity Model," in *Motivational Aspects of Prejudice and Racism (Nebraska Symposium on Motivation)*, ed. Cynthia Willis-Esqueda (New York: Springer, 2007), 111–133.

10. M. A. Hogg, "A Social Identity Theory of Leadership," *Personality and Social Psychology Review* 5 (2001): 184–200.

11. Tajfel and Turner, "An Integrative Theory of Intergroup Conflict."

12. R. J. Crisp, C. H. Stone, and N. R. Hall, "Recategorization and Subgroup Identification: Predicting and Preventing Threats from Common Ingroups," *Personality and Social Psychology Bulletin* 32 (2006): 230–243.

13. R. D. Putnam, "*E Pluribus Unum*: Diversity and Community in the Twenty-First Century, The 2006 Johan Skytte Prize Lecture," *Scandinavian Political Studies* 30 (2007): 137–174.

14. A. L. Antonio et al., "Effects of Racial Diversity on Complex Thinking in College Students," *Psychological Science* 15 (2004): 507–510.

15. S. R. Sommers, "On Racial Diversity and Group Decision Making: Identifying Multiple Effects of Racial Composition on Jury Deliberations," *Journal of Personality and Social Psychology* 90 (2006): 597–612.

16. A. Mummendey and M. Wenzel, "Social Discrimination and Tolerance in Intergroup Relations: Reactions to Intergroup Difference," *Personality and Social Psychology Review* 3 (1999): 158–174.

17. C. Steele and J. Aronson, "Stereotype Threat and the Intellectual Test Performance of African Americans," *Journal of Personality and Social Psychology* 69 (1995): 797–811.

18. Gaertner and Dovidio, *Reducing Intergroup Bias.*

19. Y. J. Huo et al., "Leadership and the Management of Conflicts in Diverse Groups: Why Acknowledging versus Neglecting Subgroup Identity Matters," *European Journal of Social Psychology* 35 (2005): 237–254.

20. Ibid.

21. R. Brown and M. Hewstone, "An Integrative Theory of Intergroup Contact," in *Advances in Experimental Social Psychology*, vol. 37, ed. M. P. Zanna (San Diego, CA: Academic Press, 2005), 255–343.

22. John F. Dovidio, Samuel L. Gaertner, and G. Kafati, "Group Identity and Intergroup Relations: The Common In-Group Identity Model," in *Advances in Group Processes*, vol. 17, ed. S. R. Thye, E. J. Lawler, M. W. Macy, and H. A. Walker (Stamford, CT: JAI Press, 2000), 1–34; C. S. Ryan et al., "Multicultural and Colorblind Ideology, Stereotypes, and Ethnocentrism among Black and White Americans," *Group Processes and Intergroup Relations* 10 (2007): 617–637; M. Verkuyten, "Multicultural Recognition and Ethnic Minority Rights: A Social Identity Perspective," in *European Review of Social Psychology*, vol. 17, ed. W. Stroebe and M. Hewstone (New York: Psychology Press, 2006), 148–184.

23. R. Y. Bourhis, L. C. Moïse, and S. Perrault, "Towards an Interactive Acculturation Model: A Social Psychological Approach," *International Journal of Psychology* 32 (1997): 369–86.

24. Dovidio, Gaertner, and Kafati, "Group Identity and Intergroup Relations."

25. M. J. Lamoreaux et al. "Reducing Intergroup Bias: When Intergroup Contact Is Instrumental for Achieving Group Goals" (manuscript in preparation, Department of Psychology, University of Delaware, Newark, 2007).

26. Brown and Hewstone, "An Integrative Theory of Intergroup Contact."

27. Lamoreaux et al., "Reducing Intergroup Bias."

2

From Group Conflict to Social Harmony

Leading Across Diverse and Conflicting Social Identities

Michael A. Hogg

Claremont Graduate University
School of Behavioral and Organizational Sciences

HISTORY REVEALS countless examples of the challenge of effective intergroup leadership. Successful examples of intergroup leadership and cooperation in the twentieth century include the Western alliance in World War II, the North Atlantic Treaty Organization, the Association of Southeastern Nations, and the European Union. Examples of inadequate intergroup leadership might include Italy's continual quest for a stable government of national unity and the division of postcolonial India into largely Hindu India, led by Nehru, and largely Muslim Pakistan, led by Jinnah.

There are numerous more recent examples. As I was writing this chapter, National Public Radio buzzed with debate about leadership in Iraq, the 2008 U.S. presidential election, and the change of prime minister in the United Kingdom. Effective leadership in Iraq needed to transcend a long history of vicious conflict between Sunnis, Shiites, and Kurds. In the United States, there was talk of a nation divided on ideological grounds into red and blue: what does a presidential candidate have to do to be seen to represent both groups and yet not be seen to betray his or her party base? For a decade, Tony Blair had kept the British Labour Party in power after eighteen years of Conservative domination by steering an avowedly centrist line; could Gordon Brown, the new prime minister and leader of the Labour Party, repeat his accomplishment?

The organizational and management sciences, where most leadership research is done, tend to focus on leader-member transactions, the transformational nature of leadership, and the role of charisma and the CEO.[1] Perhaps it is this corporate and organizational focus that deflects attention from the fact that leaders, particularly in the public sphere, almost always must provide leadership for a constituency that encompasses not merely diverse *individuals* but also diverse *groups* that in many cases simply do not get on. More often than not, the great challenge of leadership is in being an effective *intergroup leader*—providing effective leadership across multiple groups. For example, providing leadership for a psychology department in a university entails not only reconciling individual differences among department members but also, and more significantly, reconciling and transcending sometimes stark intergroup differences between, for example, social psychologists, developmental psychologists, cognitive psychologists, methodologists, and so forth.

Another feature that is often underplayed in conventional leadership research is the *identity function* of leadership. A significant role of leaders, particularly public leaders, is to provide their constituency with a shared identity; followers look to their leaders to provide them with a sense of who they are, what they should think, how they should behave, and how interaction with other groups will go. For example, in the run-up to the 2008 presidential election in the United States, there was much debate about how different presidential contenders could speak to what it is to be an American—how they could capture, express, or perhaps reconfigure U.S. identity. Another example, starker and more extreme, is how leaders of totalitarian regimes (e.g., Pol Pot in Cambodia) or religious cults (e.g., David Koresh and the Branch Davidians) embody and promulgate (often through extreme practices) a single monolithic identity for their group.

Taken together, these ideas suggest that to varying degrees effective leadership hinges on the ability to forge a shared identity embodying a single vision and common set of values, attitudes, goals, and practices. The shared identity is made from multiple identities representing different social groups (not merely different individuals) that not only differentiate themselves from one another but also quite often distrust and despise one another. More often than not, effective leadership involves being an effective intergroup leader: being able to construct and promote an overarching, or *superordinate*, identity that transcends subgroup identities, without making subgroups feel that they are losing their own distinctive subgroup identities. For example, effective leadership of Sri Lanka as a unified nation hinges on forging an identity and a set of associated national goals, values, and practices that are acceptable as self-defining national attributes to both Tamils and Singhalese (two groups that have committed appalling atrocities against one another for almost forty years), without either subgroup feeling it is losing its own distinctive identity. One can clearly see that effective intergroup leadership is not easy, because it rests on resolving intergroup conflicts.

This chapter explores the dynamics of intergroup leadership from the perspective of *social identity theory*, a social psychology theory that explores the psychological relationship between self-conception and the behavior of people within and between groups.[2] Specifically, the focus is on the *social identity theory of leadership*, which describes how leaders who are considered by the group's members to best embody the group's defining attributes are most effective.[3] However, because the key challenge of intergroup leadership is that a group may not actually agree on a single set of defining attributes—different subgroups may profoundly disagree— this chapter goes on to focus on broader social psychological principles governing resolution of intergroup conflict and the construction of superordinate identities.[4]

There are two overall aims. The first is to show that psychological processes associated with social identity and intergroup behavior make effective intergroup leadership very difficult. The second is to show that this scientific knowledge allows us to specify conditions that, if strategically implemented, will make effective intergroup leadership less difficult to achieve. A case will be made for pluralism as just such a condition; to be effective, intergroup leaders need to construct, and need to be considered to embody, an inclusive superordinate identity that does not threaten the independent integrity of subgroup identities.

Social Identity Theory

Social identity theory was introduced in the early 1970s and has since been elaborated and developed so that it is now one of the most significant social psychological explanations of group processes, intergroup relations, and self-conception as a group member.[5]

At the core of the theory is the premise that a fundamental function of social groups is to provide members with a social identity—a specification of who they are and of associated perceptions, attitudes, values, feelings, and behaviors that are shared with fellow group members and distinguish them from members of other groups. Thus, the social group Republican provides its members, Republicans, with an identity that they and others recognize and with a prescription to think, feel, and act in certain ways.

A sense of who we are, how we should behave, and how others will treat us is fundamental to adaptive social conduct; it satisfies a basic human need to reduce uncertainty about self and thus to be able to program our own behavior, plan action, and reliably predict the behavior of others.[6] Because groups not only define but also evaluate self and because people like to evaluate themselves favorably and to be evaluated by others favorably, groups and their members struggle resolutely to be not only distinct from but also better than other groups; intergroup behavior is a struggle for status, prestige, moral superiority, and so forth.[7] Thus identity processes are tightly associated with basic human motivational and cognitive processes. People seek, promote, and protect valuable self-describing social identities and the social groups that define such identities.

To deal with the enormous diversity of humanity, the mind represents the social world in terms of categories of people (e.g., Republicans, Canadians, economists, Latinos, Hindus). These representations are prototypes: a *prototype* is a set of attributes (e.g., attitudes, behaviors, dress, customs) that we believe characterizes one group and distinguishes it from relevant other groups. Typically people in one group agree on the prototype of their own group (in-group) and of relevant other groups (out-groups). In addition people almost always exaggerate differences between their own group and relevant out-groups and exaggerate the degree of similarity among members of a specific out-group. This is psychologically adaptive, because it accentuates category distinctiveness and brings into sharp relief the social world and one's place in it.

Group memberships are *salient* when, for example, we are involved in a group activity or intergroup encounter, when we meet a stranger we know little about, or when we feel proud of our own group or despise a particular out-group. When group memberships are salient, we automatically categorize people as group members and assign them the attributes of our prototype of their group; we stereotype them and treat them as embodiments of their group rather than as unique individuals, a process that social identity theorists call *depersonalization*.

For example, we are familiar with popular media stereotypes of people who use Macintosh computers and those who use PCs and perceive people as being passionately loyal to one computer system or the other. Thus, Mac users might agree that PC users are boring, dull, and "stiff" and certainly more boring, dull, and stiff than Mac users. When a Mac user meets a PC user, he categorizes her as a PC user—rather than, for example, a Democrat or a personal friend named Kate—and assigns the category attributes to her. The ensuing interaction is structured in terms of intergroup relations between the two categories—Mac users and PC users—rather than between two individuals or between a man and a woman.

A core tenet of social identity theory is that the process of depersonalization can apply to oneself; we categorize ourselves in precisely the same way we categorize others and thus assign to ourselves the prototypical attributes of our group. The implication of this is clear. Self-categorization transforms our perceptions, beliefs, attitudes, feelings, and behaviors to conform to the prescriptions of the prototype we have of our own group.

Because prototypes define and evaluate groups and their members, people are vigilant in obtaining prototype-relevant information, particularly about their own self-defining group. There are many sources of in-group prototype information. Among them, the most immediate and reliable is the behavior of fellow in-group members who one has already learned are generally highly prototypical group members. In many group contexts, the group leader is viewed by followers to be just such a highly prototypical member. This is precisely why under certain circumstances leaders play a fundamental identity-defining role for groups.

Social Identity and Leadership

The social identity theory of leadership describes how social identity processes influence leadership.[8] The key point, following directly from the processes described earlier, is that the more strongly one identifies with a group and the more important a group is to one's identity and sense of self (i.e., group membership is salient), the more one is influenced by leaders who are perceived to be prototypical of the group. To be an effective leader under these circumstances rests heavily on being perceived by members as being prototypical of the group; less-prototypical leaders have a much more difficult time providing effective leadership.

Psychologically, the process of leadership under these circumstances rests on the fact that in salient groups people pay substantial attention to the group prototype and to what and who is more prototypical. People take their lead in defining themselves as group members, and thus in knowing what to think and how to behave, from those fellow members who they consider to best embody the group's identity. Prototypical people are disproportionately influential, and thus able to be effective leaders, for at least four social identity reasons.

First, the basic cognitive process of depersonalization ensures that group members conform to the group prototype. Because highly prototypical members already embody the prototype, they appear, paradoxically, to be less influenced than are less-prototypical members; prototypical members are the source of influence—the influencers—rather than the target of influence—the influencees.

Second, group members view the in-group prototype favorably (after all, it defines self and group) and thus view more-prototypical members more favorably and like them more, as group members, than less-prototypical members. It is well documented that being liked makes it much easier to influence people.[9] Furthermore, because there is usually significant agreement on the prototype, the group as a whole likes prototypical members; they are consensually popular in group terms. This consensus crystallizes an evaluative status difference between leaders and followers in which the leader is able to influence the rest of the group.

Third, prototypical members typically find the group more central and important to self-definition and therefore identify more strongly with it. They have a greater investment in the group and thus are more likely to behave in ways that serve the group. They embody group norms, favor the in-group over out-groups, treat in-group members fairly, and act in ways that promote the in-group. These behaviors confirm their prototypicality and membership credentials and encourage group members to trust them to act in the best interest of the group even when it may not appear that they are; prototypical members are furnished with legitimacy.[10] Thus, followers invest their trust in prototypical leaders, something that paradoxically allows such leaders to diverge from group norms and be less conformist and more innovative and transformational than non- or less-prototypical leaders. Innovation and transformation are fundamental to effective leadership.[11]

Finally, because members pay close attention to prototype-relevant information and the leader best embodies this information, the leader and his behavior stand out perceptually against the background of the rest of the group. It is well documented in social psychology that this perceptual prominence accentuates the general human tendency to see a greater correspondence between someone's behavior and her underlying personality than is perhaps warranted.[12] In the context of leadership, this *correspondence bias*, as it is called, causes followers to build a charismatic leadership personality for their leader; after all, the behaviors that are being attributed to personality include being the source of influence, being able to gain compliance from others, being popular, having higher status, being innovative, and being trusted. The perception of charisma on the part of the group further facilitates effective and innovative leadership on the part of a prototypical leader.[13]

The social identity-based leadership processes just discussed extend leaders considerable power to maintain their leadership position. Because they are trusted, afforded latitude to be innovative, and invested with status and charisma, they are highly effective prototype managers who can define both what the group stands for and the social identity of its members. They can consolidate an existing prototype, modify it, or dramatically reconstruct it. One of the key attributes of effective leadership is precisely this visionary and transformational activity, in which leaders are able to change what the group sees itself as being. Such leaders can be considered *entrepreneurs of identity*.[14] For example, they talk up their own prototypicality or talk down aspects of their own behavior that are nonprototypical; they identify deviants or marginal members to highlight their own prototypicality or to construct a particular prototype for the group that enhances their own prototypicality; they secure their own leadership position by vilifying contenders for leadership, casting the latter as nonprototypical; and they identify as relevant comparison out-groups those that are most favorable to their own in-group prototypicality.

It is important to remember that social identity processes only, or more strongly, influence leadership in groups that members identify with more strongly. As people identify less strongly with a group or the group becomes less central to self-definition, social identity dynamics and associated leadership processes weaken. Here, effective leadership is less about identity and is less strongly based on group prototypicality; it is, rather, more strongly influenced by other factors, such as charismatic personality and schemas of good leadership. One implication of this is that leaders can

engage in discourse that raises or lowers salience. If they are highly prototypical, then raising salience provides the leadership benefits of high prototypicality; if they are not very prototypical, then lowering salience
protects them from the leadership pitfalls of not being very prototypical.
Generally, if leaders feel they are not, or are no longer, prototypical, they
strategically engage in a range of group-oriented behaviors to strengthen
their membership credentials.[15]

Overall, the social identity theory of leadership has solid empirical
support from laboratory experiments and more-naturalistic studies and
surveys.[16]

Social Identity and Intergroup Leadership

The challenge of intergroup leadership is to transcend group differences
and build a shared sense of "us" by bridging deep identity divisions, or *cultural divides*, within a group and focusing members on shared values, attitudes, practices, and goals.[17] If this can be accomplished, then social
identity leadership processes come into play to ensure successful leadership, but it is contingent on members seeing themselves as a single, united
group with a leader who is prototypical and representative of the group as
a whole.

There are many obstacles to building a shared sense of belonging that
transcends group differences. Generally when a group contains subgroups
(for example, as described earlier, Iraq contains Shia, Sunni, and Kurdish
subgroups), the leader comes from one of the subgroups and therefore
may not be viewed as prototypical of all; indeed because of subgroup diversity there is not likely to be a clear overall group prototype. For example,
Duck and Fielding report studies of subgroups nested within a superordinate group, in which the overall leader was markedly downgraded and dis-
liked if he was a member of a subgroup to which participants did not
belong, and upgraded and liked if a member of a subgroup to which participants did belong.[18] This finding mirrors the well-established observa-
tion that organizational mergers and acquisitions often fail precisely
because the leader of the new organization is viewed by a significant por-
tion of the merged organization's membership as belonging to a subgroup
to which they do not belong.[19]

The problem of subgroups is amplified in the common situation
wherein the subgroups are of unequal status, one subgroup having majority

status and the other minority status; Sunnis and Shiites in Iraq are, again, an excellent example. What tends to happen here is that the majority subgroup projects its defining attributes, its identity, onto the superordinate group and thus sees, and often promotes, the superordinate group as reflecting its attributes more completely than the minority's attributes.[20] Under these circumstances, the minority group, which often has the larger number of group members, can feel that its own cherished identity and distinctiveness are being erased and invalidated, replaced by the other subgroup's identity. This situation is highly threatening. At best it produces alienation and a sense of disidentification; at worst it creates a profound schism and a desperate and disenfranchised minority that may ultimately destabilize the group through various forms of protest—leading to a situation in which effective superordinate leadership becomes a significant challenge.

Although not capturing quite such an extreme state of affairs, a recent study by Hohman, Hogg, and Bligh provides some relevant findings.[21] We took the situation of Democratic and Republican subgroups (the latter the majority status group at the time) within the superordinate identity of American, with George W. Bush (the incumbent president) as the superordinate group leader. We had participants listen to a speech by Bush designed to strengthen U.S. identity. We found that under these conditions Republicans identified more strongly both as Republicans and as Americans, whereas Democrats identified more strongly as Democrats but less strongly as Americans; U.S. identity was seen to reflect Republican identity more than Democratic identity, and for this reason an attempt by a Republican subgroup leader to strengthen superordinate identity backfired in the case of the Democratic subgroup.

Transcending Incompatible Identities to Improve Intergroup Leadership

Social identity-based leadership is effective if members identify strongly with a group that has a common identity and if the leader is considered prototypical. The challenge of intergroup leadership is for the leader to construct a single identity out of multiple, often conflicting, identities in such a way that none of the conflicting identities feels marginalized or disenfranchised. This is of course part of the important topic of how to resolve social conflict in society—one of the main foci of social psychological research.[22] This research has identified one promising avenue—pluralism.[23]

In intergroup leadership, the overall objective is to construct a super-ordinate identity that does not threaten the status or existence of sub-group identities. Subgroups need to feel that their distinct identities are genuinely valued and preserved while they are working closely together with other groups in the service of shared superordinate values and goals. At the national level, many countries have pursued this general strategy by adopting a more or less explicit policy of *multiculturalism* or *cultural plural-ism* to try to build a tolerant and cohesive society in which diverse ethnic groups preserve their ethnic identity but also identify strongly with the values, goals, and customs of an overarching national identity. Canada and Australia explicitly lay claim to adopting this policy, but other countries such as the United Kingdom have also gone down this route to some extent.

The principles of social identity and intergroup relations discussed earlier suggest some general principles that inform strategies that intergroup leaders could adopt to optimize their leadership. First, leaders should play down their subgroup credentials and subgroup prototypicality and em-phasize their superordinate group credentials and prototypicality. They need to make sure that all members of the wider group see them as "one of us" and therefore to be trusted to act in the group's best interest, rather than as promoting a hidden agenda that actually serves the out-subgroup. It is not easy to engender this perception. The act of publicly distancing oneself from one's subgroup can be seen as disloyal by one's own subgroup and as self-interested by other subgroups. Both situations undermine trust and leadership potential. The strategy is more successfully implemented by a leader who is not too strongly affiliated with one subgroup.

Second, the leader needs to take great care to construct a superordi-nate identity that does not appear to overrepresent one subgroup or to contain elements that conflict with deeply entrenched core values and prac-tices of any subgroup. For example, in a group encompassing Muslims and Christians, core values of the superordinate group cannot include eating pork, something that would make Muslims feel excluded, or wearing the chador, something that would make Christians feel excluded.

Third, leaders should explicitly value distinctive subgroup identities but at the same time identify and highlight a shared superordinate identity that transcends most group differences. Such an identity might focus on widely shared human values and practices that most people subscribe to—for example, values relating to honesty, compassion, and responsibility.

Another take on this same strategy is to play up the idea that subgroups occupy different but equally valuable and essential roles in the larger group. In a task-oriented group context (e.g., an organization or a wartime alliance), this is the notion that different subgroups need to work cooperatively to achieve shared goals that cannot be achieved alone—perhaps to fend off a shared threat or combat a common out-group. Such a strategic alliance of convenience among disparate groups may help members focus on shared rather than incompatible identities and attributes.[24] If the subgroup identities are important, the challenge would revolve around issues of ideological hegemony and the choice of the subgroups and their leaders to actually lead the alliance. However, these task-oriented alliances can be fragile. A classic example is the World War II alliance between Britain, the United States, and the Soviet Union. Once that alliance had completed its shared task—combating and defeating Germany, Italy, and Japan—profound ideological differences emerged among the members. The alliance dissolved, and the ensuing cold war pitted the Soviet Union against Britain and the United States.

Finally, at a practical level, a leadership clique that contains genuine representation from all subgroups will strengthen the perception of equality of voice in the superordinate identity. An example of this is the European Union, whose leadership strives to have representation from the many diverse countries that make up the EU. Genuine representation creates a perception of fair treatment that has been shown to play an important role in strengthening group identification and in consolidating a perception that the leader is trustworthy.[25] As discussed earlier, trust is a critical variable in leadership; trusted leaders are more effective than distrusted leaders.

Together, these and other related strategies help, under the right conditions, to create an environment conducive to the development of a shared identity, an environment in which social identity and prototype-based leadership can thrive and in turn strengthen bonds that transcend subgroup divisions. To place it in context, imagine the common alternative situation, wherein one subgroup provides overall leadership and is overrepresented in the superordinate identity. Because of the sense of alienation, distrust, and identity threat experienced by the other subgroups, leadership here often requires a degree of coercion that can quickly regress into dictatorial leadership, with all its attendant inefficiencies and human suffering.

Conclusion

This chapter has focused on intergroup leadership as a situation in which identity conflict is the main obstacle to effective overall leadership. It argues that leadership often serves an identity function; members look to their leaders, to varying degrees, to define, crystallize, and express their identity in society. Identity plays a particularly important role in public leadership and ideology-based groups.

Social identity theory provides an integrated social psychological analysis of the role of the self-concept in processes within and between groups; it shows that people passionately protect and promote important social identities grounded in groups they belong to. To be effective, leaders of such groups need to be perceived as prototypical members who embody core aspects of the group. Various social psychology and social identity processes underpin this need. Social identity processes ensure effective leadership of salient self-defining groups.

The problem, however, is that in intergroup leadership the group embraces two or more competing and often conflicting identities. In these situations, leaders typically come from one subgroup, and this can mean that many members do not view them as at all prototypical, because they are effectively out-subgroup members. This situation compromises trust in the leadership, and without trust it is difficult to lead. In addition, the superordinate group's identity can be seen as disproportionately representative of the dominant subgroup's identity, a situation that can be highly threatening to other subgroups and can make them feel disenfranchised, alienated, or even oppressed.

The challenge, from an identity point of view, is for an intergroup leader to construct a common superordinate identity that transcends but does not threaten subgroup identities. This is not easy to do, but social psychology research, particularly a focus on the potential benefits of pluralism, suggests a number of leadership strategies that might promote the perception of a common identity and thus facilitate effective social identity and prototype-based leadership. To the extent that intergroup leaders can focus members on nonthreatening identity commonalities, they can then benefit from the significant leadership advantages of perceived prototypicality, consensual positive regard, and group-based trust.

Notes

1. Gary Yukl, *Leadership in Organizations*, 5th ed. (Upper Saddle River, NJ: Prentice Hall, 2002).

2. For an overview, see Michael A. Hogg, "Social Identity Theory," in *Contemporary Social Psychological Theories*, ed. Peter J. Burke (Palo Alto, CA: Stanford University Press, 2006), 111–136.

3. For an overview, see Michael A. Hogg and Daan van Knippenberg, "Social Identity and Leadership Processes in Groups," in *Advances in Experimental Social Psychology*, vol. 35, ed. Mark P. Zanna (San Diego: Academic Press, 2003), 1–52.

4. For an overview, see Michael A. Hogg, "Intergroup Relations," in *Handbook of Social Psychology*, ed. J. Delamater (New York: Kluwer Academic/Plenum, 2003), 479–501.

5. Henri Tajfel and John C. Turner, "An Integrative Theory of Intergroup Conflict," in *The Social Psychology of Intergroup Relations*, ed. William G. Austin and Stephen Worchel (Monterey, CA: Brooks/Cole, 1979), 33–47; and John C. Turner, Michael A. Hogg, Penelope J. Oakes, Stephen D. Reicher, and Margaret S. Wetherell, *Rediscovering the Social Group: A Self-Categorization Theory* (Oxford, UK: Blackwell, 1987). See also Hogg, "Social Identity Theory"; and Michael A. Hogg and Dominic Abrams, *Social Identifications: A Social Psychology of Intergroup Relations and Group Processes* (London: Routledge, 1988).

6. Michael A. Hogg, "Uncertainty-Identity Theory," in *Advances in Experimental Social Psychology*, vol. 39, ed. Mark P. Zanna (San Diego: Academic Press, 2007), 69–126.

7. Tajfel and Turner, "An Integrative Theory of Intergroup Conflict."

8. Michael A. Hogg, "A Social Identity Theory of Leadership," *Personality and Social Psychology Review* 5 (2001): 184–200; Hogg and van Knippenberg, "Social Identity and Leadership Processes in Groups."

9. Ellen Berscheid and Harry T. Reis, "Attraction and Close Relationships," in *The Handbook of Social Psychology*, 4th ed., vol. 2, ed. Daniel T. Gilbert, Susan T. Fiske, and Gardner Lindzey (New York: McGraw-Hill, 1998), 193–281.

10. Tom R. Tyler, "The Psychology of Legitimacy: A Relational Perspective on Voluntary Deference to Authorities," *Personality and Social Psychology Review* 1 (1997): 323–345.

11. Bruce J. Avolio and F. J. Yammarino, eds., *Transformational and Charismatic Leadership: The Road Ahead* (New York: Elsevier, 2003).

12. Daniel T. Gilbert and P. S. Malone, "The Correspondence Bias," *Psychological Bulletin* 117 (1995): 21–38.

13. Avolio and Yammarino, *Transformational and Charismatic Leadership*.

14. Stephen Reicher and Nick Hopkins, "On the Science of the Art of Leadership," in *Leadership and Power: Identity Processes in Groups and Organizations*, ed. Daan van Knippenberg and Michael A. Hogg (London: Sage, 2003), 197–209.

15. For example, Michael J. Platow and Daan van Knippenberg, "A Social Identity Analysis of Leadership Endorsement: The Effects of Leader Ingroup Prototypicality and Distributive Intergroup Fairness," *Personality and Social Psychology Bulletin* 27 (2001): 1508–1519.

16. For a recent review, see Daan van Knippenberg, Barbara van Knippenberg, David De Cremer, and Michael A. Hogg, "Leadership, Self, and Identity: A Review and Research Agenda," *Leadership Quarterly* 15 (2004): 825–856.

17. Deborah A. Prentice and Dale T. Miller, eds., *Cultural Divides: Understanding and Overcoming Group Conflict* (New York: Russell Sage, 1999).

18. Julie M. Duck and Kelly S. Fielding, "Leaders and Subgroups: One of Us or One of Them?" *Group Processes and Intergroup Relations* 2 (1999): 203–230; and Julie M. Duck and Kelly S. Fielding. "Leaders and Their Treatment of Subgroups: Implications for Evaluations of the Leader and the Superordinate Group," *European Journal of Social Psychology* 33 (2003): 387–401.

19. For example, Deborah J. Terry, C. J. Carey, and Victor J. Callan, "Employee Adjustment to an Organizational Merger: An Intergroup Perspective," *Personality and Social Psychology Bulletin* 27 (2001): 267–280; and Daan van Knippenberg, Barbara van Knippenberg, L. Monden, and F. de Lima, "Organizational Identification after a Merger: A Social Identity Perspective," *British Journal of Social Psychology* 41 (2002): 233–252.

20. Michael Wenzel, Amelie Mummendey, Ulrich Weber, and Sven Waldzus, "The Ingroup as Pars Pro Toto: Projection from the Ingroup onto the Inclusive Category as a Precursor to Social Discrimination," *Personality and Social Psychology Bulletin* 29 (2003): 461–473.

21. Zachary P. Hohman, Michael A. Hogg, and Michelle C. Bligh, "Identity and Intergroup Leadership: Asymmetrical Political and National Identification in Response to Uncertainty" *Self and Identity* (in press).

22. Hogg, "Intergroup Relations"; and Prentice and Miller, *Cultural Divides: Understanding and Overcoming Group Conflict.*

23. Fathali M. Moghaddam, *Multiculturalism and Intergroup Relations* (Washington, DC: American Psychological Association, 2008); and Maykel Verkuyten, "Multicultural Recognition and Ethnic Minority Rights: A Social Identity Perspective," *European Review of Social Psychology* 17 (2006): 148–184.

24. Muzafer Sherif, *In Common Predicament: Social Psychology of Intergroup Conflict and Cooperation* (Boston: Houghton Mifflin, 1966).

25. Tyler, "The Psychology of Legitimacy: A Relational Perspective on Voluntary Deference to Authorities."

3

On the Social Psychology of Intergroup Leadership

The Importance of Social Identity and
Self-Categorization Processes

Michael J. Platow

The Australian National University

Stephen D. Reicher

University of St. Andrews

S. Alexander Haslam

University of Exeter

THERE ARE at least two ways of getting people to do things. One is to force them against their will—to use coercion to secure compliance. The other is to shape their will—to use social influence to secure conversion. In exploring leadership, we work from the premise that leadership is all about social influence. In our analysis (as well as in much of the social psychology literature), the ability to influence others is the defining feature of leadership.[1] We develop our analysis of leadership from the principles of self-categorization theory.[2] *Self-categorization theory* hypothesizes that people are influenced by others to the extent that they are representative of a currently salient psychological own-group membership. In other words, we are influenced by fellow in-group members, and not by out-group members. There is strong evidence to support this theory.[3]

In one illustrative laboratory study, university science majors were recruited for a study on responses to a painful stimulus.[4] Students participated individually, placing a hand into a bucket of ice water for as long as possible until they could no longer tolerate the pain. Simultaneously, the researchers measured each participant's physiological arousal as a nonreactive measure of anxiety. After doing this once, some participants encountered another student claiming to have been a previous participant in this same study; other participants encountered no one. The second student, actually a confederate of the researchers, described herself as either a fellow science major or an arts major. This was the critical experimental manipulation of group membership. Then the confederate, regardless of supposed group membership, offered reassurance to the real participants that "the second trial is much easier." The critical issue was whether the science-major participants would be influenced by this reassurance. Consistent with predictions, participants were physiologically calmer after receiving reassurance from a fellow in-group member than they were after receiving reassurance from an out-group member or receiving no reassurance at all. In fact, out-group reassurance was no better in influencing participants than not being reassured by anyone.

In regard to our analysis of leadership, note what was really being studied here. The influence attempt was about shaping people's attitudes and behaviors and defining a reality that was, in our example, physically painful. Moreover, the influence attempt was in a domain that had substantive personal consequences (known pain), with the outcomes likely not to be under conscious control (physiological arousal), suggesting true internalization and conversion and not mere compliance. Of course, in the world at large, we are likely to be interested in leadership on a larger scale, but the fundamental point that such studies make is that the process of influence is bound up with perceptions of shared group membership.

Problems of Intergroup Leadership:
Striving to Cross Group Boundaries

It should be clear now that the potential for *intergroup leadership*—of leadership across group boundaries—is a difficult prospect from the outset. This is because of the apparently intractable problem of achieving social influence across group boundaries. To the degree that our analysis of leadership focuses on social influence, and to the degree that social influence is a uniquely in-group process, the prospect of intergroup leadership may in fact seem doomed. As a second example of this difficulty, David and Turner showed that extreme environmentalists had little effect in shaping the actions of moderate groups, and radical feminists had no sway over those who identified with moderate positions.[5]

Does the theoretical and empirical knowledge thus imply that intergroup leadership is simply not possible? Fortunately, the answer is no; this is because psychological group memberships are not fixed, but fluid and context dependent. Continuing our example, David and Turner also showed that, in contexts in which a broader out-group was salient (loggers for environmentalists, men for feminists), the relative inclusiveness of the psychological group membership shifted. Militants were no longer an out-group to the moderate majority, but rather became part of the broader in-group. Indeed, they even came to typify the in-group insofar as their very radicalism now represented not what made them different from moderates but rather what made environmentalists or feminists different from loggers or men. In this context, the militant voice was able to lead the broader movement. Former out-group members were now in-group members, and influence and leadership were possible.

The Importance of Creating a Shared Group Membership

At this point, one way to address the difficulties of intergroup leadership becomes apparent. It may be that, although a leader can influence only in-group members, the in-group can also be defined more inclusively to include those previously excluded from membership and hence from influence. Gaertner, Mann, Murrell, and Dovidio developed this basic idea in their analysis of prejudice reduction.[6] They argued that prejudice could be reduced if people were induced to *recategorize* out-group members as fellow in-group members at a higher level of category inclusiveness. The authors tested this idea experimentally and indeed showed a decrease in evaluative in-group favoritism. Importantly for our current analysis, when participants were asked whom they would like to lead the common group, in-group members were much more likely to be chosen when the intergroup distinction was maintained, but participants actually displayed a preference for erstwhile out-group members when the common group was made salient.

Of course, group members do not simply wait for recategorization to occur and then assume the mantle of leadership. Rather, would-be leaders often actively seek to define categories as broadly as possible in order to influence all those they seek to reach. One of the major skills of leadership is drawing category boundaries so as represent oneself as at one with the broad audience that one seeks to influence. As we have put it, leaders are *entrepreneurs of identity*.[7]

Reicher and Hopkins demonstrated this in their analysis of speeches to the respective parties (Conservative and Labour) of Margaret Thatcher and Neil Kinnock during the British miners' strike of 1984.[8] Both leaders sought to position themselves and their party as representative of an inclusive in-group set against a tiny minority that included the rival. A critical part of the argument involved extending the boundaries of the in-group to include all the electorate and, correspondingly, to diminish the boundaries of the out-group. For Thatcher, the strike was about Britishness (exemplified by working miners and the government) under attack from an alien revolutionary minority (supported by Labour). For Kinnock, the strike was about the lives of ordinary people (exemplified by striking miners and the Labour Party) under attack from an uncomprehending elite (notably Margaret Thatcher herself).

More generally, Reicher and Hopkins suggest that the predominance of the concept of "nation" in the politics of liberal democracies relates more to the audience from which politicians seek approval than to the content of politics.[9] By framing policies in relation to national values and characteristics, leaders can appeal to all those in a given territory who have the right to vote, and not only subsections. Accordingly, what varies between parties is the meaning given to national categories. Each party defines nationhood in a way that accords with its own proposals. Thus, in Scotland, the use of Scottishness is not restricted to the independence-minded Scottish Nationalist Party. It is equally predominant in the pronouncements of the Unionist Conservative Party. It is just that the Scottish Nationalist Party equates Scottishness with independent mindedness, whereas the Conservatives see Scottishness as centered on entrepreneurial values best pursued as part of Britain.

But there are constraints; categories cannot simply be drawn at will. Although recategorization offers an exciting prospect for intergroup leadership, there remain at least two qualifications to any conclusions we draw from the research. First, simply saying, "We're all Americans" or "We're all humans" may have behind it good intentions, but it also is likely to carry unintended consequences if naïvely pursued. If practitioners high-light people's common American group membership, for example, while doing nothing to change the real subgroup status differentials, then the subgroup status differences simply remain. In other words, if the *only* thing we do is emphasize the common superordinate group membership, then we will end up hiding real subgroup intergroup differences. Our rhetoric would say, "We're all Americans," but Anglo as well as, say, Hispanic Americans would know that Hispanics remained the lower-status subgroup and would behave in a manner that reflected this knowledge. This situation, of course, does not take us any further (and may even move us backward) in our quest to bridge the intergroup divide.

Second, there are at least two additional social psychological realities that leaders must come to terms with when emphasizing the shared group membership of people in different subgroups: (a) group members value their subgroup memberships and do not want them ignored, and (b) successful group life that does, in fact, recognize the diversity of subgroup memberships requires the additional commitment of all group members. We consider these two points next.

The Perils of Ignoring Subgroup Memberships

Eggins, Haslam, and Reynolds examined the consequences of respecting or ignoring subgroup identities in the context of an intergroup negotiation, a search to find common ground.[10] The groups in this experiment were based on participants' sex, with participants being asked to negotiate patterns of university health funding for men and women. Participants were expected to approach the negotiation more favorably when each subgroup's (i.e., men's and women's) social identities and interests were first recognized.

This is, in fact, what happened. When the social identities of men and women *as men and women* were first made salient and accorded appropriate respect, they approached the larger intergroup negotiation with relatively high expectations of intergroup consensus, low expectations of out-group bias, and (upon completion) high perceptions of negotiators working well together. This pattern of expectations and perceptions was reversed, however, when the subgroup social identity was ignored, as may happen in naïve attempts to emphasize a common superordinate category. In similar work,

Hornsey and Hogg showed that ignoring subgroup identities actually promoted in-group favoritism rather than reduced it.[11]

Valuing Subgroup Diversity

But what do leaders do once they have emphasized the common super-ordinate identity and respected subgroup identities? Is simple recognition of identities now sufficient for the larger group to push forward? Our research suggests the answer is no. Van Knippenberg, Haslam, and Platow examined this in a survey of working people's attitudes toward gender diversity in their workplace.[12] Here, among gender-diverse work groups, social identification with the superordinate work group increased to the extent that employees had favorable attitudes toward gender-based subgroup diversity. In other words, when people were employed in a group made up of gender-based subgroups, they identified *less* with the overall superordinate group when they did not value subgroup diversity; caring about the overall superordinate group was low when caring for subgroup diversity was low. Again, this result implies that leaders who naïvely emphasize common superordinate group membership run the risk of lowering identification with that superordinate group if they fail to instantiate respect for subgroup diversity.

When leaders try to cross the intergroup divide by emphasizing the shared, superordinate group memberships, they may be successful at reducing previous intergroup hostilities. However, they may also simply obscure real subgroup intergroup differences and even exacerbate intergroup hostilities if they do not display appropriate respect for the subgroups and ensure that the subgroup members actually value the intergroup diversity at the superordinate level.

Leading and Crossing Boundaries by Being Representative of "Us"

We began this chapter by noting that leadership is all about being "one of us" and that it is fellow in-group members whom we are most likely to follow. But will we follow all members of our group equally? The answer, of course, is no, and self-categorization theory provides a concept for understanding relative differences in leadership and social influence. This concept is referred to as *relative in-group prototypicality*.

In simple terms, *prototypicality* is the degree to which, in a particular salient psychological group membership in any given context, group members display behaviors and attitudes that best capture the essence of "us" and what it is that makes us different from "them." The relative prototypicality gradient represents degrees of how "in-group-like" group members are. The more in-group-like people are—the more they capture in their attitudes and behaviors what we are and what we are not—the more influential they will be. So being one of us is important, but that is only a starting point; the more people can capture the essence of us, the better their prospects for leadership.

Relative In-Group Prototypicality and Intragroup Leadership

To explore the importance of a people's in-group prototypicality for their ability to exert influence over others, van Knippenberg and Wilke presented Dutch university students with arguments for and against the use of university entrance exams.[13] Prior to this, however, they experimentally created an in-group-prototypical position along this attitude dimension by giving the students (false) information that support or opposition to the exams was, or was not, representative of their in-group. As expected, greater conformity was obtained from the in-group-prototypical position, whatever it was said to be.

The concept of relative in-group prototypicality can even help explain such seemingly mysterious qualities as charisma. Platow, van Knippenberg, Haslam, van Knippenberg, and Spears, for example, experimentally manipulated the in-group prototypicality of a student leader by describing this person as being either central or peripheral on a series of *unspecified* characteristics defining the in-group.[14] As expected, and despite knowing neither the leader nor the actual characteristics, student participants attributed greater levels of charisma to the in-group-prototypical leader (the one with central in-group characteristics) than to the nonprototypical leader.

In practice, leaders deploy many devices to establish themselves as prototypical of their groups. One device is biography. Whenever leaders talk or write of their pasts, they tend to select (or even invent) episodes that merge individual history with the identity of the groups they seek to guide. For instance, John Major—the most recent British Conservative prime minister—was famously described as the son of a failed circus entertainer. In this way, Major could be seen as experiencing the hardships of ordinary British people, overcoming the accusation that Conservatives were out of touch with the population.

The converse process can also apply. When the leader acquires status as a symbol of the nation and people seek to define the national identity in different ways to promote a different political course of action, one way to do that is to create different histories for the leader. Lodge, for instance, analyzes the different biographies of Nelson Mandela, showing that those promoting an Africanist agenda stress that the formative period in his life was his traditional African childhood.[15] Conversely, those pursuing a modernizing, nonracial agenda focus on Mandela's "rebirth" when he came to be a lawyer in Johannesburg.

Another set of devices surrounds the way in which leaders can draw upon symbolism to liken themselves to iconic figures, real or mythical, of the group's past. For example, the Indonesian leader Sukharno sought to portray himself as Bima, the legendary hero and demigod of Javanese and Balinese mythology. This effort included publishing biographies stressing Sukharno's embodiment of Bima's key qualities of bravery and will. It also included the use of pictures emphasizing the parallel between Sukharno's muscularity and Bima's. It even included Sukharno's use of a booming voice, a low Javanese dialect, and brutal gestures, all of which violated the norms of Indonesia's political class but resonated with both Bima and the broader populace. Sukharno even took on Bima's association with the color black by always being seen with a black baton, often seen as a sacred repository of power.[16]

In sum, the quest for prototypicality does not occur in only one aspect of leadership or another. It needs to be a coherent performance encompassing all that the leader says, does, and is—encompassing even hairstyle (Margaret Thatcher adopted a less feminine style to associate herself with a harsher, more masculine image of Britishness) and dress. Indeed, dress is a particularly important domain, whether it be George W. Bush's all-American leather jackets and cowboy boots or Yasser Arafat's head scarf—the symbol of the Palestinian peasantry and a means of tying Palestinian identity to Palestinian land.[17]

Relative In-Group Prototypicality
and Intergroup Leadership

Platow and van Knippenberg sought to extend the analysis of relative in-group prototypicality to intergroup leadership, asking whether relatively high in-group prototypicality would provide leaders with some leeway in their attempts to bridge the intergroup divide.[18] Participants were presented with an unnamed leader whose unspecified characteristics either were central to those defining the in-group (i.e., relatively high in in-group prototypicality) or were peripheral. Moreover, the leader was described as distributing valued resources either fairly or unfairly between the in-group and a relevant out-group.

Among participants for whom the group really mattered (i.e., among those who psychologically identified with the group), highly prototypical leaders were supported no matter how they distributed the resources between the two groups. However, among this same sample of participants, when leaders were relatively in-group nonprototypical, they *had* to favor the in-group over the out-group in the resource distribution. Thus, in-group-prototypical leaders receive relatively strong support overall from people who value their group membership. But leaders who fail to capture the essence of "us" relative to "them" along some dimension must work much harder to prove their group credentials and are afforded much less latitude to stray from the path of in-group favoritism. Before they can bridge the intergroup divide, leaders must first ensure that they are seen unequivocally as one of us, and not one of them.

Platow et al. followed this study by describing a leader according to *specific* characteristics that were in-group defining and not out-group defining, or out-group defining and not in-group defining.[19] Thus, the leader was said to be quite like the in-group or quite like the out-group. At the same time, participants were presented with a letter supposedly from the leader emphasizing either participants' individuality ("you" and "me") or the group as a whole ("us"). As expected, in-group-prototypical leaders were seen as more charismatic than nonprototypical leaders, although this time the charisma of nonprototypical leaders was enhanced if they emphasized the importance of the group as a whole. Again, being in-group prototypical is a basis for leaders to be seen as charismatic. However, if leaders are, for some reason, in-group nonprototypical, then they must, to be seen as charismatic, work hard to emphasize the collective that they are seeking to lead, thereby establishing their credentials as "one of us."

On the one hand, this research suggests that when there are questions about the degree to which leaders are one of us (i.e., when they are less prototypical), they must do far more to establish their credentials and therefore have far less leeway for action, especially when it comes to making overtures to out-groups and healing intergroup conflicts. It is notable, for instance, that in Northern Ireland, it was the most uncompromising leaders of Loyalist and Republican traditions—Ian Paisley and Martin McGuinness—who emerged as first minister and deputy first minister of the new Northern Ireland Assembly after the Good Friday Agreement had formalized power-sharing arrangements in 1998.[20] More notable still is the fact that they succeeded in this venture when many before them had failed.

On the other hand, however, this research suggests that leaders are not simply fated to succeed or fail as a function of their given level of proto-typicality. Thus far we have argued that even if leaders cannot help who they are, they can alter the extent to which they speak and act in group terms. One can take this argument one step further. Effective leaders can play a part in determining their own prototypicality. Indeed, we suggest that one of the prime skills of leadership lies in describing oneself, one's actions, and one's group so as to make one's leadership appear as the embodiment of a shared social identity. Again, leaders are entrepreneurs of social identity.[21]

Conclusion

We have presented a social-psychological analysis of leadership that places strong emphasis on psychological group memberships. In our view, leadership is all about the ability to influence fellow group members. It is not enough for those seeking leadership positions to hold great visions of future directions, and it is not enough for them to be able to communicate and manage these visions. If no one follows these visions, then would-be leaders remain only on personal quests, and, as initiators of collective projects, they are destined to fail. For it is only when group members are able to elicit the followership of others that leadership emerges. And this ability obtains only when a shared sense of "us" exists between the leader and those followers. For this reason, leadership hinges critically on the management of this sense of shared social identity.[22]

With this as our foundation, we can see that prospects for intergroup leadership are hampered from the outset. Nevertheless, the theoretical analysis provided by self-categorization theory shows that leaders are able to promote intergroup leadership by exploiting the fact that psychological group memberships are highly fluid and context dependent, and that all intergroup relations are actually nested in a common, higher-order group. Thus, an important strategy that leaders can pursue when seeking to bridge the intergroup divide includes emphasizing shared, superordinate group membership. Yet this first step is not sufficient in itself, because isolated (and naïve) implementations of it can (a) ignore (and obscure) real intergroup differences in status, (b) fail to accord appropriate respect that group members demand for their subgroup memberships, and (c) compromise identification with the superordinate group if a shared value of subgroup diversity is not adequately established.

At the same time, would-be leaders who are not sufficiently representative of their group—those who are relatively in-group nonprototypical—will be treated with suspicion and must work to establish more fully their in-group credentials, often by engaging in behaviors counterproductive to the reduction of intergroup hostilities (e.g., by engaging in clear in-group favoritism). In-group-prototypical leaders, by contrast, are accorded greater leeway by their fellow group members in their intergroup overtures.

Finally, we have noted throughout that leaders are not passive in-group members but actively work to construct and reconstruct the actual meaning of the group, often positioning themselves as highly in-group prototypical. Through their rhetoric, would-be leaders can actively create a shared sense of "us" by giving meaning and psychological substance to the group itself.

In sum, then, we see that leadership is all about the way that this sense of shared social identity is created, managed, maintained, and embedded. This, we believe, is the foundational insight of a new psychology of leadership.[23] It takes us beyond the sense of leadership as an individual-level property or process and enables us to see leadership as a group-level phenomenon that is grounded in the dynamic relationship between individuals and groups in a changing and changeable world.

Notes

1. S. Alexander Haslam, *Psychology in Organizations: The Social Identity Approach*, 2nd ed. (London: Sage, 2004); E. P. Hollander, *Leaders, Groups and Influence* (New York: Oxford University Press, 1964).

2. John C. Turner, Michael A. Hogg, Penelope J. Oakes, Stephen D. Reicher, and Margaret S. Wetherell, *Rediscovering the Social Group: A Self-Categorization Theory* (Oxford: Blackwell, 1987).

3. See, for example, John C. Turner, *Social Influence* (Buckingham, UK: Open University Press, 1991).

4. Michael J. Platow, Nicholas J. Voudouris, Melissa Coulson, Nicola Gilford, Rachel Jamieson, Liz Najdovski, Nicole Papaleo, Chelsea Pollard, and Leanne Terry, "In-Group Reassurance in a Pain Setting Produces Lower Levels of Physiological Arousal: Direct Support for a Self-Categorization Analysis of Social Influence," *European Journal of Social Psychology* 37, no. 4 (2007): 649–660.

5. Barbara David and John C. Turner, "Studies In Self-Categorization and Minority Conversion: Is Being a Member of the Out-Group an Advantage?" *Journal of Social Psychology* 35, no. 3 (1996): 179–199.

6. Samuel L. Gaertner, Jeffrey Mann, Audrey Murrell, and John F. Dovidio, "Reducing Intergroup Bias: The Benefits of Recategorization," *Journal of Personality and Social Psychology* 57, no. 2 (1989): 239–249.

7. Stephen D. Reicher, S. Alexander Haslam, and Nick Hopkins, "Social Identity and the Dynamics of Leadership: Leaders and Followers as Collaborative Agents in the Transformation of Social Reality," *Leadership Quarterly* 16, no. 4 (2005): 547–568.

8. Stephen D. Reicher and Nick Hopkins, "Self-Category Constructions in Political Rhetoric: An Analysis of Thatcher's and Kinnock's Speeches Concerning the British Miners' Strike (1984–5)," *European Journal of Social Psychology* 26, no. 3 (1996): 353–371.

9. Stephen D. Reicher and Nick Hopkins, *Self and Nation* (London: Sage, 2001).

10. Rachael A. Eggins, S. Alexander Haslam, and Katherine J. Reynolds, "Social Identity and Negotiation: Subgroup Representation and Superordinate Consensus," *Personality and Social Psychology Bulletin* 28, no. 7 (2002): 887–889.

11. Matthew J. Hornsey and Michael A. Hogg, "Subgroup Relations: A Comparison of Mutual Intergroup Differentiation and Common Ingroup Identity Models of Prejudice Reduction," *Personality and Social Psychology Bulletin* 26, no. 2 (2000): 242–256.

12. Daan van Knippenberg, S. Alexander Haslam, and Michael J. Platow, *Unity Through Diversity: Value-in-Diversity Beliefs, Work Group Diversity, and Group Identification*, ERIM Report Series Reference No. ERS-2007-068-ORG (Rotterdam, The Netherlands: Erasmus Research Institute of Management, 2007).

13. Daan van Knippenberg and Henk Wilke, "Prototypicality of Arguments and Conformity to Ingroup Norms," *European Journal of Social Psychology* 22, no. 2 (1992): 141–155.

14. Michael J. Platow, Daan van Knippenberg, S. Alexander Haslam, Barbara van Knippenberg, and Russell Spears, "A Special Gift We Bestow on You for Being Representative of Us: Considering Leader Charisma from a Self-Categorization Perspective," *British Journal of Social Psychology* 45, no. 2 (2006): 303–320.

15. Tom Lodge, *Mandela: A Critical Life* (Oxford: Oxford University Press, 2006).

16. Ann R. Wilner, *The Spellbinders: Charismatic Political Leadership* (New Haven, CT: Yale University Press, 1984).

17. Ted Swedenburg, "The Palestinian Peasant as National Signifier," *Anthropological Quarterly* 63, no. 1 (1990): 18–30.

18. Michael J. Platow and Daan van Knippenberg, "A Social Identity Analysis of Leadership Endorsement: The Effects of Leader Ingroup Prototypicality and Distributive Intergroup Fairness," *Personality and Social Psychology Bulletin* 27, no. 11 (2001): 1508–1519.

19. Platow et al., "A Special Gift We Bestow on You for Being Representative of Us."

20. Ed Cairns, *Northern Ireland: Power Sharing, Contact, Identity and Leadership* (lecture, Andrew W. Mellon Sawyer Seminar Series on Power-Sharing in Deeply Divided Places, University of Pennsylvania, September 20, 2007).

21. Reicher et al., "Social Identity and the Dynamics of Leadership"; and Reicher and Hopkins, *Self and Nation*.

22. Haslam, *Psychology in Organizations*.

23. S. Alexander Haslam, Stephen D. Reicher, and Michael J. Platow, *The New Psychology of Leadership: Identity, Influence and Power* (New York: Psychology Press, in press); Stephen D. Reicher, S. Alexander Haslam, and Michael J. Platow, "The New Psychology of Leadership," *Scientific American Mind* 17, no. 3 (2007): 22–29.

4

United Pluralism

Balancing Subgroup Identification and
Superordinate Group Cooperation

Margarita Krochik

New York University

Tom R. Tyler

New York University

O VER THE YEARS a considerable amount of research has focused on investigating the traits and skills that produce great leaders. As some organizational scholars suggest, the idea of great leadership has often assumed a heroic, larger-than-life quality.[1] A great deal of energy is devoted to optimizing our understanding of leadership ability. This energy flows from the recognition that the effectiveness of groups, organizations, and societies depends considerably on having leaders who are able to orchestrate, unify, motivate, and coordinate collective action toward shared values and goals.

Although effective leadership is important, it is contingent on the features and qualities that define *groups themselves*, features and qualities that are equally important determinants of group efficacy and success. It is to them that we turn our attention in this chapter. We approach the formulation of an effective leadership strategy in pluralistic intergroup contexts by analyzing the larger (societal or organizational) structure linking diverse groups as well as the dynamics between the people belonging to these more-specific groups and the leaders who want to build coalitions across group divides. Specifically, we describe how fair procedures on the part of leaders foster overarching superordinate social identities and motivate intergroup cooperation without infringing on important subgroup ties.

We begin by discussing the importance of shared superordinate identity in intergroup contexts, and then we turn to its role in promoting cooperation in superordinate groups. We outline two paths to cooperation, focusing on the indirect path from identification with the group to increased attention to the relational information provided by leaders. We explain how fair treatment by leaders can meet these concerns and create a sense of unity across diverse subgroups.

After detailing specific strategies in a four-component model of procedural justice, we go on to discuss its practice in the context of pluralism. We raise questions about the usefulness of assimilationist policies, which assume a conflict between subgroup identification and superordinate identification. We then consider the implications of maintaining a strong subgroup identity vis-à-vis the intergroup cooperation cultivated by fair treatment. After a review of the empirical evidence, we conclude not only that subgroups pose little threat to superordinate identification but also that respect and recognition of these subgroups on the part of leaders may even facilitate cooperation downstream when implemented in tandem with fair treatment and superordinate identification.

The Role of Shared Identity

The people within groups, organizations, and societies are united in many ways. One way is through shared efforts to obtain desired resources. This outcome of interdependence has been widely recognized within social psychology and is central to theories of social exchange.[2] More importantly, people use the groups to which they belong to define themselves and evaluate their self-worth. This second use of groups is detailed in research on social identity and forms the basis of our discussion in this chapter.[3] Identity plays a focal role in how individuals perceive themselves in relation to others around them, in whether they see others as competitors or as members of their team, and in whether individuals internalize and promote group-level values and goals as their own. In other words, social identity—which can be defined along lines of race, class, gender, organization, culture, religion, nationality, or ideology, to name a few—lies at the core of group life.

Because shared group identity facilitates cooperation, participation, and productivity among group members, the proper implementation of identity is an indispensable tool for would-be practitioners of positive leader-follower relations.[4] Leaders are able to influence attitudes, behavior, and performance to the extent that they can engender identification with themselves as leaders and with the group they represent.[5] Moreover, by linking group members' self-esteem and self-efficacy to group well-being, leaders may promote values and behaviors that are instrumental to achieving the group's overarching goals. This use of group identity can be explicit, as when leaders of allied nations emphasize the shared history of their citizens, or it can be more subtle, as when organizational leaders use the word *we* to acknowledge collective achievements and motivate group members' dedication to group causes.

From Superordinate Group Identification to Intergroup Cooperation

Despite the presence of subgroups in society, the superordinate group provides an overarching framework that can unite the subgroups that compose it. Depending on the situation, people may choose to see themselves (i.e., identify) in terms of their gender, their occupation, their political party, their nation, and so on. Yet superordinate identification provides a way to overcome potential subgroup divisions, inspiring various forms of intergroup cooperation.

Research in social psychology consistently finds that the success of the superordinate group is intertwined with personal success and that the well-being of other group members is personally relevant for highly identified individuals. Whether it be young people and old people who identify with each other as members of the same community or Democrats and Republicans who share concerns about global warming, those who identify with superordinate groups are more willing to make voluntary sacrifices to aid their community during a crisis, defer to legal authorities, and work on behalf of their organization.[6] Thus, the first principle for leaders who wish to unite and mobilize the progress of societal or organizational subgroups toward a set of shared societal goals is to emphasize the interdependence and similarity between them.

Fair Treatment as a Path to
Cooperation Across Subgroups

Although a direct path from group identification to cooperation exists (i.e., highly identified individuals cooperate more), this chapter focuses on the indirect path to cooperation because it offers leaders a wider array of action possibilities. The indirect path often begins with some initial basis for group identification (e.g., status as a U.S. citizen), which directs group members' focus to *relational concerns*, such as their status in the larger group—whether they are respected by authorities and group members— and the status of the group itself.[7]

Shifting the focus to these concerns is important, because it changes the information people use to determine whether to cooperate. When deciding whether to cooperate with a decision or policy, members of superordinate groups may focus on instrumental aspects—personal or subgroup outcomes—or relational aspects—procedural justice. Superordinate group leaders may thus motivate cooperation either by providing outcome information—promising individuals or groups material rewards or threatening them with punishment—or by providing treatment that communicates status and respect.

Studies of groups, organizations, and societies make clear that it can be quite difficult for leaders to motivate group members with sanctions or rewards alone.[8] To illustrate this point, one need only conjure the unavoidable difficulty of maintaining motivation in a work environment where people do not know (or care to know) each other by name, regardless of the size of one's paycheck. It is easy to imagine, as well, how severe threats and Orwellian *1984*-style surveillance of employees, citizens, or neighboring nations can backfire by communicating a lack of trust, making group members feel marginalized and ultimately leading to subversive behavior.

Hence, when alternative, noninstrumental bases of cooperation are available, it is to leaders' benefit to implement them. High superordinate identification facilitates the potential for group leaders' fair treatment and fair procedures to inspire group members' cooperation. Some of the most effective electoral campaigns, for example, acknowledge the importance of each individual who pays taxes, casts a vote, or makes an effort to recycle; they also applaud the contributions of the various groups and organizations in society that donate to those in need, lobby government officials, or contribute to the cultural diversity of the nation. Such expressions of respect, evenhandedness, and group pride are even more effective when paired with identity-building strategies, such as inspirational speeches that unify crowds of strangers by referring to a shared experience of historical events or appealing to a universally cherished vision.

From the perspective of leaders, it is preferable that people link their reactions to the group with these noninstrumental criteria or relational issues. Leaders cannot always deliver rewards, nor can they always ensure an environment in which surveillance can effectively detect wrongdoing. In fact, they are especially unlikely to be able to do so during times of crisis or change, when member support is most needed. It is during transitions or downturns that having a cohesive and cooperative group is most central to group success, and yet it is at exactly these times that leaders are the least able to provide resources. Providing relational information, on the other hand, is an economical way for leaders to inspire group cooperation. Asking group members to provide their input when solving a problem or making a decision, for instance, is a surprisingly powerful way to secure their support and invest them in the group outcome—not to mention that it is usually free.

Research supports the idea that identification motivates a relational perspective in the superordinate group—a focus on the fairness of group procedures. For example, advantaged Americans who identify with their nationality are found to be more willing to support policies to help disadvantaged groups when those policies are fairly enacted.[9] In addition, employees are more likely to cooperate with a new company following a merger when the merger is fairly conducted *and* when employees identify with the new company.[10]

Implementing Fair Procedures to Build Identification and Boost Cooperation

Leaders should harness superordinate identification, because people who are highly identified cooperate more and because identification encourages cooperation based on relational rather than instrumental goals (see figure 4-1). How, then, can leaders create and maintain shared group identity if it is not initially high?

Interestingly, the very use of procedural justice can build identification and thus reciprocally boost cooperation. Studies show that one way to increase identification is by treating people fairly. This route to cooperation

FIGURE 4-1

Cooperation resulting from effects of prior identification on procedural justice concerns

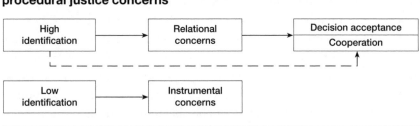

influences the identity and status judgments of group members through the implementation of just decision-making procedures and the maintenance of just interpersonal treatment (see figure 4-2). By applying fair procedures in the intergroup context, such as neutrality in the treatment of various subgroups, leaders motivate group members to identify with the superordinate group. For example, by giving all superordinate group members an equal opportunity to voice their opinions in group discussions regardless of the status of their subgroup, leaders convey a sense of unity and communicate a shared identity that stretches across various subgroup divides. Once superordinate identification is in place, leadership is easier because people attend to how leaders make decisions rather than how favorable those decisions are. As a result, evaluations of leaders, acceptance of their decisions, and cooperation with their group will be determined more by the quality of group procedures and treatment by authorities than by the outcomes subgroups receive from superordinate group leaders.[11] Thus, both procedural justice and identification are necessary facets of the cycle of positive relational feedback and cooperation.

The Four-Component Model of Procedural Justice

Research in organizational settings consistently reveals that evaluations of leaders and the groups they represent are heavily influenced by judgments of the fairness of the procedures used, regardless of the favorability or fairness of the outcomes that result from those procedures.[12] This means that contrary to conventional wisdom, practicing procedural justice in the workplace is more productive than threatening sticks or promising car-

FIGURE 4-2

Cooperation as a function of the interplay of procedures and identification

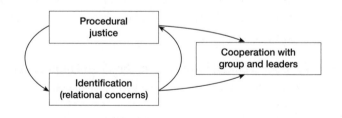

rots. Thus, encouraging employees to provide input into important decisions and avoiding favoritism should, in the long term, facilitate more productivity and compliance than do looming warnings or bonuses in current corporate incentive systems.

Similarly, emphasizing transparency in the process of appointing public officials should be a more effective means of boosting volunteerism than promising to support pork barrel policies for specific people or groups. In fact, even traffic control is likely to be more effective if drivers perceive that tickets for speeding violations and other infractions are issued fairly, based on observed facts, rather than haphazardly, depending on a driver's appearance or ability to sweet-talk an officer out of writing a ticket.

Recent work identifies a four-component model of procedural justice and outlines four significant criteria that practitioners can readily use in crafting a procedurally just leadership strategy. Two aspects of organizational processes and two sources of information about procedures constitute the four-component model and contribute to group members' global procedural-justice judgments. Each or these four components speaks to group members' relational concerns and thus impacts their willingness to cooperate.[13]

- *The quality of leaders' decision-making procedures* is one aspect of organizational processes that group members use to evaluate the procedural justice of their superordinate group. Are decision makers neutral, objective, and factual when they create, implement, and enforce laws, rules, and regulations? Are rules applied consistently across situations and individuals?

- Although it is not directly linked to the decisions being made through the procedure, *the quality of people's treatment by organizational leaders* is an equally important aspect of procedural-justice evaluations. Are interactions with authorities characterized by politeness and dignity? Are leaders concerned about the rights of group members?

Two sources of procedural information, direct and indirect, can inform evaluations of these two aspects of organizational processes.

- The *leadership of the organization* is one source, with leaders providing formal statements of the organization's rules, structure, and values. Does the organization have formal grievance procedures that allow people to voice complaints? Do organizational leaders provide vision statements or emphasize formal laws and rules? Whether by enacting laws that reflect societal values or by emphasizing vision statements that reiterate the values of an organization, leaders can use this component of procedural justice to speak to the relational concerns of group members without having to interact with them directly. This type of information may be especially useful in the context of large groups, such as nations or multinational corporations. Although the president of the United States does not have a personal relationship with most Americans, for example, the president can use these kinds of formal communication to articulate group goals and values, thus providing citizens with a shared basis for identification and cooperation.

- The second source of procedural information is *the quality of direct interpersonal interaction* with delegated authorities who implement the general principles and rules of the organization in the context of particular communities or work groups. Although they are generally constrained by formal rules and procedures, police officers, judges, managers, teachers, mediators, and other officials exercise considerable discretion when implementing these procedures and when resolving specific issues not covered by formal rules.[14] Further, these authorities are often afforded a great deal of flexibility in how they treat the group members with whom they interact. Do managers implement formal procedures rudely and dismissively, or do they emphasize the dignity of the employees involved?

Each of the four components defined along these two dimensions plays an important role in shaping overall procedural-justice evaluations. Each has the potential to communicate positive identity-relevant information and thus to encourage positive evaluations of the superordinate group and its leaders. Because it is part of a coherent whole, however, any one component is insufficient if it is not developed in tandem with the others. For example, even a celebrated bill of rights would do little to soothe minority subgroups whose everyday lives are beleaguered by racist police or sexist managers.

The upshot of this multifaceted procedural-justice strategy—when it is properly implemented—is that group members will increasingly base their evaluations on noninstrumental, nonmaterial concerns, and these concerns will encourage them to continue to identify and cooperate with the superordinate group. Given these substantial benefits, leaders are urged to incorporate procedural-justice principles into their dealings with group members and to consider the potential role of such strategies in reducing reliance on material incentives, which can result in subgroup competition rather than superordinate cooperation, in addition to being financially costly.

Practicing Procedurally Just Leadership in the Context of Pluralism

Fostering superordinate identification and cooperation through procedural justice may be straightforward in some contexts, such as a basketball game, but most real-world intergroup contexts are much more complex. In multicultural societies and organizations, group members often experience strong ties to cultural, racial, religious, or political subgroups, which constitute an essential part of their identity.

The presence of such diversity poses special problems for superordinate group leaders to the extent that it highlights subgroup boundaries in the context of a larger group. If people are loyal to their subgroups, they may focus on the specific concerns those groups represent, diverting attention from the larger group. For this reason, policy makers historically have favored practices and arrangements that attempt to fold marginalized groups into the mainstream. Such policies, referred to as *assimilation*, involve encouraging people to minimize their loyalty to subgroups in order to emphasize the superordinate group.

Assimilation Versus Biculturalism

Hailed by playwrights and politicians alike, the idea of assimilation holds a defining presence in U.S. history and continues to influence contemporary prescriptions for minority engagement in the superordinate U.S. enterprise. However, although the idea of mending long-standing rifts between subgroups by eliminating perceptions of difference may be intuitively appealing, research in social psychology suggests that doing away with subgroups does little, if anything, to improve superordinate group identification and cooperation. In fact, there is empirical reason to believe that subgroup identification may actually supplement superordinate group identification; further, neglecting the relevance of such subgroup identification may even dampen the superordinate identity-enhancing effects of procedural justice, resulting in reduced cooperation with the superordinate group.

Assimilation and the Illusion of Group Identity Conflict

Why are subgroups seen to pose a threat to the cohesion of the superordinate group? According to the assimilationist perspective, if ethnic minorities in the United States do not abandon their ethnic ties in exchange for heightened superordinate group membership, the defining values and institutions that enable U.S. viability will be jeopardized. With regard to the procedural-justice strategies advocated in this chapter, one concern might be that leaders will not be able to engage superordinate group members by treating them with neutrality and respect if those group members identify with the subgroup *instead of* with the superordinate group. If this were the case, it would be futile to try to address the relational concerns of superordinate members, because one's relationship with the group (e.g., one's status in the group) is less relevant when identification with that group is low.

However, there is no reason to assume that subgroup and superordinate group identification are diametrically opposed. Strong identification with one's nation does not necessarily imply a weak relationship with, for example, one's ethnic group. Subgroup and superordinate group identification are not polar opposites on a single continuum but rather two independent identities that can be maintained simultaneously, so that the extent to which one identifies with one's work group is not inherently related to how much one identifies with the company—or with one's country. The fact that two individuals belong to two different linguistic subgroups (e.g., one speaks Spanish and the other Portuguese) does not mean that they cannot both identify with being American. People of different church denominations can still find a shared identity in being Christian, and people belonging to different racial subgroups may still feel bound to the same local community. Thus, because subgroup differences do not necessarily interfere with a shared superordinate identity, the impact of fair procedures on cooperation should not be diminished by acknowledging that these differences exist.

Research in social psychology is consistent with this reasoning. Work on social cognition has shown that people's cognitive representations of themselves are made up of more than one identity.[15] Meanwhile, justice and groups researchers have examined the viability of procedurally just leadership in a pluralistic context and have found that strong identification with a subgroup was not related to the strength of identification with the superordinate group. In addition, the extent to which people identified with a racial or ethnic subgroup was not found to influence the relationship between how identified people were with their superordinate group and how much relational cues about fairness from leaders representing the superordinate group mattered to them. Assimilators, who identified only with the superordinate category, and biculturalists, who identified with both the subgroup and the superordinate group, attended equally to the way their leaders treated them.[16]

These findings suggest that cooperation with societal regulations, norms, and values is quite plausible in a pluralistic context where loyalties to subgroups run high, at least when the values endorsed by the subgroups do not inherently conflict with those of the superordinate group. This type of societal cooperation is best achieved by means of respectful and impartial treatment of the members of all subgroups on the part of leaders. The psychological bottom line is that if superordinate identification is strong, leaders can appeal to that level of identification to effectively manage a pluralistic group.

Subgroup Respect as a Catalyst for Superordinate Group Success

Many individual-level and group-level benefits have been attributed to the presence of diversity in the superordinate group, ranging from higher self-esteem to increases in innovation and improvement in workplace performance. On the other hand, when the superordinate identity is pit-ted against and framed as superior to other subgroup identities, as is the case with assimilationist policies, the sources of identity that are relevant to the individual are implicitly devalued. Such threats to the value of one's subgroup can exacerbate social conflict and antagonize minority or low-status groups.[17] Because individuals strive to achieve the optimal balance between being a part of groups and being different from other group mem-bers, subgroup identification may satisfy the need to be distinct from one's superordinate group without forcing members to disidentify with it.[18]

In line with this idea, research on institutional messages of assimilation has found that these messages can backfire and lead to disengagement and withdrawal from the institution's goals and values.[19] Respect for the sub-group by leaders encourages subgroup members to make a positive evalu-ation of the superordinate group, as well as of its leaders and its justice system.[20] These findings imply that people will disregard identity-relevant cues, such as fair treatment and respect, from leaders who represent the superordinate group if these cues suggest that leaders do not respect their specific subgroup. Subgroup members should not be put in a position in which they feel that endorsing the superordinate group means that they are endorsing disrespect for their subgroup.

Thus, if the procedural-justice approach is to be harnessed to advantage and used to cultivate cooperation among superordinate group members, a dual-identity approach must be adopted. When leaders acknowledge a val-ued aspect of the self instead of simply ignore it, followers are more pre-disposed to imbue the leaders and their actions with trust and legitimacy.

Conclusion

The policy message is clear. Rather than encourage people to stop identi-fying with their respective subgroups, leaders are advised to shift the focus of the group to the level of superordinate identity. This practice creates a common basis for shared group membership. In doing so, the leader facil-itates the merger of self and group, shifting the emphasis from outcomes to the quality of the decision making and interpersonal treatment pro-vided by the authorities representing the superordinate group. The leaders can use fair procedures to both create and maintain superordinate group identification and to foster cooperation between subgroup members.

Two specific elements of procedures are important: (a) decision mak-ing—whether or not a voice is given to the individual by neutral and consistent authorities, and (b) interpersonal treatment—whether the leader is courteous, respectful, and supportive. The presence of these two elements should increase both cooperation and reciprocal identification with the superordinate group.

Notes

1. James R. Meindl and Sanford B. Ehrlich, "The Romance of Leadership and the Evaluation of Organizational Performance," *Academy of Management Journal* 30, no. 1 (1987): 91–109.

2. John W. Thibaut and Harold H. Kelley, *The Social Psychology of Groups* (Oxford: Wiley, 1959).

3. Henri Tajfel and John Turner, "The Social Identity Theory of Intergroup Behavior," in *The Psychology of Intergroup Relations*, ed. Stephen Worchel (Chicago: Nelson-Hall, 1986), 7–24.

4. Tom R. Tyler and Steven L. Blader, *Cooperation in Groups: Procedural Justice, Social Identity, and Behavioral Engagement* (New York: Psychology Press, 2000).

5. Barbara van Knippenberg, Daan van Knippenberg, David De Cremer, and Michael A. Hogg, "Research in Leadership, Self, and Identity: A Sample of the Present and a Glimpse of the Future," *Leadership Quarterly, Special Issue: Leadership, Self, and Identity* 16, no. 4 (2005): 495–499.

6. Tom R. Tyler and Peter Degoey, "Collective Restraint in Social Dilemmas: Procedural Justice and Social Identification Effects on Support for Authorities," *Journal of Personality and Social Psychology* 69, no. 3 (1995): 482–497; Tom R. Tyler and Yuen J. Huo, *Trust in the Law: Encouraging Public Cooperation with the Police and Courts* (New York: Russell Sage, 2002); and Tyler and Blader, *Cooperation in Groups.*

7. Tom R. Tyler and Allen E. Lind, "A Relational Model of Authority in Groups," in *Advances in Experimental Social Psychology*, vol. 25, ed. Mark P. Zanna (San Diego: Academic Press, 1992), 115–191.

8. Tom R. Tyler, "Psychological Perspectives on Legitimacy and Legitimation," *Annual Review of Psychology* 57 (2006): 375–400.

9. Heather J. Smith and Tom R. Tyler, "Justice and Power: When Will Justice Concerns Encourage the Advantaged to Support Policies Which Redistribute Economic Resources and the Disadvantaged to Willingly Obey the Law?" *European Journal of Social Psychology* 26, no. 2 (1996): 171–200.

10. Tom R. Tyler and David De Cremer, "Process-Based Leadership: Fair Procedures and Reactions to Organizational Change," *Leadership Quarterly, Special Issue: Leadership, Self, and Identity* 16, no. 4 (2005): 529–545.

11. Tom R. Tyler, "Social Justice: Outcome and Procedure," *International Journal of Psychology, Special Issue: Diplomacy and Psychology* 35, no. 2 (2000): 117–125.

12. Tyler and Blader, *Cooperation in Groups.*

13. Steven L. Blader and Tom R. Tyler, "A Four-Component Model of Procedural Justice: Defining the Meaning of a 'Fair' Process," *Personality and Social Psychology Bulletin* 29, no. 6 (2003): 747–758.

14. Tyler and Huo, *Trust in the Law.*

15. Marilynn B. Brewer, "The Social Self: On Being the Same and Different at the Same Time," *Personality and Social Psychology Bulletin* 17, no. 5 (1991): 475–482.

16. Yuen J. Huo, "Procedural Justice and Social Regulation Across Group Boundaries: Does Subgroup Identity Undermine Relationship-Based Governance?" *Personality and Social Psychology Bulletin* 29, no. 3 (2003): 336–348.

17. Matthew J. Hornsey and Michael A. Hogg, "Assimilation and Diversity: An Integrative Model of Subgroup Relations," *Personality and Social Psychology Review* 4, no. 2 (2000): 143–156.

18. Brewer, "The Social Self," 475.

19. Jennifer Crocker, Brenda Major, and Claude Steele, *Social Stigma* (New York: McGraw-Hill, 1998).

20. Yuen J. Huo, Ludwin E. Molina, Rina Sawahata, and Josephine M. Deang, "Leadership and the Management of Conflicts in Diverse Groups: Why Acknowledging Versus Neglecting Subgroup Identity Matters," *European Journal of Social Psychology* 35, no. 2 (2005): 237.

5

Imaginative Leadership

How Leaders of Marginalized Groups
Negotiate Intergroup Relations

Jolanda Jetten

University of Queensland/University of Exeter

Frank Mols

University of Queensland

WE ARE OFTEN fascinated with leadership. We can feel inspired by effective leaders, we look to them as role models, and we wish that we too could command such fervor. We are captivated by leaders who have achieved positive outcomes, such as Martin Luther King, Jr., and Mahatma Gandhi, and we buy autobiographies written by influential leaders in the hope we can learn from them. In our admiration we often put effective leaders on a pedestal, because there seems to be something special about them. At the same time, we are horrified by the influence of leaders who have been able to mobilize others to turn their destructive ideas into reality, such as Adolf Hitler and Joseph Stalin.

There is a difference, however, between the great leaders of this century, leaders of the caliber of Nelson Mandela or Mahatma Gandhi, and the leaders who are described in the many "how to become an effective leader" guidebooks we find in every airport terminal. Keys that describe effective leadership in such guidebooks include having vision and passion, inspiring others, setting and achieving goals, and possessing charisma. Although these characteristics may describe world leaders such as Mandela and Gandhi, the key to understanding their leadership is that they represented groups that were marginalized, powerless, and discriminated against by those in power (whites in South Africa, and the British colonizers in India).

What made their leadership different from other types of leadership is that they were able to lead despite persecution, imprisonment, and other obstacles. Their reality stands in contrast to the implicit assumption often found in leadership research: that leaders can choose from a wide range of strategies. We argue that this is why existing leadership models are inadequate for understanding leadership of groups that are marginalized: leaders of marginalized groups are seldom in a position to choose what course of action to take to achieve group goals.

We argue that Gandhi and King became exceptional leaders because they intrigued us with the mysterious way they managed to mobilize their groups and the fact that they succeeded against all odds, and with minimal material resources, as exemplified by Gandhi's salt marches in India. Despite the lack of material resources, these leaders managed to draw the attention of the world to the devalued status and the illegitimate treatment their group was receiving. This, we argue, was possible because their understanding of the needs of the group became their main resource—a resource they were able to harness effectively.

Indeed, we argue that the fact that actions of leaders of devalued groups are constrained by the context in which they operate is crucial in understanding the leadership style of such leaders. Whereas the success of presidents, prime ministers, and CEOs is often measured in terms of how well the leader chose between different tools and methods to achieve group goals, the leadership success of marginalized groups is unique in that its success is often judged solely on the basis of whether leaders managed to bring about social change and status improvement for their group.

The question that emerges is, Why was Mandela's and Gandhi's leadership so effective? How could they achieve so much with so little? We argue that the study of leadership in devalued groups makes clear that leadership must be studied in context.[1] The examples of Gandhi and Mandela illustrate that effective leadership depends on leaders harnessing their relationship with the group (i.e., their followers).[2] In our analysis of leadership, we rely on recent theorizing derived from the social identity approach.[3] In this view, leadership is made possible when leaders build a sense of shared identity with those who follow.[4] The extent to which groups and their leaders share identity determines the extent to which leaders can change, influence and steer the group, and manage intergroup relations. The idea that leadership is a property of the group, and not of the individual, is now well understood and provides an influential analysis of leadership.[5] It allows us to move beyond individualistic accounts of leadership and to conceive of leadership as an outcome of shared social identity.

In this chapter, we discuss leadership strategies that leaders of marginalized groups can consider, and we give examples to illustrate our point. We start from the assumption that it is not simply a coincidence or a matter of fate that determines whether leaders are perceived as representative of their group. Those who have leadership aspirations are not passive in this process, but actively maneuver in such a way that their behavior appears to be aligned with the goals of the group. Indeed, leaders are very much *entrepreneurs of identity*, in the sense that they proactively steer this process.[6] Leaders read the situation, decide what is required, and position themselves accordingly.

Leaders' Responses to Marginalization

Our analysis assumes that leadership strategies are affected by the nature of group processes. That is, leaders' actions are shaped, fueled, and also at times restricted, by the nature of intergroup relations. Central to our reasoning is the idea that the strategy leaders adopt is largely determined by what the intergroup context affords. Whereas leaders of powerful high-status groups are able to change the actual social, economic, political, or organizational landscape, leaders of powerless, marginalized groups are forced to resort to very different and more-creative strategies.

In particular, we predict that leaders will be sensitive to perceptions of whether there are alternative ways to achieve group goals (so-called cognitive alternatives).[7] We argue that leaders who have no access to conventional means to bring about social change do not have to accept defeat; there are alternative routes.[8] Being able to imagine another, more equitable future appears to be the catalyst that triggers important social change.

For instance, stating that there were alternative ways to think about race relations lies at the core of Martin Luther King, Jr.'s 1963 "I have a dream" speech. In this famous speech, King described a future that is radically different from the present: "I have a dream that one day on the red hills of Georgia the sons of former slaves and the sons of former slave owners will be able to sit down together at the table of brotherhood." By imagining a future where black and white live peacefully together, as equals, he moved the group's agenda to thinking about ways that would allow this dream to become reality, providing the group with a redefined self-understanding, a new frame of reference for judging the appropriateness of responses and collective action. When Rosa Parks questioned whether she had to sit in the back of the bus, she did more than question the fairness of a rule; she questioned the validity of an entire belief system about race relations. We now recognize that this event was an important trigger for the civil rights movement.

In the sections that follow, we map out the ways in which the perceptions of alternatives to perceived group relations affect the strategies leaders may engage in to represent their group and achieve important group goals. Key to our reasoning is the idea that leaders' perceptions about the various ways group goals can be achieved will affect their leadership style. There are two further points that are important. First, perceptions of alternatives do not come out of the blue. Indeed, actions such as those of Martin Luther King, Jr., and Rosa Parks should be perceived in the context of their group's broader struggle. Their actions were consequential and could take root only at a time when the group as a whole was ready to imagine a different future.

Second, we argue that the perception of alternatives is not necessarily triggered by changes to the group itself; often, these alternatives are perceived because marginalized group members and their leaders feel that there is instability in the broader group landscape and that change is in the air. For example, witnessing the fall of the communist government in Hungary in the late 1980s raised awareness among citizens of other East European countries that they did not have to think of themselves as citizens of nations loyal to communist Moscow. This arguably was one factor that led to the fall of the Berlin wall in 1989.

We focus on two changes in the broader intergroup context that open up possibilities for marginalized groups to conceive of an alternative future (see figure 5-1 for an overview). In particular, we predict that there is ample scope for leaders to redefine the group's self-understanding when it is possible to imagine an identity alliance (a) with a more powerful group or (b) with another marginalized group.

FIGURE 5-1

Social context affecting perceptions of alternatives and leadership strategies

Opportunities afforded by
the intergroup context   Leadership strategies

Many alternatives for marginalized group

(a) Alliance formation with a more powerful group
(b) Alliance formation with another marginalized group

Social creativity strategies

Few alternatives for marginalized group

(a) Development of rebel or dissident identity
(b) Schisms within the marginalized group

Social change strategies

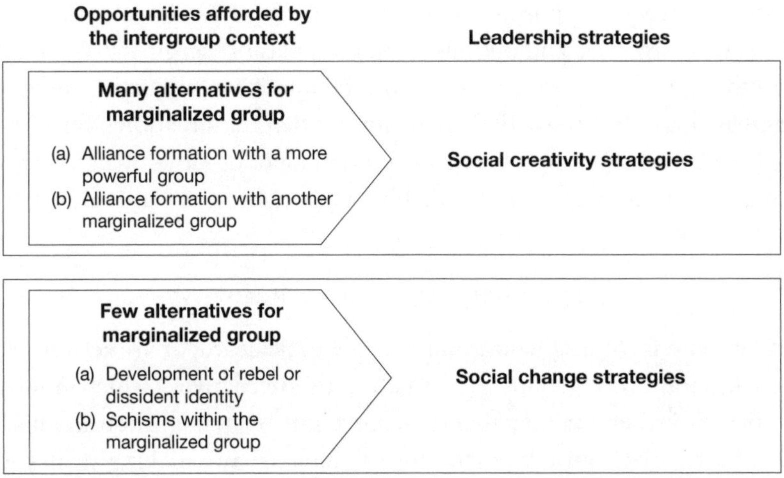

Of course, it is also possible that there are no opportunities to pursue alliance formation. In that case marginalized groups and their leaders must go it alone and challenge the status quo directly. Faced with a lack of potential alliance partners, leaders of such groups are more likely to resort to more-extreme responses to achieve group goals.[9] In that context, marginalized groups may set themselves apart from the dominant group by developing a rebel or dissident identity. It is also likely that, under these conditions, tension will increase about how to achieve group goals. Differing opinions about how to best represent the marginalized group may lead to a schism within the group in which some factions embark on a more radical agenda to achieve group goals.

The strategies identified in figure 5-1 should not be seen as a typology of leadership strategies. We warn against this because the list of strategies is not exhaustive, and leaders can use a combination of strategies to achieve group goals. Moreover, leaders of marginalized groups may abandon one strategy in favor of another as soon as intergroup relations change or when addressing different audiences. For instance, although Welsh intellectuals called themselves Welsh–European in the 1980s, this alliance-formation strategy became less popular after Wales was granted devolved powers by the central British government.

As we indicated earlier, leaders of marginalized groups do not simply reflect existing intergroup power relations. Instead, they negotiate these relations and actively push for a certain representation of reality. Whether there are alternatives and options to realize goals of marginalized groups is therefore very much in the eye of the beholder—a subjective judgment that may not reflect the actual opportunities that the situation affords.[10] Indeed, leaders may decide to emphasize certain options rather than others and to pursue certain strategies afforded by the social context and not others.[11]

When There Are Many Alternatives

Leaders who face marginalization, struggle to be heard, or are actively sidelined by dominant groups are sensitive to alternatives, which hold the promise that they may be able to achieve greater recognition in another way. Alternatives can take many forms, such as laws making it illegal to discriminate on the basis of race or gender, which open up opportunities for members of these marginalized groups. We focus here on ways that other groups' actions and alliances with other groups can increase the perception that there are alternative ways to conceive of the future.

In particular, by forming an alliance with other groups, marginalized groups are likely to feel stronger in their struggle for recognition, and alternative futures become possible (i.e., "standing strong together"). The nature of the allied group is important, because it affects the way goals of marginalized groups are achieved. We distinguish and discuss two types of alliance strategies: alliance with a more powerful group and with another marginalized group.

Alliance Formation with a Powerful Group

Leaders of marginalized groups often try to form alliances with powerful external groups as a way to achieve group goals and enhance the status of the marginalized group. One could argue that the special relationship between the United Kingdom and the United States, which has characterized British foreign policy for many decades, has been fueled in part by the United Kingdom's "awkward partnership" with the European Union and its reputation as a reluctant EU member on the EU's western periphery.[12] This strategy provides the marginalized group clear benefits. By associating itself with a more powerful group, the marginalized group feels protected. It gains not only material benefits in terms of having access to opportunities that otherwise would not be available (e.g., financial and material resources) but also can turn its back on the groups that marginalized it.

Arguably, there is a price to be paid for forming an alliance with a dominant group. Because of the power asymmetry, it is likely that the norms and rules of the powerful partner will overshadow those of the less powerful group. For example, political commentators have accused former British prime minister Tony Blair of being uncritical of the U.S.–led "war on terror," portraying Blair as George W. Bush's "poodle." Another downside of forming an alliance with a powerful partner is that alienation from other groups is often inevitable. In the case of British foreign policy, it could be argued that precisely because the British government felt secure in its strong alliance with the United States, it did not feel much need to consult its European Union partners. This may have led to loss of voice on the European Union stage.

Forging an alliance with a powerful group typically involves portraying the marginalized group's identity as naturally compatible with the identity of the more powerful group. For example, when Yasser Arafat addressed the UN General Assembly in 1988, he stated, "The State of Palestine is an Arab State; its people are an integral part of the Arab nation [. . .], its civilization, and its aspiration to attain its goals of social progress, unity and liberation."[13] A similar dynamic was witnessed in research into EU attitudes among politicians in peripheral regions in the United Kingdom.[14] Not only did these politicians portray their regional identity and European identity as naturally compatible, but also they portrayed the EU as an ally in the struggle for greater regional autonomy.

Alliance Formation with Another Marginalized Group

Although it is easy to understand why marginalized groups would like to forge an alliance with a powerful group, it is more difficult to explain why, at times, marginalized groups form alliances with each other. Consider, for example, the "identity alliance" between Yasser Arafat and Saddam Hussein in the lead-up to the first Gulf War. Arafat mentioned in his January 1990 address at a rally in Baghdad that "Iraq and Palestine represent a common will. We will be together side by side and after the great battle, God willing, we will pray together in Jerusalem."[15] It is likely that alliances typically are formed with other marginalized groups when there is no opportunity to form an alliance with a more powerful group. Such alliances may also be formed when marginalized groups perceive that they share negative views of the dominant groups and when the alliance is expected to force powerful out-groups to take notice. For instance, Hitler's decision to form an alliance with Stalin can be seen as his message to the victorious allied forces of World War I that Germany was still a force to be reckoned with. As these two cases illustrate, this kind of alliance formation can backfire, certainly if it unites rather strange bedfellows. However, it can also be effective, as can be seen in the World Social Forum, which brings together fringe movements such as human rights activists and environmentalists under the banner of "antiglobalization."

Although the two types of alliances—with a powerful group and with another marginalized group—are associated with slightly different leadership strategies, what they have in common is that they represent leaders pursuing a so-called social creativity agenda.[16] Characteristic of social creativity alliance strategies is that leaders work within the confines of the social reality, reinterpret it, but do little to actively change it. Because direct confrontation with the dominant group is not feasible, these leaders do not question the other group's right to dominate. Instead, they try to achieve their goals indirectly by creatively reinterpreting the social reality, by subtly bypassing the dominant group, or by strengthening bonds with like-minded groups that face similar challenges. Paradoxically, it thus appears that the greater the scope for alliance formation, the less likely it becomes that groups will challenge intergroup relations, and the more likely it is that groups will work *with* the system to achieve goals. This reasoning is compatible with social identity theory, reasoning that marginalized groups will explore all options that the context affords to improve their fate.

When There Are Few Alternatives

In line with social identity theory reasoning, we predict that revolutionary movements take root only when groups perceive that there are few other groups with which to form an alliance (i.e., when there are few alternatives). This perception can emerge for a number of reasons. For example, alliances that worked in the past may break down or simply may not bring the improvement of status that the marginalized group was hoping for. Alternatively, forming alliances with other groups may never have been an option. In these circumstances, a sense of isolation is likely to emerge, forcing those who aspire to social change to revert to more-confrontational tactics. In sum, when social creativity (alliance) strategies are not an option, then members of marginalized groups experience a sense of frustration and isolation, and the group leader is forced to become more radical and to pursue an agenda of social change.[17]

In what follows, we discuss two ways in which leaders of marginalized groups may challenge the status quo when they perceive there to be few alternatives to the current status relations. The first strategy focuses on situations wherein conflict with the dominant group becomes overt. In such situations, marginalized groups and their leaders may decide to call for collective action to address the legitimacy of their marginalized status. In this process, leaders of marginalized groups may take on the role of rebels or dissidents to achieve group goals.

Second, we predict that the lack of alternatives may lead to internal tension in the group. The comparison with a pressure cooker comes to mind: the more the steam is trapped in the cooker, the more pressure in the system builds up because there are no ways to vent the system. Along similar lines, a lack of options for achieving group goals increases tension in the group and may lead to discussions about how to pursue group goals. This may lead to polarization and breakdowns whereby some faction and its leaders may pursue a more radical agenda to achieve group goals (see figure 5-1).

Development of a Rebel or Dissident Identity

In response to marginalization, groups that perceive few alternatives are likely to turn their backs on the system. Leaders may set their group apart and emphasize that their group is different. Under such conditions, intergroup differences are not downplayed, but emphasized.[18] For instance, an important first step of the civil rights movement was for African Americans to emphasize that they were different from the majority. Emphasizing "us versus them" raises awareness of the group's status and its unique concerns. It facilitates the development of a sense of common fate, and this is often an important first step toward the development of a "politicized identity" in which groups respond to their devalued status collectively rather than individually.[19]

Leaders may cultivate and exaggerate perceptions of intergroup differences to raise collective awareness—a point illustrated in the following interchange between a (white) court judge and the black activist Steve Biko during South Africa's apartheid period:

JUDGE BOSHOFF: But now why do you refer to your people as blacks?
Why not brown people? I mean you people are more brown than black.

BIKO: In the same way as I think White people are more pink and
yellow and pale than white.

[General laughter in the court]

JUDGE BOSHOFF: Quite . . . but now why do you not use the word
brown then?

BIKO: No, I think really, historically, we have been defined as Black
people, and when we reject the term non-White and take upon ourselves the right to call ourselves what we think we are, we have got
available in front of us a whole number of alternatives . . . and we
choose this one precisely because we feel it is most accommodating."[20]

This excerpt illustrates how leaders themselves can create a dissident
identity by setting the group apart and by making clear that they do not
want their group to be subjected to the rules imposed by the dominant
group. Standing on the side allows them to comment and criticize the actions of the dominant group without being bound by its rules and norms.
Dissidents' actions are aimed at provoking the dominant group, and, by
demanding that it justify its actions, the leaders of the marginalized group
become a force to be reckoned with.[21]

Interestingly, these leaders are perhaps the best example of creatively
working within the constraints provided by the social context. Rather than
engage in a social creativity strategy—such as redefining the situation as
one where "we have to make the best of it"—they take a more militant
stance. As a result these leaders can be highly influential, because, by scru-
tinizing the actions of dominant groups and by questioning the legitimacy
of their actions, they often become the moral consciousness of a society or
act as devil's advocates (e.g., the crusade against political correctness and
cultural relativism by Theo van Gogh, Pim Fortuyn, and Ayaan Hirsi Ali
in the Netherlands). This influence not only gives these leaders authority
and followers, but it also increases their power to channel raised collective
awareness to change group relations. Importantly, rebel leaders may lose
their influence after the status of the marginalized group is raised. Their
appeal lies in challenging the status quo, and not necessarily in their ability to lead a group when collective action has been effective and the mar-

ginalized group has obtained more voice (examples include Mikhail Gorbachev and Leon Trotsky in the former Soviet Union).

Schisms in Marginalized Groups

Just as there are different ways to represent marginalized groups, there may be opposing forces, divisions, and heated debates in these groups about how to pursue group goals. On the one hand, some may pursue a conciliatory agenda and remain willing to work with the dominant group to achieve the marginalized group's goals. Even though this strategy may be effective, there is an associated cost, because, implicitly, the legitimacy of the power of the dominant groups is recognized.

On the other hand, others may favor radical ways of challenging the status quo and undermining the power of the dominant groups. In extreme cases, such behavior leads to violence against dominant groups and even terrorism.

Schisms in marginalized groups are quite common.[22] For example, once the Irish Republican Army (IRA) laid down its weapons and allowed its more-moderate leaders (Sinn Fein) to negotiate a peaceful resolution to the Northern Ireland conflict, a small group of more-militant IRA members separated itself from the IRA. This group called itself the "Real IRA" (RIRA) and carried out a series of terrorist attacks to underscore its aspirations—a united Ireland.

Marginalized groups' leaders can choose to downplay disagreements about strategies to achieve group goals, or alternatively they can exaggerate differences. When they choose to highlight differences between factions, they often present the issue as one requiring fundamental debate about what the group stands for and argue that the opposing faction is morally weak, willing to sell out to the enemy, and subverting the true identity of the group.[23] However, leaders are aware that schisms involve considerable opportunity cost, because, at least temporarily, they reduce the power of the subgroup and divert attention from the collective cause.

Conclusion

When we think of great leaders, we tend to think of leaders who gained worldwide fame for the mysterious way in which they managed to lead a marginalized group out of marginalization. Indeed, they become iconic examples of exceptional leadership because they are able to achieve the unthinkable, or rather, because they are able to imagine the unthinkable. Given the abundance of examples, it is somewhat surprising that an analysis of leadership of marginalized groups is lacking. We argue that the study of leaders of marginalized groups reveals that to understand leadership, one must understand the broader social context in which leaders operate.[24] Effective leadership is not about personality or access to resources but instead resides in individuals who understand group needs, become one with the group, and strategically use the opportunities the social context affords.

We argue that leadership strategies are shaped by the extent to which alternative ways of conceiving of intergroup relations is possible. We argue that alternatives often take shape when marginalized groups form alliances either with other, more powerful groups or with groups that are equally marginalized. Often, forming an alliance with other groups means that marginalized groups feel that there are alternative ways to achieve group goals because the ally will help in the pursuit of group goals. However, we also point out that by forming an alliance, marginalized groups run the danger that the pursuit of their own goals can be sidetracked or become diluted. In particular when an alliance is sought with a more powerful group, marginalized groups implicitly accept the status quo; if they achieve group goals they do so by playing by the rules of the dominant system and by not actively challenging status relations. Many developing countries find themselves in this situation when they accept aid and resources from more-developed Western countries.

Interestingly, when we think of the great leaders of the twentieth century, it becomes clear that these individuals often did not have powerful allies to assist in their struggle. These leaders and their groups often fought a battle in which they were on their own, isolated, and rejected by all. We argue that despite the lack of material resources and allies, these leaders were effective because they understood that the goals of the group could be achieved by speaking to the imagination of their followers. Indeed, the future may have looked bleak, but these leaders were able to paint a picture of the future that matched processes that were set in motion by the group as a whole (e.g., overthrowing apartheid in South Africa).

Often, effective leadership is portrayed as a matter of personality and the ability to choose wisely among alternative courses of action. However, our analysis shows that exceptional leadership is characterized by imaginative leadership—the leader's ability to redefine the nature of a conflict and to persuade the group of the feasibility of a brighter future.

Notes

Authors' note: This chapter was supported by a large grant from the Economic and Social Research Council. We would like to thank Alex Haslam, Matthew Hornsey, and Michael Wohl for helpful comments on a previous draft of this chapter.

1. Alexander S. Haslam, *Psychology in Organizations: The Social Identity Approach* (London: Sage, 2001).

2. Edwin P. Hollander, "Organizational Leadership and Followership," in *Social Psychology at Work: Essays in Honour of Michael Argyle*, ed. Peter Collett and Adrian Furnham (London: Routledge, 1995), 69–87.

3. Henri Tajfel and John C. Turner, "An Integrative Theory of Intergroup Conflict," in *The Social Psychology of Intergroup Relations*, ed. William Austin and Stephen Worchel (Monterey, CA: Brooks/Cole, 1979), 33–47.

4. Michael A. Hogg, "A Social Identity Theory of Leadership," *Personality and Social Psychology Review* 5 (2001): 184–200.

5. Haslam, *Psychology in Organizations.*

6. Stephen D. Reicher and S. Alexander Haslam, "On the Agency of Individuals and Groups: Lessons from the BBC Prison Experiment," in *Individuality and the Group: Advances in Social Identity*, ed. Tom Postmes and Jolanda Jetten (London: Sage, 2006), 237–257.

7. Henry Tajfel, *Differentiation Between Social Groups: Studies in the Social Psychology of Intergroup Relations* (London: Academic Press, 1978).

8. Reicher and Haslam, "On the Agency of Individuals and Groups."

9. Tajfel and Turner, "An Integrative Theory of Intergroup Conflict."

10. Naomi Ellemers, "The Influence of Socio-Structural Variables on Identity Enhancement Strategies," *European Review of Social Psychology* 4 (1993): 27–57.

11. Reicher and Haslam, "On the Agency of Individuals and Groups."

12. Stephen George, *An Awkward Partner: Britain in the European Community* (Oxford: Oxford University Press, 1988).

13. "1968 Palestinian National Covenant," English rendition, in *Basic Political Documents of the Armed Palestinian Resistance Movement*, ed. Leila S. Kadi (Beirut, Lebanon: Palestine Research Centre, December 1969),137–141.

14. Frank Mols and S. Alexander Haslam, "Understanding EU Attitudes in Multilevel Governance Contexts: A Social Identity Perspective," *West European Politics* 31, no. 3 (2008): 442–463.

15. Yasser Arafat, quoted in *International Herald Tribune,* January 8, 1991.

16. Tajfel and Turner, "An Integrative Theory of Intergroup Conflict."

17. Bernd Simon and Bert Klandermans, "Politicized Collective Identity: A Social Psychological Analysis," *American Psychologist* 56 (2001): 319–331.

18. Jolanda Jetten and Nyla R. Branscombe, "Seeking Minority Group Memberships: Responses to Discrimination When Group Membership Is Self-Selected," in *Coping with Minority Status: Responses to Exclusion and Inclusion*, ed. Fabrizio Butera and John Levine (New York: Cambridge University Press, in press).

19. Simon and Klandermans, "Politicized Collective Identity."

20. Stephen B. Biko, *I Write What I Like* (London: Penguin, 1978), 121.

21. Jetten and Branscombe, "Seeking Minority Group Memberships."

22. Fabio Sani and Stephen Reicher, "When Consensus Fails: An Analysis of the Schism Within the Italian Communist Party (1991)," *European Journal of Social Psychology* 28 (1998): 623–645.

23. Ibid.

24. John C. Turner, "Explaining the Nature of Power: A Three-Process Theory," *European Journal of Social Psychology* 35 (2005): 1–22.

PART II

Tools and Pathways

6

Creating Common Ground

Propositions About Effective
Intergroup Leadership

Rosabeth Moss Kanter

Harvard Business School

*Intergroup leadership is finding common ground and helping everybody
enter with similar opportunity. This, ironically, allows people to differentiate
themselves as individuals. Because individuals are part of a whole that
can work together effectively, their differences can be enriching.*

—Rosabeth Moss Kanter

THE DYNAMICS of divisiveness are well known. Identities of individuals and groups are formed, in part, by contrast to "others" who are viewed as "different." People feel that they belong "inside" a relationship because others are "outside" of it, constituting strangers to be feared, lesser beings to be shunned, or enemies to be battled. In-groups enjoy privileges that are withheld from out-groups. Out-groups sometimes organize to retaliate and reverse the flow of privilege. Such dynamics account for a wide range of social phenomena: women as the "second sex"; racial minorities stereotyped as inferior; "clashes of civilizations" in international conflicts; or problems in corporate mergers that reduce shareholder value.[1]

The forces producing collaboration to achieve shared purposes have received less attention. This chapter provides a perspective on collaboration at many system levels, derived from a continuous stream of quantitative and qualitative studies of social and organizational behavior conducted over decades. These research projects include the study of successful (long-lived) nineteenth-century utopian communities and the entry of women into the formerly all-male ranks of a major corporation.[2] Also studied were innovators and the conditions that produce leadership for change in organizations; the factors producing financial value in the first years following corporate mergers; and the dynamics of strategic alliances across companies.[3] Other research covered the correlates of continuing success, winning streaks, and the actions of leaders to turn around losing streaks.[4] Still other studies examined key national leaders who increase intergroup harmony and productivity, particularly President Nelson Mandela of South Africa, and, in progress, the characteristics of exemplary global companies.[5] Drawing on this diverse array of studies, I offer six propositions for effective intergroup leadership.

Definitions

Effective intergroup leadership involves mobilizing and motivating people whose identities are rooted in one particular group to work and live harmoniously and productively with those initially seen as different. Peaceful coexistence is only a starting point; *productivity* involves getting all to do more together than they could do alone. At best, effective intergroup leadership promotes productive use of differences, whatever their origin and nature.

Intergroup leadership is at the heart of social order. Yet the world at the beginning of the twenty-first century is a testament to the social tensions and armed conflicts that arise because people are aware of their differences from one another as individuals, members of informal groups, and members of organizations that stand in varying positions with respect to other groups. Majorities and minorities, races and nationalities, in-groups and out-groups, legacy groups or newly associated groups (e.g., via immigration or business mergers) are all groups or subgroups by which people signify their inclusion or exclusion in accessing desirable resources.

Effective intergroup leaders find the unifying force that unites a diverse population under an overarching purpose, focus on the future rather than history, and help people acknowledge that membership in the whole is as important as identification with any one part. Leaders divide the labor or create subgroups, but with an understanding that subgroups will not be hostile, unproductive, or permanent. *E pluribus Unum* (one out of many), the Latin phrase associated with U.S. founders, is the model for intergroup leadership that emerges from my diverse research and underlies the six propositions described in this chapter.

A consistent thread runs through organizations and social systems of all sizes examined in the studies referenced earlier—nineteenth-century utopian communities, corporate mergers, sports teams, Nelson Mandela's presidency in South Africa. Low performance is associated with fragmentation into factions—in-groups and out-groups—whose enmity leads to hoarding, defensiveness, and passivity, requiring resources to be spent policing boundaries. High performance is associated with collaboration across groups (identity, ethnicity, task) and thus with effective intergroup leadership—across subgroups in a bounded system, or across boundaries.

What is the essence of effective intergroup leadership? I set forth six propositions, illustrated with leader actions. Many of the examples are drawn from turnaround situations, because that is when leadership is most crucial and identifiable.

Proposition 1: Convening Power

Effective intergroup leaders convene people whose initial affiliations or commitments differ and structure conversations to find common ground across subgroups.

Global companies promote intergroup communication when they choose a corporate language (often English) and offer common protocols and templates for operating (increasingly Web-based and thus highly accessible) that are universal across countries. Rather than cause differences to disappear, a common platform makes it easy to acknowledge differences and use them to make productive connections. Similarly, for religious communities, rituals are a common vocabulary that identifies people as fellow believers and thus transcends other differences. Divisiveness occurs when groups not only speak different languages but also create forms of expression to which only insiders are privy—the mode of secret societies. Effective intergroup leadership thus requires leaders who facilitate common forms of expression and then bring people to the table and get them talking.

Convening power, or creating occasions at which people across groups engage in conversation, is an underrecognized but highly valuable power that leaders possess. Once convened, conversations begin that tend to continue beyond the occasion itself. Rick Haythornthwaite, turnaround CEO of Invensys, said, "The only thing I really do is lead conversations. Any group is a network of conversations. I continuously thrust people into situations that force them to challenge the current conversation they're holding, to get beyond that conversation to one that's more productive." Haythornthwaite formed nine strategy teams comprising people from across the divisions, focusing each team on a different customer segment. The company launched this initiative by involving the top three hundred ranked people and one hundred additional participants, called "ambassadors for change," thus including employees below the managerial ranks in the conversation.

Sometimes convening power forces collaboration. The combative senior managers of Turkey's GarantiBank were "invited" by CEO Akin Ongor to attend leadership development seminars to aid the bank's transformation to a collaborative mode; those managers who did not participate after three invitations were fired. During Jim Kilts's first day as Gillette's turnaround CEO, he laid out a schedule of mandatory executive team meetings, larger management meetings, and off-site retreats.

Small teams as well as large systems can become divided over differences. Sports teams characterized by winning streaks have higher levels of cooperation; everyone understands that the job includes helping teammates. In contrast, teams on losing streaks tend to fall apart over individual differences, divide into factions by task, and breed a culture of isolation and weak accountability in which players play for their own records only, whether the team wins or loses (so they lose). To turn around the performance of the Chicago Cubs, a professional U.S. baseball team, new manager Dusty Baker said, "I want my pitching coach talking to my hitters and my batting coach talking to the pitchers, because if the pitcher doesn't know how the hitters think, he's not going to get them out." Intergroup communication improves performance.

Leaders must not let differences harden. In traditional intentional communities, fixed subgroups were destructive to commitment to the whole; people could too easily engage in conflict and fragment the entire community, threatening common ground. Leaders tried to ensure that no one in the community had an exclusive set of ties—particularly to marriage and family—so strong that he could not work effectively with other people. Israeli kibbutzim provided common dining halls and raised children in group nurseries; Shakers required celibacy; and the Oneida colony encouraged "free love" that involved many overlapping relationships across the community. Interestingly, in utopian communities, celibacy and open marriage were functionally equivalent.

But even though those communities suppressed differences within their boundaries, they isolated themselves from larger entities to preserve their own group, thus reflecting intragroup rather than full intergroup leadership. Intergroup leaders encourage conversations across boundaries of groups characterized by recognizable differences, because the inevitable clash of ideas often produces innovation. This is why innovation is more likely to come from cosmopolitans than locals, and why today's innovation-seeking global enterprises widen employees' social and business networks.

Proposition 2: Transcendent Values

Effective intergroup leaders identify a collective definition of success and provide an overarching goal or motivational framework that encompasses different groups.

Nelson Mandela's leadership in South Africa demonstrates effective intergroup leadership under extreme circumstances. Imprisoned for twenty-seven years for his actions against apartheid in South Africa—a political system in which a white minority separated and oppressed a black majority and ghettoized a small intermediate group, largely from India, called "colored"—Mandela emerged from prison in 1990 and proclaimed a message of common humanity. His rhetoric stressed a shared interest in development of the nation to benefit all; he became South Africa's first democratically elected president.

Gordon Bethune's leadership of Continental Airlines also demonstrates this principle: when achievement both depends on everyone's efforts and rewards everyone, then subgroup goals become linked to one transcendent purpose, creating alignment, as the current jargon goes, but also creating meaning. Factions, divisiveness, low morale, and poor service had characterized the financially troubled airline. Bethune's most important move was to define a transcendent purpose—why people fly—and embody it in a collective definition of success: on-time arrivals. Customers *and* employees cared about this goal, and achieving it would avoid the costs associated with delayed or canceled flights. For every quarter in which Continental was among the top four airlines in on-time arrivals, Bethune promised to share half the cost savings equally with everyone in the company. The symbolism of a truly shared purpose meant more than the money, which amounted to a mere $65 per person.

IBM leaders consider its values an essential ingredient in enabling the company to work effectively across boundaries in partnerships with communities and governments worldwide. CEO Sam Palmisano recently led a reinvention of the values for the twenty-first century through a Web-based chat session with more than three hundred thousand employees. "Innovation that makes a difference for the world" emerged as a core value and facilitated collaboration among diverse national groups.

Consider one set of projects. The IBM Technology Development Center in Cairo was aware that IBM had digitized the treasures of the Hermitage Museum in St. Petersburg, Russia. Knowing that preserving Egypt's cultural heritage was a government priority, leaders proposed the Eternal Egypt project to digitize not only museum contents but also ancient structures such as the pyramids. These artifacts could then be experienced virtually, thereby boosting tourism and contributing to economic development.

IBM Egypt sought funding from U.S. corporate officials to partner with the Egyptian government to create new technology for a Web site (www.eternalegypt.org) in three languages, software programs to download information from handheld devices at tourist sites, and a school curriculum. Innovation came from ideas exchanged between engineers in Cairo and Chicago. The Egypt team also relied on IBM's Israel research lab, ignoring political and religious hostilities between the countries.

Eternal Egypt became a model for IBM China's Forbidden City project. Visiting Beijing in November 2006, Palmisano announced to IBMers worldwide that a global "Innovation Jam" (a Web dialogue among one hundred forty thousand IBMers) had identified virtual worlds as a top priority, which he demonstrated by showing his own avatar entering the Forbidden City. Such IBM initiatives show how overarching values can transcend national intergroup differences.

Proposition 3: Future Orientation— Building a New Identity

Effective intergroup leaders involve people from differing groups in creating a new entity focused on a future in which they all can share, without eliminating their individual histories. This broadened entity must bring rewards sufficient for people in the favored in-group to suspend or share some of their privileges with a perceived out-group.

Nelson Mandela reflected this principle when he established the Truth and Reconciliation Commission, granting amnesty for perpetrators who confessed crimes committed under apartheid, which acknowledged but moved beyond the past. Mandela also created a new constitution for South Africa through a series of public dialogues, including town meetings, which involved everyone possible in envisioning the future. History solidifies identities that can become enshrined in rivalries and tensions that last well beyond the original causes. But effective intergroup leaders stress the future and, in so doing, create the basis for a new overarching identity that produces collaboration.

In U.S. business, it is well known that most mergers fail to create value for many years, in part because of continuing tensions among formerly distinct groups who never forget the past. But for Shinhan Financial Group in Korea, a strong emphasis on the future facilitated successful merger integration under difficult circumstances.

Here is how it happened: Shinhan Bank, a small, entrepreneurial bank established in the 1980s to serve the middle market, bought Chohung, a much larger bank that was more than one hundred years old and served large Korean industrial associations (chaebols). Chohung had proud traditions but poor performance; after the Asian financial crisis of 1997, it was bailed out by the government. When Chohung's sale to Shinhan was announced, thirty-five hundred members of the Chohung union (in the Korean system, this includes managers) protested by shaving their heads and piling up the hair in front of Shinhan headquarters.

Following this dramatic instance of intergroup conflict, Shinhan leaders agreed to union demands to maintain pay levels, have equal board representation by each company, maintain a separate identity for Chohung, and postpone a formal merger for three years. But rather than let divisiveness stand, Shinhan leaders on the new board began a stream of activities to unite members of both the former banks and plan the future. They convened interbank task forces for three tracks: "dual bank," "one bank" (which I cover in proposition 5), and "new bank."

"Dual bank" acknowledged differences. Each bank operated separately under its own name but as an equal partner; task forces met to understand each other's procedures and best practices. Gradually, as people heard from one another, the dual banks became more alike. Meanwhile, "new bank" was emerging, starting with the creation of a holding company, Shinhan Financial Group, an overarching new entity unidentified with either previous bank. High-talent employees from each bank were given a series of planning tasks that were aspirational and future oriented. Putting "new bank" on the agenda immediately, even while still operating as a "dual bank," made intergroup tensions seem foolish. Attention became focused on a bigger prize—to create the bank of the future. Three years after the acquisition, the group had enjoyed three years of positive growth in profit and revenues and a big leap in stock price, outperforming the Korean market.

Proposition 4: Important Interdependent Tasks

Effective intergroup leaders unify people with different initial affiliations by offering challenging tasks with major consequences and a chance to succeed by working together. Task interdependence can facilitate positive intergroup relationships.

Large responsibilities and deadlines are classic focusing mechanisms to turn potential conflict to collaboration, especially in high-risk situations when people depend on one another. This proposition holds particularly for task-oriented groups. Early in their tenure as turnaround leaders of Seagate Technology, CEO Steve Luczo and COO Bill Watkins made an assignment to a cross-functional team called Factory of the Future. It was an apparently unachievable goal: to raise plant productivity dramatically. The engineers came from different parts of the company that held strongly negative views of the others. Seagate's culture was characterized by divisiveness, antagonism, and intergroup tensions among functions. Previous efforts to use cross-functional and cross-division task forces to solve problems had failed.

Rather than single out culture change as a goal in itself, Luczo and Watkins initiated a huge task that people grumbled was impossible. When Luczo and Watkins insisted, making jobs contingent on successful innovations, the engineers, forced to collaborate, did achieve the impossible: they raised productivity by a factor of 4. This clear win, with enormous positive financial consequences, modeled a new culture for Seagate, involving routine use of teams from across many subgroups to innovate. Initiatives assigned to cross-functional teams were real and important. Hard-nosed engineers became sold on collaboration, because it was a practical way to get bigger wins.

Every turnaround leader must ask for extraordinary effort—more practices, longer hours, more sacrifices. When people know that the work is important and challenging, they are more likely to show up to do it. Chemistry—confidence in each other—builds one win at a time: game by game, project by project. Each win helps people learn what to expect from each other and share the experience of success.

Proposition 5: Interpersonal Norms and Emotional Integration

Effective intergroup leaders articulate and demand codes of conduct and compliance with interpersonal norms. Effective intergroup leaders recognize the importance of emotional bonds and are willing to invest in activities that arouse people's positive feelings for one another across their groups of origin.

Positive intergroup relations can erode if left to purely voluntary actions. Awareness of differences seems to be built into human DNA, but what is done with that awareness is largely a matter of socialization. Effective intergroup leaders educate people to minimize those tensions and maximize positive interactions, at least in the public realm.

Intergroup leaders signal respect in how they treat people and how they expect them to treat others. Leaders set ground rules for discussion and foster the language of contribution rather than blame, insisting that people seek solutions and value each other's potential to contribute. Seagate had been characterized by macho name-calling; there was even an award, called the "dog's head" award, for the worst behavior at management meetings. Luczo and Watkins no longer tolerated this behavior. They coached their executive team on respectful treatment and removed people who did not exhibit it.

Effective intergroup leaders also facilitate interpersonal bonds that solidify good feelings among people. This is why business deals are solidified over cocktails or golf, or some strategic alliances are triggered by CEOs bonding as though "falling in love."[6] Successful turnaround leaders who have connected warring groups keep the social events even while cutting other costs. The coach of a successful women's college soccer team "tolerated" social chitchat before practices because he knew that solidarity depended on emotional bonds and not only a common task.

Shinhan Financial Group invested heavily in emotional integration. "Dual bank" helped people with continuity, "new bank" built the future, but "one bank" created emotional ties that facilitated relationships, the social capital that enabled groups to work together productively. When an interbank task force proposed to top leaders that the missing ingredient in most mergers was emotional integration, arguing that culture clashes persisted well after acquisitions, the leadership invested many millions of dollars on powerful experiences. At a summit early in the process, fifteen hundred managers from both banks attended a conference where they climbed a mountain at one of Korea's most historic spots. The very size of the group aroused emotions—the collective spirit of a crowd at a large rally. To form "one bank," Shinhan offered similar events for groups well down the ranks.

Proposition 6: Inclusiveness and Evenhandedness

Effective intergroup leaders often arise from one of the groups in the intergroup relationship. Such leaders succeed by making gestures of generosity to the other groups, even at the risk of backlash from their former peer or identity group.

When Nelson Mandela rose to leadership in South Africa with a clear intergroup agenda—to bridge the racial divide that was the negative legacy of apartheid—some people in his own party, the African National Congress, wanted him to get revenge by oppressing the white population and favoring the black population. Mandela instead signaled inclusion and tried to hold the former in-group accountable without making it an outgroup. Even before he was elected president, he went on television to soothe a tense nation when a black leader was assassinated by a white man, making it clear that isolated criminal acts did not have to set group upon group. Once elected, he formed a cabinet that was highly inclusive of the population. He visited the widow of a former apartheid-era prime minister, showing his willingness to engage with the former enemy. And when South Africa's all-white rugby team, which had been banned from the sport under apartheid, won the world championship in Johannesburg, Mandela, wearing the team colors, strode out to the field and embraced them. His recognition gave the black population permission to celebrate what was essentially a white victory, but on behalf of the nation; later, white people could celebrate the victory of a formerly all-black team.

Effective intergroup leaders make it clear that everyone belongs, regardless of individual or subgroup differences. One way to do this, and to get people to invest in each other, is for leaders to invest resources in material changes that benefit all. To stress inclusiveness, some leaders get everyone a new item or new offices. To help integrate Gillette into Procter & Gamble after it was acquired by P&G, the head of P&G moved everyone, not only former Gillette employees, to a new office. Turnaround leaders hired to heal rivalries and antagonisms at the BBC (where radio and television divisions had faced acrimonious conflict) renovated rundown buildings or refurbished dingy offices. Improvements in something tangible that people see every day reinforce the message that everyone is important.

Such actions help reverse characteristic patterns in losing streaks: decisions made in secret behind closed doors; inequalities reflecting favoritism, not fairness; exclusionary practices. Jim Kilts of Gillette was lauded for not playing favorites, for giving everyone the same objective measures and holding everyone to the same standards. Steve Luczo of Seagate Technology removed assigned seats from top executive meetings and added new meeting rooms with round tables. The symbolism of the round table works everywhere; Akin Ongor of GarantiBank in Turkey replaced rectangular tables with round ones. To lead his turnaround of the Chicago Cubs, manager Dusty Baker began with inclusion. He purposefully did not let on that he knew who the stars were. Reported Sonny Jackson, Baker's special assistant, "The first thing you do is make sure that players understand that everybody's in this thing together: coaches, players, the minor league people. Dusty has us call some of the minor players so they get a chance to play and show their stuff."

Conclusion: Intergroup Leadership as Leadership

In a sense, all leadership is intergroup leadership, because the potential for differentiation exists in any social unit larger than two.[7] Thus, these propositions resonate at many system levels for many kinds of teams, organizations, and social groupings, as my widely varying examples make clear. All leadership is about mobilizing, organizing, involving, and inspiring followers in collective action. The leaders who are most respected, and often ultimately the most effective, are not purely partisan, not purely the creatures of one identity group or one set of interests or one organization. They speak to higher principles that build common ground across groups. That is why Nelson Mandela became one of the most-admired leaders of the twentieth century; his advocacy of racial justice united highly diverse sectors of a once oppressively divided nation.

The six propositions constitute core leadership principles: convening on a common platform, stressing values, orienting people to the future, investing in emotional bonds that include norms of respect, and stressing inclusiveness. It is easier to take these actions in relatively small groups that begin with relatively few dimensions of difference, in which people are located near one another, and for whom the spoils of success are close at hand; people are already standing on corners of common ground. It is harder to do so—and a true test of leadership—in large, complex, multidimensional systems in difficult times. That is when the temptation arises to set group against group by blaming one for the troubles of others, or to maintain social order by suppressing some groups in the interest of others. Acting on the positive principles I have identified requires a long-term orientation on the part of leaders and a willingness to ignore instinctive human impulses to fear or fight others and to embrace instead meaning-making visions of a better, united future.

Leaders must be convinced of the benefits of collaborative intergroup relationships, and they must be able to convince others. They do this through what I call the "MEs" of leadership: the messages they espouse; the model they exemplify; and the mechanisms they establish—what leaders say, do, and enable others to do.[8] By their words, their own example, and the structures and processes they put in place, leaders can turn differences into sources of strength, so that people from different places or different identities can indeed work together on common ground.

Notes

1. Allusions are to books that have become motifs for divisive intergroup relationships: Simone de Beauvoir, *The Second Sex*, trans. and ed. H. M. Parshley (New York: Random House, 1993); Samuel Huntington, *The Clash of Civilizations and the Remaking of World Order* (New York: Simon and Schuster, 1996). See also Ralph Ellison, *Invisible Man* (New York: Modern Library, 1952).

2. Rosabeth M. Kanter, *Commitment and Community: Communes and Utopias in Sociological Perspective* (Cambridge, MA: Harvard University Press, 1972); and Kanter, *Men and Women of the Corporation* (New York: Basic Books, 1977).

3. Rosabeth M. Kanter, *The Change Masters: Innovations for Productivity in the American Corporation* (New York: Simon and Schuster, 1983); and Kanter, *When Giants Learn to Dance* (New York: Touchstone Book, 1990). See also a series of Harvard Business School case studies: Shinhan, Publicis. Rosabeth M. Kanter, *World Class: Thriving Locally in a Global Economy* (New York: Simon and Schuster, 1995).

4. Rosabeth M. Kanter, *Confidence: How Winning Streaks and Losing Streaks Begin and End* (New York: Crown Business, 2004), chapter 10.

5. Rosabeth M. Kanter, *America the Principled: 6 Opportunities for Becoming a Can-Do Nation Once Again* (New York: Crown, 2007). For a first report on exemplary nations, see Rosabeth M. Kanter, "Transforming Giants," *Harvard Business Review* (January 2008).

6. Rosabeth M. Kanter, "Collaborative Advantage: The Art of Alliances," *Harvard Business Review* (July–August 1994).

7. Georg Simmel, *The Sociology of Georg Simmel*, trans. Kurt H. Wolff (New York: Free Press, 1950).

8. Kanter, *Confidence: How Winning Streaks and Losing Streaks Begin and End*, chapter 11.

7

Boundary-Spanning Leadership

Tactics to Bridge Social Identity Groups in Organizations

Chris Ernst

Center for Creative Leadership

Jeffrey Yip

Center for Creative Leadership

As structural and technological boundaries are dismantled, a flat world of boundaryless organizations gives rise to a different type of boundary found in intergroup relations. In organizations worldwide, leaders are challenged to bridge social identity boundaries between groups of people with different histories, perspectives, values, and cultures.[1] For instance, in South Africa, leaders work to transform deep-rooted social tensions between Afrikaners and black Africans in a financial-services firm. In Southeast Asia, the CEO of a faith-based organization attempts to bridge differences between religious fundamentalists and nonbelieving staff regarding how best to align the organization with the needs of a pluralistic, multifaith community. In a manufacturing facility in the United States, line managers struggle to create an environment in which Native Americans,

African Americans, European Americans, and Hispanics can work productively together on the assembly line.

As these examples make clear, groups of people who have historically
remained apart are now increasingly working together. In this chapter we
focus on the role of *boundary-spanning leadership*: leadership that bridges
boundaries across groups in service of a broader vision, mission, or goal.
Specifically, we provide a detailed description of four boundary-spanning
tactics—suspending, reframing, nesting, and weaving—that leaders can
use to span differences across groups of people in organizational settings.

The Challenge of Leadership Across
Social Identity Boundaries

Boundaries are a basic aspect of organizational life. *Social identity boundaries* refer to aspects of our identities that have to do with the various
demographic groups to which we belong (e.g., gender, religion, age, nationality, and ethnicity).[2] In varying cultures and contexts, social identity
group membership is also expressed through other forms of identification,
such as educational background, generational differences, sexual orientation, physical disability, job level, function, caste, and tribe.

Management scholars Dora Lau and Keith Murnighan propose that
social identity boundaries in groups are analogous to geological faults in
Earth's crust: they are always present, and they create various levels of
friction as boundaries rub together, pull apart, grind, and collide.[3] In the
same way that geologists cannot prevent faults from cracking open in
Earth's surface, leaders are constricted in their ability to manage and solve
points of friction in intergroup relationships.

Specifically, the challenge for leaders to effectively bridge social identity boundaries is fraught with peril in at least three ways. First, leaders are
often pulled in multiple directions between conflicting values, viewpoints,
and beliefs. Second, they are commonly pushed to one side. A leader is, of
course, a member of some social groups and not a member of other social
groups. Despite a leader's best efforts to be impartial and fair, members of
social groups will form perceptions based solely on the social grouping
of the leader. And third, leaders are frequently caught out of the loop. In
part, this stems from the natural tendency for information to be filtered
as it moves up the organizational hierarchy. However, another reason is
that more often than not, leaders are representatives of traditionally ad-

vantaged and dominant social groups. In these instances, leaders often lack critical awareness of the inequities and challenges faced by less-advantaged groups.

Given these sizable challenges, how do leaders bridge the social identity boundaries that exist in their places of work? As members of a global research project at the Center for Creative Leadership, we surveyed and interviewed leaders from for-profit and nonprofit organizations in twelve countries to identify a broad range of boundary-spanning tactics in the workplace.[4] In this chapter, we describe a specific subset of four tactics for effective intergroup leadership: suspending, reframing, nesting, and weaving.

Tactics for Boundary-Spanning Leadership

Boundary-spanning leadership is the term we use to recognize the increasingly important and necessary role that leaders play in bridging social identity boundaries in service of a larger organizational vision, mission, or goal. Boundary spanning lies in creating the necessary links between groups in order to move ideas, information, people, and resources where they are needed most.[5] Each of the tactics we describe helps leaders establish these links by altering the nature and composition of intergroup boundaries. These tactics are well established in the social psychology literature.[6] The research supporting them is described elsewhere in this book.

Our aim in the sections that follow is to detail examples of these tactics from a variety of countries and contexts, thereby connecting theories from research with evidence from practice. We provide specific definitions, share relevant cases, and consider strengths as well as potential blind spots characteristic of each tactic. It is our hope that leaders can use this knowledge to incorporate boundary-spanning tactics in their daily work with functional units, project groups, task forces, or virtual teams. A summary of each boundary-spanning tactic can be found in figure 7-1.

Suspend: Create a Third Space

The tactic of *boundary suspending* seeks to create a neutral zone where social interactions are person-based rather than based on identity group. In the literature, this tactic is referred to as *decategorization*, because the emphasis is on individuals rather than on social categories.[7] In creating a third space, leaders establish a suspended neutral zone where personal relationships can be developed, assumptions can be brought to the surface,

FIGURE 7-1

Boundary-spanning leadership tactics

	Suspend Create a third space	Reframe Activate a shared identity	Nest Embed groups within larger whole	Weave Cross-cut roles and identity
Action	Create a neutral zone where social interaction is person-based rather than indentity-group-based.	Activate a shared or superordinate identity that is inclusive across social groups.	Embed and affirm groups in larger wholes so that groups have both distinct and interdependent identities.	Cross-cut work-group roles with social-group membership in a systematic way.
Schematic				
Example	A leader in a multinational financial-services firm organizes frequent after-work activities to encourage interaction between individuals of different national origins.	Teachers in a school in Israel bring together Israeli and Palestinian teenagers to work together on preserving common natural resources, thereby identifying one another as stewards of a shared natural resource.	A global technology company creates affinity groups for nondominant groups in which employees have a voice as a unique group *and* contribute input to broader, strategic goals.	A bank in South Africa uses a mentoring strategy in which previously advantaged white supervisors are paired with black South Africans to cross-cut layers of management and social identity membership.
Specific leadership practices	• Organization-sponsored events • After-work activities • Organizational hot spots or creativity labs	• All-inclusive organizational mission or goal • Third-party competitor • Larger calling or societal value	• Affinity groups • Communities of practice • Cross-boundary strategy planning	• Job rotations • Cross-cutting mentoring • Virtual or dispersed teams

values can be safely explored, and new language can be created. The Japanese notion of *ba* proposed by philosopher Ikujiro Nonaka is a related concept.[8] *Ba* is considered to be a shared space that serves as a foundation for emerging relationships and knowledge creation. This space can be physical (e.g., an office, a dispersed business space), virtual (e.g., e-mail, a teleconference), mental (e.g., shared experiences, ideas, ideals), or any combination of these.

Consider the case of Mr. Yamada, a Japanese project manager we studied whose work requires him to work for short stints in countries throughout the Asia Pacific. His role as a boundary spanner demands that he quickly build productive and task-oriented cross-national teams to launch new information technology (IT) initiatives. On assignment in Korea, Yamada frequently created neutral zones through after-work events for his team members from Australia, Indonesia, Korea, and New Zealand. Over time, team members discovered that the cultural stereotypes they held did not apply to members of the team. By providing space for personal relationships to develop, Yamada was able to build the level of trust needed to launch IT projects in a timely fashion.

Although establishing such practices seems straightforward at first glance, this is not always the case. Yamada also described an experience in which he managed a new project in Hong Kong. Here Yamada's efforts to organize after-work activities were met with resistance. He found that even though his expatriate colleagues from Europe enjoyed going to an Irish pub, his local Chinese colleagues preferred the karaoke bar. These intergroup boundaries were reinforced in the workplace. Project delays, work-arounds, and behind-the-scenes in-group conversations were the norm. The actual technical work was not the problem. The problem, according to Yamada, was that the different national groups were never able to get along. "It was a clash of civilizations between East and West . . . and I found myself stuck in the middle." Ultimately, Yamada struck upon an elegant solution. Hong Kong is a city blessed with some of the finest cuisine from all corners of the globe. By organizing weekly "Dine Around the World" events, Yamada used food as a medium to develop personal relationships across cultures, which in turn created a more positive and collaborative work environment in the office.

Bridging entrenched social identity boundaries is something that few leaders have been trained to do, and yet for people like Yamada, it is an integral aspect of their leadership role. Boundary-suspending tactics allow leaders to create a third space where people can interact not as members of distinct groups but rather as unique individuals. Other examples of third spaces include storytelling sessions where individuals are encouraged to share personal life events and lessons; "creativity labs" or "hot spots" where diverse teams can hold dialogues and solve problems; or off-site retreats designed to take advantage of the third-space qualities of a neutral location.

A potential blind spot in applying the tactic of boundary suspending is that in-groups may feel a sense of threat or resistance when brought into contact with out-groups with which they have a history of tension or mistrust. In the Yamada example, the expatriate workers enjoyed going to the

Irish pub because it reconnected them to their European identity, just as the Chinese locals valued their cultural singing tradition. Had Yamada required the Europeans to sing karaoke, or the Chinese to cheer for the favored rugby team at the pub, it most likely would have been a recipe for disaster. Only by thoughtfully creating a neutral, third space did Yamada enable his subordinates to develop productive cross-boundary relationships. Equally important, Yamada recognized that the tactic of boundary suspending is not a quick fix, but rather a tactic that must be nurtured and cultivated over time.

Reframe: Activate a Shared Identity

The tactic of *boundary reframing* is designed to activate a common category or superordinate identity that is inclusive across social groups. In the social identity literature, this tactic is known as *recategorization* or the *common in-group identity model* because it attempts to break down group identity by uniting people under a superordinate identity.[9]

In the workplace, boundary reframing works to increase the salience, relevance, and importance of belonging to the organization as a higher-level social category. Thus, the organization itself and its mission and goals become the all-inclusive identity group. In this regard, boundary reframing has much in common with visionary or charismatic leadership models.[10] Although such models emphasize the qualities of the leader (e.g., persuasive, articulate, and inspiring), boundary reframing focuses on the process of creating a shared and inclusive identity across social groups.

A powerful example of boundary reframing comes from Child's Rights and You (CRY), a nongovernmental organization (NGO) in India that is transforming itself from an agency for child relief to an agency for child rights. The grassroots organization spans seventeen of the twenty-eight Indian states and is a microcosm of the diversity of the vast nation, including intergroup differences in gender, religion, region, language, ethnicity, and caste. Members of the CRY management committee recognized that the transformation would succeed only if all the social groups of the organization reframed their differences and identified with the organization's broader mission. Becoming an advocacy-based organization for child rights meant having to come to terms with intractable social identity issues that play out in the broader society. As one senior leader put it, "We can't create a movement with over a billion people in India until we first create that movement and that understanding within our own diversity."

To create its vision for the future, the organization is using a number of practices including whole-systems methodologies. As described by organizational development pioneer Marvin Weisbord, these methodologies require representatives of whole systems to be present in the discussion, planning, and action cycle of key organizational initiatives.[11] For CRY, bringing cross-boundary groups together allows key decisions to be broadly informed and discourages development of an "us versus them" mind-set. When North or South regional divisions or rifts between the Brahmin and Dalit castes become apparent, they can be addressed in the moment. This process allows for common ground to be identified, which in turn creates the needed momentum for CRY to reframe a galvanizing cross-boundary vision for its future.

A compelling mission or vision found in nonprofit organizations, such as CRY's vision concerning children's rights, creates a built-in superordinate goal to bridge disparate social groups. In the corporate arena, however, superordinate goals often focus on competitive dimensions, such as winning market share, hitting financial targets, or being first to market with an innovative product or service. These practices serve to bridge social identities by focusing on interorganizational competition and by emphasizing what is positive and distinctive about the organization compared with its competitors. Typically, reframing practices such as these are particularly effective in tightly contested industries such as finance and technology. In education, nursing, or other helping professions, however, leaders may find that reframing works better if they call on a shared professional identity. A professional calling, such as caring for those in need, can provide a binding identity that transcends other social identity differences.

The boundaries that separate social identity groups are rooted in group membership and are charged with emotion and meaning. Boundary-spanning leaders are well advised to be attentive to these differences and not to attempt to eliminate them. Nor should they deliberately put members of social groups in a position where they must abandon core aspects of their social identity on behalf of the organizational identity. Not only would this raise basic issues of ethics, but also it is a strategy that cannot sustain itself over time.

Although boundary-spanning leaders should be mindful of these blind spots, it is also the case that an inclusive shared vision can be a powerful means to bind groups together. As observed in an environmental organization in Israel, boundary reframing is one of our most hopeful tactics for the future. A school brings together Israeli and Palestinian teenagers to work on preserving common natural resources. Through these interactions, members of the two groups are able to identify with one another as stewards of a shared natural resource. Because this practice appeals to a larger societal value that improves the world condition, the outline for a new, inclusive identity can be found in the next generation of leaders in the Middle East.

Nest: Embed Groups Within the Larger Whole

The tactic of *boundary nesting* seeks to structure interactions so that social groups have distinct roles that are embedded in a larger mission, goal, or objective. In the literature, this tactic is known as *subcategorization* or *mutual intergroup differentiation*, because members of different groups are considered to have distinct but complementary roles to contribute toward a common goal.[12] This tactic draws on decades of psychological and adult-learning research that demonstrates that humans have strong needs for both distinctiveness and belonging.

Research by psychologists John Dovidio, Sam Gaertner, and Ana Validzic has verified through a series of experiments that intergroup bias can be decreased when group identities are made salient and subgroup identities are part of a larger shared identity.[13] In addition, Michael Hogg and Deborah Terry of the University of Queensland propose that when the group is large and the shared identity amorphous, subgroup members might view imposed assimilation (e.g., boundary reframing) as an identity threat. Hogg and Terry suggest that an effective strategy for managing such situations is to make subgroup and shared group identity simultaneously salient.[14]

As residents of Singapore, we have witnessed firsthand how the nation's first prime minister, Lee Kuan Yew, and subsequent generations of government leaders have used boundary nesting to remarkable effect. As leader of a highly multicultural, multiethnic, and multifaith society, Lee Kuan Yew has stressed since Singaporean independence in 1965 that the nation's strength lies in the diversity of its many cultures. Diverse ethnic and religious identities are respected for maintaining their unique traditions while concurrently contributing to the whole of the nation. This culture of respect is evidenced in social practices ranging from the celebration of each religion's primary holidays to spectacular annual events, such as the New Year's Parade and National Day, in which diverse groups are given equal time on center stage. Such practices prevent dominant identity groups from asserting their identities over others and allows minority groups to practice their unique identities.

The tactic of boundary nesting has functioned as a powerful force against ethnic discrimination in Singapore, and its success is evident in the ease with which citizens of different ethnic backgrounds interact. Singaporeans, by and large, value the state of their multiethnic society in terms of the quality of interethnic relationships and the stability they provide. Consequently, these relationships are often cited as one of the key drivers of what has become one of the world's most dynamic, successful, and diversified economies.[15]

Returning to the organizational arena and CRY, the India-based NGO has adopted an innovative strategy-planning process that uses the concept of boundary nesting. Many are familiar with traditional strategic planning, in which a strategy is developed by the senior team and then cascaded down through the chain of command. Each functional and geographic unit must then attempt to fit itself into this prescribed box. In sharp contrast, CRY wanted to develop a strategy process that recognized and valued the distinct regional identities across the organization. As one travels north to south and east to west, India encompasses vast differences in everything from dialects to social attitudes to the amount of spice in the food. Even though the organization recognized these differences, however, it also knew it needed an integrated long-term plan to provide an overarching blueprint. The solution is a process whereby each regional group collectively works on the strategy after having broken it into smaller actionable steps. With this approach, the final version is what emerges after the groups cooperate to reconcile regional variations in support of an integrated strategy.

Other common examples of boundary nesting in organizations include the creation of affinity groups and of communities of practice. Both methods seek to foster the development of a shared identity while also keeping groups connected to the broader organizational strategy. As discussed earlier, research demonstrates that nesting groups within larger wholes can be an effective means to reduce intergroup threat and anxiety. Yet putting nesting into practice can be difficult. Given the often territorial nature of organizational life, it is a serious challenge for leaders to balance in-group cohesion with cross-group identification with the organization as a whole.

To help manage these tensions, boundary-spanning leaders can take several additional steps. First, they can structure interdependent tasks so that each group's expertise is equally valued. Second, they may find benefit in using a tiered approach in which subgroup members first engage in activities that affirm their identity, and then different groups are brought together to work toward a shared understanding.[16] Boundary-spanning leaders also can help manage these intergroup dynamics by actively speaking out concerning both the unique perspectives brought by various groups and their contributions to larger organizational goals. These additional steps help ensure that smaller subgroups, like well-crafted Russian dolls, retain unique meaning and integrity while being nested within a larger organizational whole.

Weave: Cross-Cut Roles and Identity

The final tactic of boundary weaving seeks to *cross and intersect social and organizational identities* in an interdependent manner so that they are less tightly coupled. The concept of weaving speaks to the practice of interlacing social identities across roles and levels in the organization, a tactic that in turn facilitates opportunities for increased cross-boundary collaboration and creativity. This is an extension of Marilyn Brewer's concept of cross-cutting.[17] Brewer, a professor of psychology at Ohio State University, argues that social categories in the broader society become problematic when they are related to subcategories within the organization. For example, social categories often overlap with functional groups, as when employees are categorized as male executives and female secretaries. In that case, boundary weaving is particularly relevant in bridging the diversity gap between dominant and minority groups in the organization.

In the United States, especially in the corporate sector, organizations typically use multilayered initiatives to ensure greater cross-boundary representation and contact across levels. One practice involves actively hiring and promoting underrepresented social groups to particular job titles or occupations. A second practice uses formal job rotation programs to broaden employee skills and ultimately to increase the number of underrepresented groups within a specified occupation or role. A third practice includes cross-cutting mentoring, such as pairing a supervisor and an employee who are members of different identity groups and levels. Each of these practices is consistent with the tactic of boundary weaving in that they cross-cut work-group boundaries with social identity membership.

Taking boundary weaving a step further, leaders can strategically use this tactic as a catalyst for cross-boundary collaboration, learning, and innovation. Consider the example of a corporate leader (we will call her Siritina) whose job requires her to lead virtual teams in implementing regional financial services across countries having widely differing infrastructures. She describes a typical team as having as many as thirty members consisting of men and women, of various ages, with multiple nationality backgrounds, and representing a range of organizational levels and functions. The strength of these teams, Siritina explains, is that through mixed functional and social identity representation, she increases the likelihood of creating relevant, market-sensitive services. The blind spot, however, is a sharply increased potential for intergroup fault lines and conflict, as various subgroups line up around shared demographic or functional attributes.

In an interesting twist on conventional wisdom, Siritina emphasizes a task orientation to a greater extent than a team orientation when she is in the early stages of working with a new team. She draws up detailed monthly timetables, clearly communicates performance goals, and ensures that required team budgets and resources are obtained. Her rationale is to build quick and visible momentum for the project. "When diverse teams experience early success, potential areas of conflict fade into the background," she reasons. "But when things start off on the wrong track, differences will quickly derail your efforts." Later, as her teams move into the formal execution of their tasks, Siritina switches to emphasize a greater interpersonal orientation. "I increasingly focus on relationships and make sure everyone on the team feels included and has voice around the work." This practice helps ensure that the best ideas come forward across demographic and functional boundaries, something that in turn creates feelings of commitment and buy in over time.

By demonstrating flexibility in her leadership style and a keen awareness of group composition, Siritina is able to proactively weave multiple layers of intergroup boundaries.[18] For leaders like Siritina, intergroup differences are not thought of as a challenge to solve, but rather as the very means to solve the challenge. By weaving social groups with organizational level and roles, boundary-spanning leaders unlock creativity within individuals and within the organization as a whole.

Conclusion

In this chapter, we have outlined four tactics leaders can use to span boundaries across groups of people with different histories, perspectives, values, and cultures. As illustrated in the examples, leaders incorporate these tactics according to their strengths and potential blind spots in daily work projects, meetings, activities, and initiatives. By suspending intergroup differences, reframing a shared and inclusive identity, nesting diverse groups within a larger organizational goal, and weaving organizational and social identities, boundary-spanning leaders can generate effective intergroup contact in service of a larger organizational mission, vision, or goal.

As dynamics in our broader society increasingly appear in organizational settings, the workplace serves as a place where historical and emerging intergroup boundaries can be bridged. Our hope is that if people of different social groups are provided opportunities for positive cross-boundary contact in the workplace, their experiences can spill over into local communities. Framed in this way, boundary-spanning leadership can serve as a catalyst for positive change in organizations—and in the broader communities they serve.

Notes

1. Thomas Friedman, *The World Is Flat* (New York: Farrar, Straus and Giroux, 2005); and Ron Ashkenas et al., *The Boundaryless Organization: Breaking the Chains of Organizational Structure* (San Francisco: Jossey-Bass, 1998).

2. Boundary spanning has a long tradition in organization theory. Although the concept has focused on spanning structural and information boundaries in organizations, we address the role of leadership in spanning social identity boundaries. See Howard Aldrich and Diane Herker, "Boundary Spanning Roles and Organization Structure," *Academy of Management Review* 2, no. 2 (1977): 217–230. See also Ralph Katz and Michael Tushman, "A Longitudinal Study of the Effects of Boundary Spanning Supervision on Turnover and Promotion in Research and Development," *Academy of Management Journal* 26, no. 3 (1983): 437–463.

3. For a comprehensive analysis of demographic fault lines, see Dora Lau and Keith Murnighan, "Interactions Within Groups and Subgroups: The Effects of Demographic Faultlines," *Academy of Management Journal* 48, no. 4 (2005): 645–659; and Lau and Murnighan, "Demographic Diversity and Faultlines: The Compositional Dynamics of Organizational Groups," *Academy of Management Review* 23, no. 2 (1998): 325–340.

4. The Leadership Across Differences project is a multicountry, multimethod study of leadership in the context of social identity differences. The project is housed at the Center for Creative Leadership. For more information, visit the project Web site at http://www.ccl.org/lad.

5. Deborah Ancona and David Caldwell, "Bridging the Boundary: External Activity and Performance in Organizational Teams," *Administrative Science Quarterly* 37 (1992): 634–665.

6. Donna Chrobot-Mason, Marian Ruderman, Todd Weber, Patricia Ohlott, and Maxine Dalton, "Illuminating a Cross-Cultural Leadership Challenge: When Identity Groups Collide," *International Journal of Human Resource Management* 18, no. 11 (2007): 2011–2036.

7. Marilynn M. Brewer and Norman Miller, "Beyond the Contact Hypothesis: Theoretical Perspectives on Desegregation," in *Groups in Contact: The Psychology of Desegregation*, ed. N. Miller and M. M. Brewer (New York: Academic Press, 1984), 281–302.

8. Ikujiro Nonaka and Noboru Konno, "The Concept of 'Ba': Building a Foundation for Knowledge Creation," *California Management Review* 40, no. 3 (1998): 40–54.

9. Samuel L. Gaertner and John F. Dovidio, *Reducing Intergroup Bias: The Common Ingroup Identity Model* (Ann Arbor, MI: Sheridan Books, 2000).

10. Bernard M. Bass, *Leadership and Performance Beyond Expectations* (New York: Free Press, 1985).

11. Marvin Weisbord, *Discovering Common Ground* (San Francisco: Berrett-Koehler, 1992).

12. Miles R. C. Hewstone and Rupert J. Brown, "Contact Is Not Enough: An Intergroup Perspective on the Contact Hypothesis," in *Contact and Conflict in Intergroup Encounters*, ed. M. R. C. Hewstone and R. J. Brown (Oxford: Blackwell, 1986), 1–44.

13. John Dovidio, Sam Gaertner, and Ana Validzic, "Intergroup Bias: Status, Differentiation, and a Common In-Group Identity," *Journal of Personality and Social Psychology* 75 (1998): 109–120.

14. Michael A. Hogg and Deborah J. Terry, "Social Identity and Self-Categorization Processes in Organizational Contexts," *Academy of Management Review* 25 (2000): 121–140.

15. Beng-Huat Chua, *Communitarian Ideology and Democracy in Singapore* (London: Routledge, 1995).

16. Alexander Haslam and Naomi Ellemers, "Social Identity in Industrial and Organizational Psychology: Concepts, Controversies, and Contributions," in *International Review of Industrial and Organizational Psychology*, vol. 20, ed. Gerard P. Hodgkinson and J. Kevin Ford (Hoboken, NJ: John Wiley & Sons, 2005), 39–118.

17. Marilynn M. Brewer, "Managing Diversity: The Role of Social Identities," in *Diversity in Work Teams*, ed. Sharon E. Jackson and Marian N. Ruderman (Washington, DC: American Psychological Association, 1995), 47–68.

18. The techniques described in the Siritina example parallel recommendations made in a quantitative study of leadership by Lynda Gratton and her colleagues. For more on how leaders can modify their style to manage fault lines, see Lynda Gratton, Andreas Voigt, and Tamara J. Erickson, "Bridging Faultlines in Diverse Teams," *MIT Sloan Management Review* 48 (2007): 22–29.

8

Trust Building in Intergroup Negotiations

Challenges and Opportunities for Creative Leaders

Roderick M. Kramer

Graduate School of Business, Stanford University

A N IMPORTANT and challenging task often faced by leaders is how to facilitate the development of trust between groups they represent. This task is especially challenging when a history of deep distrust or suspicion exists between the groups. In particular, this chapter focuses on several basic issues leaders must understand and address if they are to build trust successfully between groups they represent. First, how should trust be conceptualized in the context of intergroup relations? In other words, what are the special or distinctive elements of trust that operate at the intergroup level? Second, what special barriers to trust exist in such contexts? Stated slightly differently, why is it hard to cultivate and sustain trust between groups? Third, how might leaders go about creatively stimulating the development of intergroup trust, especially when climates of distrust and suspicion prevail?

In this chapter, I address these critical questions by focusing attention on how resourceful and creative leaders can facilitate the trust-building process, especially in negotiation settings. I emphasize these settings because negotiation has long been recognized as one of the primary mechanisms available to leaders to manage conflict and distrust between groups.[1] For example, negotiation processes have played a major role in recent attempts by the George W. Bush administration to broker constructive relationships with China, North Korea, and other nation-states.[2]

Negotiation can be particularly effective in addressing at least two common problems that arise in intergroup conflicts. First, when two or more groups are embroiled in conflicts regarding contested resources or issues, negotiation can help leaders forge mutually acceptable agreements, thereby avoiding costly stalemates or destructive escalation.[3] Second, negotiation may be useful when the leaders of interdependent groups perceive an opportunity for mutual gain but lack a set of shared understandings or decision rules for structuring a productive collaboration.[4]

Conceptualizing Trust in Intergroup Negotiations

Researchers have long recognized the central role that trust plays in effective negotiations.[5] For example, trust has been shown to facilitate the attainment of more-satisfactory bargaining outcomes, and the absence of trust has been shown to impede such results.[6] Providing a crisp characterization of such trust, however, has presented difficulties. Although social scientists have afforded considerable attention to the problem of defining trust, a concise and universally accepted definition has remained elusive.[7] As a consequence, the term *trust* has been used in a variety of distinct, and not always compatible, ways in the social sciences.

At one extreme are formulations that highlight the explicit beliefs and tacit assumptions that contribute to people's understanding of trust. One scholar, for instance, characterized trust as the set of "socially learned and socially confirmed expectations that people have of each other, of the organizations and institutions in which they live, and of the natural and moral social orders that set the fundamental understandings for their lives."[8] At the other end of the definitional spectrum are conceptions that emphasize the strategic or calculative dimensions of trust. For example, Pruitt and Rubin defined trust as simply the expectation that another is positively concerned about our interests.[9]

Researchers have also differed in whether they portray trust primarily as an individual, psychological characteristic or instead as an aspect of the social relationship between two or more interdependent parties. Thus, some researchers have treated trust primarily as a dispositional variable or personality characteristic of individuals.[10] In contrast, others have construed trust as an inherently relational property between the parties.[11] Whether trust is characterized as a dispositional property of social actors or an emergent feature of their relationship, however, these diverse conceptions converge in that, whatever else it encompasses, trust can be viewed as a psychological state or orientation of one social actor (the truster) toward one or more others (the prospective trustee or trustees).

When conceptualized as a psychological state or orientation, trust has been further defined as several interrelated cognitive processes. First, trust entails a state of perceived vulnerability or risk that is derived from individuals' uncertainty regarding the motives, intentions, and prospective actions of others with whom they are interdependent. As Lewis and Weigert observed along these lines, trust can be characterized as the "undertaking of a risky course of action on the confident expectation that all persons involved in the action will act competently and dutifully."[12] In the context of intergroup negotiations, such trust entails a variety of perceptions, including the belief that the other party is expected to cooperate and is prepared to engage in earnest and constructive problem solving.[13]

Extrapolating from these various distinctions, I conceptualize trust within the context of intergroup negotiations as the set of assumptions, beliefs, and expectations held by a negotiator (or negotiators) from one group regarding the likelihood that the actions of a negotiator (or negotiators) from another group will be beneficial, favorable, or at least not detrimental to one's interests.

The Benefits of Trust in Intergroup Negotiations

Support for the proposition that trust supports integrative bargaining processes and outcomes comes from a variety of studies. Trust has been shown, for instance, to facilitate the exchange of useful information between negotiators. Trust also has been found to facilitate the reaching of agreements on proposed offers.[14] Other research has demonstrated that individuals are more likely to engage in cooperative behavior when they trust others.[15]

Trust can also affect integrative behavior during negotiation by influencing the kinds of bargaining strategies and tactics leaders select when trying to influence the other party. Rothbart and Hallmark, for example, emphasized the difference between conciliatory and coercive bargaining strategies used in intergroup negotiation. Conciliatory strategies entail the use of positive inducements to elicit cooperative responses from a negotiation opponent.[16] Coercive strategies, in contrast, entail the use of threats and deterrents and are aimed at inducing compliance from a presumably recalcitrant opponent.

A leader's trust in the other party can play an important role in these strategic choices, because the selection of an influence strategy will be affected by a leader's assumptions regarding the other party's receptiveness or responsiveness to a given strategy. Negotiators are likely to employ positive influence strategies, for instance, when trust in the other's responsiveness is high. In contrast, they are likely to resort to more-coercive strategies if their trust is so low that they believe the other party will exploit cooperative or conciliatory gestures.[17]

Other social psychology research suggests that trust can affect not only negotiators' expectations before negotiation and their behavior during negotiation, but also the attributions they make after a negotiation is complete. When trust is high, individuals are more likely to give the other party the benefit of the doubt. In contrast, when trust is low, they are likely to construe the same behaviors and outcomes in more sinister terms.[18]

Barriers to Trust in Intergroup Negotiations

To build trust in intergroup negotiation contexts, leaders need to be cognizant of the psychological and social barriers that can impede the development of such trust. To this point, researchers have identified a variety of factors that can impede the development of trust.[19] For the purposes of this analysis, these factors can be discussed in terms of, first, psychological processes that undermine trust and, second, social impediments to trust.

With respect to the psychological dimension, behavioral scientists have afforded considerable attention to identifying cognitive and affective processes that impair negotiator performance. Research has demonstrated, along these lines, the existence of a variety of judgmental processes and decision biases that adversely affect integrative bargaining.[20] In identifying cognitive processes that undermine trust development between groups, the most extensive research to date has examined the deleterious effects of social categorization on social perception and judgment.[21] Early research on in-group bias demonstrated a robust and pervasive tendency for individuals to hold relatively positive views of their own group and its members but comparatively negative views of other groups and their members. Subsequent research showed that merely categorizing individuals into arbitrary but distinct groupings resulted in systematic judgmental effects, including in negotiation contexts.[22]

Insko and Schopler's research on the *discontinuity effect* points to a similar conclusion.[23] In particular, these authors provided evidence regarding the existence of a negative *out-group schema* that can lead negotiators to be distrustful and suspicious of out-group members and also to expect more-competitive bargaining behavior from them. According to Marilynn Brewer and Rupert Brown, this out-group schema has two important components.[24] The first is *schema-based distrust*, which represents "the learned belief or expectation that intergroup relations are competitive and therefore the outgroup is not to be trusted and the ingroup's welfare must be protected." Second, this anticipated competition generates a self-fulfilling dynamic. As Brewer and Brown further noted, "when one believes that the other party has competitive intent, the only reasonable action is to compete oneself in order to avoid potential loss."[25]

One manifestation of the sort of defensively based, diminished expectations injected by such biases into a negotiation surrounds the negotiating parties' beliefs regarding the responsiveness of the other party to specific cooperative or conciliatory gestures. Rothbart and Hallmark found that one consequence of social categorization is that individuals tend to believe that in-group members will be more responsive to conciliatory influence strategies, whereas out-group members will be more responsive to coercive strategies.[26] Such presumptions are likely to lead negotiators to opt for overly coercive strategies when trying to influence a presumably resistant opponent from another group. Because the other side also is judging this negotiator's motives and intentions by his actions, the result is a series of destructive action–reaction cycles, as each side responds in what it construes as a justified, defensive way to the threatening and provocative actions of the other side.[27]

All else being equal, it might seem as if these various judgmental distortions would be difficult to sustain, especially when disconfirming evidence becomes available to negotiators. Unfortunately, there are a number of psychological dynamics that may contribute to difficulties in correcting such misperceptions, especially in intergroup negotiation. Arguably, these self-sustaining characteristics of distrust and suspicion arise both from the distrustful perceiver's difficulty in learning from trust-related experiences and from the difficulty of generating useful (diagnostic) experiences. One problem that the suspicious negotiator confronts is that, because of the presumption that the other party is untrustworthy and that things may not be what they seem, the perceived diagnostic value of any particular bit of evidence regarding the other's putative trustworthiness is, from the outset, tainted.

As Weick commented in this regard, all diagnostic cues are inherently corruptible.[28] He cites an interesting historical example to illustrate this problem. The day before the Japanese attack on Pearl Harbor, a U.S. naval attaché informed Washington that he did not believe a surprise attack by the Japanese was imminent because the fleet was still stationed at its home base. As evidence for this conclusion, he noted that large crowds of sailors could be observed casually walking the streets of Tokyo. What the attaché did not know was that these "sailors" were in actuality Japanese soldiers disguised as sailors to conceal the fact that the Japanese fleet had already sailed. From the perspective of the Japanese, this ruse was a brilliant example of what military intelligence experts call *strategic disinformation*. Such strategic misrepresentations can be used in negotiation and other conflict situations to mislead an adversary about one's true capabilities or intentions.

In elaborating on the implications of this incident, Weick noted that the attaché's search for a foolproof cue made him, ironically, more vulnerable to exploitation. Weick reasoned that "the very fact that the observer finds himself looking to a particular bit of evidence as an incorruptible check on what is or might be corruptible is the very reason he should be suspicious of this evidence; for the best evidence for him is also the best evidence for the subject to manipulate."[29]

In addition to impairing leaders' ability to learn directly from their experience, situations that induce distrust may impede leaders' ability to generate the kind of diagnostic information needed to accurately calibrate the other party's trustworthiness. Learning about trustworthiness entails risk-taking.[30] People must engage in appropriate interpersonal "experiments" if they are to generate the diagnostic data necessary to learn who among them can be trusted and how much. Such experiments require that individuals expose themselves to the prospect of misplaced trust and misplaced distrust.

Any systematic bias in the generation of data samples can, of course, influence the inferences that result from these experiments. Along these lines, trust theorists such as Hardin and Gambetta have argued that asymmetries in the presumptive trust of individuals who begin with low or high trust levels may differentially impact the frequency with which they generate useful learning opportunities.[31] These asymmetries can also affect individuals' ability to extract reliable cues from those opportunities that they do generate. As Gambetta noted in this regard, it is very difficult to invalidate distrust through experience, because it either "prevents people from engaging in the appropriate kind of social experiment, or, worse, it leads to behavior which bolsters the validity of distrust itself."[32] Consequently, presumptive distrust tends to become perpetual distrust.

In addition to these psychological factors, social dynamics can contribute to asymmetries in judgment regarding trust and distrust in intergroup negotiation. For example, intragroup dynamics may impede trust development. Insko and Schopler investigated the effects of in-group discussion on trust-related judgments.[33] They had judges code tape-recorded discussions for both explicit and implicit statements of distrust. The results showed that there were significantly more distrust statements in discussions between groups compared with discussions between individuals. There was also a strong negative correlation between the level of distrust recorded in these conversations and subsequent cooperative behavior.

Another potential social barrier to generating trust-building experiences derives from various self-presentational predicaments that negotiators, as representatives for their groups, face. As Kressel observed, "Negotiators may be pressured by their constituents into presenting the constituents' demands vehemently and without backing down, while their opposite numbers across the bargaining table may expect these same negotiators to adhere to norms of moderation and compromise."[34] Thus, when individuals feel accountable to others, they are more likely to be concerned not only about the objective outcomes they obtain but also about how those outcomes are perceived and evaluated by those to whom they feel accountable. Research on the effects of perceived accountability on negotiator judgment and decision shows that such self-presentational concerns exert an important influence on negotiator judgment and behavior.[35]

What Can Leaders Do to Create and Sustain Trust in Intergroup Negotiations?

The psychological and social barriers identified in the preceding section would seem to support little optimism that trust might gain even a viable toehold—let alone endure—in intergroup negotiations. To be sure, the problem of creating and sustaining trust has proven daunting for many leaders. The difficulty, as experienced by the negotiators themselves, was nicely captured in a personal communiqué sent by Soviet premier Nikita Khrushchev to U.S. president John F. Kennedy at the height of their tense negotiations during the Cuban missile crisis. Khrushchev cautioned Kennedy that the escalating conflict between their countries could be likened to a rope knotted in the middle: "The harder you and I pull, the tighter this knot [of war] will become," he said. "And a time may come when this knot is tied so tight that the person who tied it is no longer capable of untying it."[36]

Although the barriers to trust are formidable, there is evidence that they are not insurmountable. Accordingly, I turn now to a discussion of how trust can be created and the knot of distrust can be, if not untied completely, at least loosened. I consider, first, unilateral initiatives that can be undertaken by the negotiating parties themselves and then turn to a discussion of structural approaches to building trust.

In unilateral negotiator initiatives, leaders can obviously attempt to influence each other's perceptions and behaviors when they are embroiled in a conflict or crisis. This action can include efforts to create a climate of mutual trust, both by trying to elicit cooperative behavior from the other party and by attempting to communicate their own trustworthiness and willingness to cooperate. Much of the literature on this trust-building process has been motivated by recognition of the circular relation between trust and cooperation: trust tends to beget cooperation, and cooperation breeds further trust.[37]

Perhaps the simplest and most direct way to initiate such constructive change in the relationship between two wary negotiating groups is for one of the negotiators to make a gesture that interrupts the status quo. Early studies pursuing this idea, however, produced discouraging results: unvarying or unconditional cooperation is puzzling to recipients, and the tendency is to exploit it.[38]

Although strategies of unconditional cooperation yield disappointing results, initiatives that involve *contingent* cooperation have proven more effective in eliciting and sustaining cooperative behavior.[39] Studies in this vein have identified specific patterns of reciprocation that are efficacious in such situations. Osgood's strategy of graduated reciprocation in tension reduction (GRIT) was an early model of such patterns.[40] Osgood's core insight was that a sequence of carefully calibrated and clear signals might initiate a sustainable process of mutual trust and cooperation. In an often-cited example, Etzioni used the GRIT framework to interpret the series of progressively conciliatory exchanges between President Kennedy and Premier Khrushchev in the early 1960s.[41]

Drawing on this basic idea, Lindskold and others undertook a sustained program of laboratory-based research on the dynamics of trust development.[42] Several practical recommendations emerged from this work. First, it is useful for negotiators to announce what they are doing ahead of time and to carry out the initiatives as announced. In addition, it has been suggested that conciliatory initiatives should be irrevocable and noncontingent; in this way they will be understood as efforts to resolve the conflict rather than to gain a quid pro quo. Also, they should be costly or risky to oneself so that they cannot be construed as a cheap trick or trap. They should be continued for a period of time so as to put pressure on the other party to reciprocate and to give the other party time to rethink its policy.

The GRIT strategy adopts a logic of starting small in order to jumpstart an incremental trust-building process. An alternative strategy—and one that reverses the logic a bit—involves an attempt by one party to more dramatically and quickly "break the frame" of distrust and suspicion by making a large conciliatory gesture. Because a large (risky) initiative entails obvious and severe political costs to the negotiator making the initiative, its significance is hard to discount or ignore. A notable example was the trip by Egyptian president Anwar Sadat to Jerusalem in 1978, a step that paved the way for peace between Egypt and Israel.[43] This strategy is not unconditionally effective, however, and may produce unintended effects. Such initiatives risk alienating important constituents and may undermine a negotiator's credibility and effectiveness with constituents. As Sadat's experience demonstrated, moreover, sometimes such courageous initiatives may prove fatal.

Turning now to structural approaches leaders can use to build trust, we find a large body of theory and research on institutional approaches leaders can use to create and sustain mutual trust.[44] The Standing Consultative Commission (SCC) provides one illustration of how creative leaders can employ institutional structures to potentially improve and stabilize trust in complex, recurring, high-stakes negotiations, especially when the parties are highly distrustful of each other.[45]

The SCC was a product of the Strategic Arms Limitation Talks between the United States and the Soviet Union, begun in 1969. Thus, its creation was a direct result of a specific negotiation (the ABM treaty of 1972), but its aim was more general: the commission was to contribute to the continued viability and effectiveness of negotiated agreements by resolving questions of interpretation and concerns about compliance if and when they arose. It thus created an institutional mechanism that allowed leaders and their subordinates to reach an initial agreement, even though many details had not been worked out to the parties' respective satisfaction.

Another approach involves *fractionating* a conflict by restructuring or decomposing it into numerous smaller issues so that the risk associated with reaching agreement on any one issue is relatively low.[46] In most real-world situations, a motivated and willing leader can usually make a tiny cooperative move even if trust is low and then can wait to see whether the other party reciprocates before taking the next small move. Two leaders can sometimes move toward settlement using this strategy by each making small concessions that are reciprocated by the other until they arrive at a common position. Much like GRIT, this strategy greatly reduces the perceived risk of misplaced trust. It has the additional benefit, like piecemeal reciprocity, that the leaders learn that reaching agreement is possible (i.e., that it is possible to trust the other party along at least some dimensions or with respect to some set of issues). Success on these early and comparatively easy issues may then build momentum and confidence on subsequent, thornier issues, leading over time to greater trust between the leaders.

Conclusion

The primary aim of this chapter has been to paint a constructive and optimistic picture regarding the prospects for building and sustaining trust between groups. As is evident in this review of the extant literature, leaders possess a wide array of effective strategies and tactics for enhancing trust between wary groups. With such a toolkit, they can play an assertive and consequential role in reducing distrust and suspicion between interdependent groups. Doing so, however, requires both knowledge and creativity. Trust may be fragile, but it is also viable.

Notes

Author's note: A preliminary version of these ideas was presented at the 2006 Conference on Intergroup Leadership, organized by Todd Pittinsky and held at the Center for Public

Leadership, John F. Kennedy School of Government, Harvard University. I am grateful to Todd Pittinsky and several anonymous reviewers for their comments on that earlier draft.

1. Robert Blake and Jane Mouton, "From Theory to Practice in Interface Problem Solving," in *Psychology of Intergroup Relations*, ed. Stephen Worchel and William Austin (Chicago: Nelson-Hall, 1986), 67–82.

2. Gerry Kessler, *The Confidante: Condoleezza Rice and the Creation of the Bush Legacy* (New York: St. Martin's Press, 2007).

3. Peter Carnevale and Dean Pruitt, *Negotiation in Social Conflict* (Buckingham, UK: Open University Press, 2000); Deepak Malhotra and Max Bazerman, *Negotiation Genius* (Boston: Harvard Business School Press, 2007); and Dean Pruitt and Jeffrey Rubin, *Social Conflict: Escalation, Statement and Settlement* (New York: Random House, 1986).

4. Robert Kahn, "Organizational Theory," in *International Negotiation: Analysis, Approaches, and Issues*, ed. PIN (Processes of International Negotiations) Project (San Francisco: Jossey-Bass, 1991), 148–163.

5. William Webb and Steve Worchel, "Trust and Distrust," in *Psychology of Intergroup Relations*, ed. Stephen Worchel and William Austin (Chicago: Nelson-Hall, 1986), 213–228.

6. Deborah Larson, *Anatomy of Mistrust: U.S.–Soviet Relations During the Cold War* (Ithaca, NY: Cornell University Press, 1997); and Roy Lewicki and Barbara Bunker, "Trust in Relationships: A Model of Trust Development and Decline," in *Conflict, Cooperation, and Justice*, ed. Barbara Bunker and Jeffrey Rubin (San Francisco: Jossey-Bass, 1995), 131–145.

7. Bernard Barber, *The Logic and Limits of Trust* (New Brunswick, NJ: Rutgers University Press, 1983); Russell Hardin, "The Street-Level Epistemology of Trust," *Annals der Kritikal* 14 (1992): 152–176; and John Lewis and Adam Weigert, "Trust as a Social Reality," *Social Forces* 63 (1985): 967–985.

8. Barber, *The Logic and Limits of Trust*, 164–165.

9. Pruitt and Rubin, *Social Conflict: Escalation, Statement and Settlement*.

10. Julian Rotter, "Generalized Expectancies for Interpersonal Trust," *American Psychologist* 26 (1971): 443–452.

11. Lewis and Weigert, "Trust as a Social Reality."

12. Ibid., 971.

13. Carnevale and Pruitt, *Negotiation in Social Conflict*.

14. Svenn Lindskold and Gert Han, "GRIT as a Foundation for Integrative Bargaining," *Personality and Social Psychology Bulletin* 14 (1988): 335–345.

15. Morton Deutsch, "Strategies for Inducing Cooperation," in *Psychology and the Prevention of Nuclear War*, ed. Ralph White (New York: New York University Press, 1986), 41–68.

16. Mick Rothbart and Wendy Hallmark, "Ingroup–Outgroup Differences in the Perceived Efficacy of Coercion and Conciliation in Resolving Social Conflict," *Journal of Personality and Social Psychology* 55 (1988): 248–257.

17. Svenn Lindskold, "Trust Development, the GRIT Proposal, and the Effects of Conciliatory Acts on Conflict and Cooperation," *Psychological Bulletin* 85 (1978): 772–793.

18. Marilynn Brewer and Rupert Brown, "Intergroup Relations," in *Handbook of Social Psychology*, ed. Dan Gilbert, Susan Fiske, and Gardner Lindzey (Boston: McGraw-Hill, 1998), 554–594; and Roderick Kramer, "Paranoid Cognition in Social Systems: Thinking and Acting in the Shadow of Doubt," *Personality and Social Psychology Review* 2 (1998): 251–275.

19. Svenn Lindskold, "GRIT: Reducing Distrust Through Carefully Introduced Conciliation," in *Psychology of Intergroup Relations*, ed. Stephen Worchel and William Austin (Chicago: Nelson-Hall, 1986), 305–322; and Webb and Worchel, "Trust and Distrust."

20. For an extensive overview of this literature, see Malhotra and Bazerman, *Negotiation Genius*.

21. Brewer and Brown, "Intergroup Relations"; and David Messick and Diane Mackie, "Intergroup Relations," *Annual Review of Psychology* 40 (1989): 45–81.

22. Marilynn Brewer, "Ingroup Bias in the Minimal Intergroup Situation: A Cognitive Motivational Analysis," *Psychological Bulletin* 86 (1979): 307–324; Messick and Mackie, "Intergroup Relations," *Annual Review of Psychology* 40; Jeffrey Polzer, "Intergroup Negotiations: The Effects of Negotiating Teams," *Journal of Conflict Resolution* 40 (1996): 678–698; and Leigh Thompson, Kathleen Valley, and Roderick Kramer, "The Bittersweet Feeling of Success: An Examination of Social Perception in Negotiation," *Journal of Experimental Social Psychology* 31 (1995): 467–492.

23. Chet Insko and Janet Schopler, "Differential Distrust of Groups and Individuals," in *Intergroup Cognition and Intergroup Behavior*, ed. Constantine Sedikides, John Schopler, and Chet Insko (Mahwah, NJ: Erlbaum, 1998), 75–108.

24. Brewer and Brown, "Intergroup Relations," 569.

25. Ibid.

26. Rothbart and Hallmark, "Ingroup–Outgroup Differences in the Perceived Efficacy of Coercion and Conciliation in Resolving Social Conflict."

27. Roderick Kramer, "Windows of Vulnerability or Cognitive Illusions? Cognitive Processes and the Nuclear Arms Race," *Journal of Experimental Social Psychology* 25 (1989): 79–100.

28. Karl Weick, *The Social Psychology of Organizing* (New York: Addison-Wesley, 1979).

29. Ibid., 172–173.

30. Hardin, "The Street-Level Epistemology of Trust"; Dean Pruitt, *Negotiation Behavior* (New York: Academic Press, 1981).

31. Hardin, "The Street-Level Epistemology of Trust"; Diego Gambetta, "Can We Trust Trust?" in *Trust: Making and Breaking Cooperative Relationships*, ed. Diego Gambetta (New York: Blackwell, 1988).

32. Gambetta, "Can We Trust Trust?" 234.

33. Insko and Schopler, "Differential Distrust of Groups and Individuals."

34. Keith Kressel, "Kissinger in the Middle East: An Exploratory Analysis of Role Strain in International Mediation," in *Dynamics of Third Party Intervention: Kissinger in the Middle East*, ed. Jeffrey Rubin (New York: Praeger, 1981), 227.

35. Peter Carnevale, Dean Pruitt, and Steven Seilheimer, "Looking and Competing: Accountability and Visual Access in Integrative Bargaining," *Journal of Personality and Social Psychology* 40 (1981): 111–120.

36. Robert Kennedy, *Thirteen Days: A Memoir of the Cuban Missile Crisis* (New York: W. W. Norton, 1969), 81.

37. Morton Deutsch, *The Resolution of Conflict* (New Haven, CT: Yale University Press, 1973); and Lindskold, "Trust Development."

38. Deutsch, "Strategies for Inducing Cooperation."

39. Deutsch, *The Resolution of Conflict*.

40. Charles Osgood, *An Alternative to War and Surrender* (Champaign: University of Illinois Press, 1962).

41. Amitai Etzioni, "The Kennedy Experiment: Unilateral Initiatives," *Western Political Quarterly* 20 (1967): 12–23.

42. See Lindskold, "Trust Development," and Lindskold, "GRIT: Reducing Distrust Through Carefully Introduced Conciliation," for a review.

43. Herbert Kelman, "Overcoming the Psychological Barrier: An Analysis of the Egyptian–Israeli Peace Process," *Negotiation Journal* 1 (1985): 213–235.

44. Lynn Zucker, "Production of Trust: Institutional Sources of Economic Structure," in *Research in Organizational Behavior*, ed. Barry Staw and Larry Cummings (Greenwich, CT: JAI Press, 1986), 53–111.

45. Kahn, "Organizational Theory."

46. Roger Fisher, "Fractionating Conflict," in *International Conflict and Behavioral Science*, ed. Roger Fisher (New York: Basic Books, 1964), 91–109.

9

Boundaries Need Not Be Barriers

Leading Collaboration Among Groups in Decentralized Organizations

Heather M. Caruso

Harvard University

Todd Rogers

Harvard Business School

Max H. Bazerman

Harvard Business School

M ANY EMPLOYEES in decentralized organizations note that it is harder to work with other divisions or departments within their own organization than it is to work with outside suppliers or customers. In ordinary cases, this intraorganizational coordination failure can cost substantial sums of money. In other cases, these failures can be catastrophic, as was the case when various agencies in the U.S. intelligence community (notably the CIA and FBI) neglected to integrate knowledge of the looming threats that existed prior to September 11, 2001.[1]

Often, instances of coordination failure stem from the failure to structure the organization appropriately according to the key interdependencies in the organization, whether that suggests organizing by function (e.g., sales, marketing, or manufacturing), by product group, or by region.[2] Yet even when organizations design divisions according to the appropriate interdependencies, coordination and information sharing across the resulting units often remains vital to organizational effectiveness.

When the desired collaborative activities are familiar and foreseeable, organization leaders can tailor cross-cutting, integrative organizational groups to promote the appropriate interactions at the appropriate times.[3] Unfortunately, the novel and dynamic pressures that create the demand for decentralization in the first place can place organization leaders in considerably less certain, and consequently less commanding, positions. After setting up organizational structures to coordinate those activities that are most predictable and best understood, leaders must enable their followers to fill in the gaps as necessary, sharing and coordinating information between their units whenever doing so can advance organizational goals.

Unfortunately, boundaries and bad habits make it unlikely that organization members will instinctively reach across divisional lines to appropriately integrate their knowledge and activities. This chapter aims to help leaders of decentralized organizations understand and overcome such barriers.

Barriers to Information Sharing
Across Organizational Boundaries

In the sections that follow, we identify three key barriers to effective coordination and collaborative information sharing across organizational boundaries: intergroup bias, group territoriality, and poor negotiation norms. We then recommend ways of overcoming each of the barriers to promote organizational success.

Intergroup Bias

One key barrier to cross-boundary information sharing stems from one of the very reasons organizations establish group boundaries to begin with: to construct a recognizable and meaningful distinction between groups. The basic need for self-esteem encourages members of affected groups to use such distinctions to their advantage—that is, to set themselves apart from others (by virtue of group membership) in ways that enhance their image and reputation.[4] To this end, organization members are likely to behave in ways that promote a favorable reputation for their own group relative to that of other groups, or *positive distinctiveness*.[5] This behavior sets the stage for *intergroup bias*—the systematic tendency to unfairly treat one's own group or its members better than a nonmembership group or its members.

Intergroup bias can be extreme when groups seek better outcomes for themselves because they perceive themselves to face *realistic group conflict*—competition for a scarce resource.[6] Company funding, access to markets, intellectual property rights, and numerous other organizational assets are potentially scarce resources over which organizational groups may have to (or feel they must) compete. Unfortunately, even though competition for these resources may sometimes be necessary and reasonable, research suggests that competitive urges can spill over into unnecessary intergroup hostility outside formal competition.[7]

The fog created by legitimate competition between organizational groups can even prevent group members from recognizing or taking advantage of unrelated opportunities to share mutually beneficial information and collaborate. A struggle over departmental office space, for example, may reduce department members' willingness to exchange all kinds of unrelated assets (e.g., equipment, personnel, knowledge) with "the other side." Perceived competition might also create an exaggerated fear of sabotage, predisposing group members to withhold information from other groups that might leave them vulnerable.

These dynamics may even play a role when the need for collaboration is obvious and extreme, as in counterterrorism efforts. The now-famous intelligence failures surrounding September 11 reveal a situation in which the sometimes conflicting goals of the CIA (intelligence gathering) and the FBI (criminal prosecution) created the perception of interagency competition for information, time, and access to key informants or suspects.[8] Intergroup bias arising from this perceived competition may therefore have facilitated the failure of interagency information sharing by increasing agents' investment in promoting the success of their own agency without similar regard for the success of the other, even when the two agencies' goals could have been mutually served.

Although competition is a powerful driver of intergroup bias, research has shown that it is not a necessary precondition. Intergroup bias actually arises with little more than the mere assignment of people into distinct groups.[9] In these studies, people are assigned to groups on the basis of trivial factors (such as their supposed tendency to over- or underestimate the number of dots on a page) and are simply asked to distribute money or resources between two other anonymous participants: one from the participant's own group, and the other from the participant's out-group. Even though the groups are not explicitly competing (or even interacting), participants reliably distribute more money to members of their own group than to members of another group.

A notable extension of this work suggests that people are willing to exhibit this in-group favoritism despite significant costs to themselves and their group.[10] This research has shown that people favor maximizing in-group gain *relative to* out-group gain, even when doing so prevents them from maximizing in-group gain or total distributed value in an absolute sense. As with too many real-world groups, the goal for these people becomes beating the competition rather than maximizing value, hence discouraging cooperative activity.

Group Territoriality

Organizational boundaries serve not only to distinguish groups from one another but also to define groups in a more absolute sense, identifying and circumscribing the territory each will occupy within the organization. This territory generally includes physical space and other tangible objects, as well as any number of intangible objects such as activities, roles, issues, ideas, and information.[11]

Unfortunately, the establishment of such territory can have negative implications for cross-boundary collaboration, because it affords group members a sense of *psychological ownership*—claims to, or feelings of possessiveness and attachment toward, territorial objects.[12] Groups may begin to see themselves as the sole rightful performers of certain tasks or possessors of certain knowledge, and then hold themselves to those expectations by restricting their interactions and information exchange solely to in-group members.

We classify these behaviors as instances of *group territoriality*: actions undertaken by a group, or by individuals on behalf of their group, that are designed to reflect, communicate, preserve, or restore the group's psychological ownership of its territory. Unlike intergroup bias, this preferential attention to the in-group does not stem from the desire to improve the standing of one's group relative to others. Instead, this behavior is more inward-looking; it stems from the need to respect and reaffirm the identity, efficacy, and security of the group within the organization. Nevertheless, group territoriality can constitute a significant barrier to emergent intergroup collaboration and information exchange.

For instance, group territoriality may manifest itself as the institution of barriers that discourage out-group members from even attempting to access group information. Such behaviors, called *marking*, are designed to make group territory suit and reflect the identity of its owners and to signal their ownership to others.[13] Marking—using either physical symbols (a labeled group mailbox, a group logo on letterhead, etc.) or more social ones (e.g., esoteric group "lingo" to refer to proprietary knowledge)—is often the way groups first make others aware of their territory and begin the process of negotiating acceptance of their territorial claim in the social environment.

Even more forceful territorial actions can arise when a group feels the need to defend or restore its territory. In such situations, groups seek to actually restrict territorial access to group members alone and repair breaches to that restricted access. Initially, groups are likely to enact *anticipatory defenses*—actions taken before any territorial infringement occurs—with the purpose of thwarting attempts (e.g., storing or encrypting its information on a password-protected computer). If out-group members overcome anticipatory defenses, groups are likely to enact *reactionary defenses*: reactions to territorial infringement intended to undermine the infringement and restore the territory to the group (e.g., discrediting the out-group's understanding of the information and acquiring new, higher-quality information).

Territorial behavior in decentralized organizations is sustained by three important and universal group needs. First, territoriality serves a group's need to establish, develop, and safeguard a concept of itself within the organization—a *group identity*. Group territory can be useful here, because people can simply look for those who have access to the territory as an indicator of group membership. Notably, unlike intergroup bias, the need for group identity is likely to encourage groups to cling to both high- and low-status territory, as long as that territory clarifies its membership and its relationships with other organizational entities.

The second group need that undergirds group territoriality is the need to establish and maintain a sense of group efficacy in organizationally relevant domains. This form of efficacy refers to a group's belief in its collective ability to organize and perform the activities necessary to achieve desired goals.[14] At the broadest level, identification and protection of group territory help groups identify the goals they should aspire to achieve. Moreover, when a group's territory is widely recognized by others, such recognition can serve as an implicit endorsement of the group's efficacy in related domains.

The last need served by group territoriality is the need for security within the organizational environment—the need for a relatively stable and familiar "place" from which to solicit, access, and interact with the rest of the organization. When a group feels secure in its environment, it can more easily develop expectations of and predictions about its environ ment, facilitating the planning and execution of activities. Moreover, it can relax or eradicate any fears about expulsion from the environment, so its members can make longer-term investments in their work and set more-ambitious goals.

Poor Negotiations Across the Organization

The final barrier to effective cross-boundary information sharing we discuss involves the poor strategies used by members of different organizational divisions when they negotiate with one another. In one often-used classroom simulation, two divisions of a realistic (yet fictional) organization (El-Tek) negotiate over the transfer of technology.[15] The two divisions can enter into a transaction that will create value for the company, and the nature of the agreement affects the actual levels of profitability that each division and the organization will obtain.

The simulation tests students' abilities to simultaneously create a bigger pie to divide within the corporation and claim a larger slice of the pie for their division. Nevertheless, both parties commonly focus only on the claiming aspect, destroying value for themselves and their organization. These failures are caused both by faulty cognitive assumptions and by the absence of skills and strong situational forces needed to promote more-effective negotiations.[16] Perhaps the three most important errors made concern the myth of a "fixed pie" in negotiations, the failure to carefully consider the decision processes of one's negotiation partner, and the failure to recognize opportunities to negotiate in the first place.

As parties enter into a negotiation, they often assume that their task is to divide up a fixed pie of resources. Researchers have described this tendency to view competitive situations as purely win–lose as the "mythical-fixed-pie" mind-set.[17] This common belief comes from negotiators' experience with vivid types of competition that *are* purely distributive, such as sporting events, university admissions, and some types of corporate promotion systems.[18] In fact, purely distributive negotiations are rare in negotiation across organizational boundaries. What might initially appear to be a fixed pie can, in fact, expand to incorporate many other interests and issues. For example, negotiations might also incorporate parties' interests in the timing of information or of product sharing, consideration of short-term versus long-term needs, or the distribution of credit for joint outcomes. When the negotiators identify a broader set of interests and issues, it becomes easier for them to make mutually beneficial trade-offs that enlarge the pie of value.

Related to the myth of a fixed pie is the cognitive failure to fully consider the perspective and decision processes of the other party. Although many people recognize the importance of putting yourself in the shoes of others, ample research shows that most of us fail to do so. The price we pay for this failure is poorer negotiation outcomes. To best identify areas where mutually beneficial trades are possible, negotiators need to understand how and in what domains their negotiation partners value issues differently from themselves. By incorporating these value asymmetries into integrative trades, both parties can do better than they would have by simply compromising across the board on all issues. In contrast, when organization members from one division do not consider or inquire about the underlying interests of the other division's negotiator, it becomes more likely that mutually beneficial trades will never be discovered and that the organization will consequently suffer.

A last cognitive barrier to effective cross-divisional negotiations is that the parties fail to recognize that they are involved in a negotiation at all, thus missing the accompanying opportunity for value creation. Because many (mistakenly) view the primary function of a negotiation as the distribution of a fixed pie, negotiation is often stigmatized as a hostile endeavor. Accordingly, when interacting with members of other divisions, many well-intentioned agents feel that they should not approach the interaction as a negotiation.[19] In the process, though, they forgo opportunities to create value for the organization as a whole and for their respective divisions.

Beyond cognitive biases, cultural norms can also powerfully influence cross-divisional negotiations. Consider the intelligence community's failure to share information across agencies that might have helped connect the dots before 9/11. Investigations after the terrorist attacks revealed that members of the intelligence community (specifically, FBI agents) wrongly believed that they were not permitted to share certain information with members of other divisions of the intelligence community (specifically, the Department of Justice). This misunderstanding of the 1978 Federal Intelligence Surveillance Act (FISA) was widely referred to as "the Wall," and it contributed to a culture in the FBI that discouraged cross-divisional information sharing. If such norms could have been dismantled, members of the different intelligence community agencies would likely have recognized more opportunities to coordinate their information and actions and thus potentially to prevent the 9/11 attacks.[20]

Strategies for Leading Collaboration Across Boundaries

The challenges we have identified for effective collaboration in decentralized organizations have a number of implications for effective leadership. Accordingly, we focus this section on three key recommendations leaders can explore to overcome the threats of intergroup bias, group territoriality, and poor negotiation norms.

Link Group Interests to Superordinate Interests

Approaches to overcoming intergroup bias often focus on diminishing the existence or salience of differences between groups.[21] If one can replace divergent group goals with a common goal, the thinking goes, groups are likely to find that they have little basis for hostility. Indeed, they may find that they have no substantive basis for continuing to see each other as distinct groups.[22] A similar approach manipulates group identity directly to improve cooperation, encouraging groups to replace subordinate (us and them) group identities with superordinate (we) identities.[23] Such recategorization can heighten attention to group members' similarities and decrease attention to their differences, thereby successfully reducing bias.[24]

In decentralized organizations, however, it can be important to retain and even emphasize the salience of distinct group goals and identities so as to facilitate the efficient discovery of related resources and expertise. Focusing group members exclusively on superordinate organizational identities or goals may also distract them from thinking and acting in ways that are consistent with their group membership, diminishing their ability to provide the localized focus, perspective, and actions on which a decentralized organizational structure depends.

We therefore suggest that organizations may reap the greatest benefit not only by accentuating superordinate interests but also by simultaneously highlighting the ways in which those interests depend on subordinate group goals and identities. Such efforts do not require merely that managers make both group and superordinate interests salient; managers must also clearly and somewhat specifically articulate the vital contribution of each group's goal to organization goals, and of each group's identity to the organization's identity. It should be made clear that no one group can achieve the superordinate goals, nor can one group give the organization sufficient richness and depth. Group members can thus be encouraged to see themselves as fundamentally linked to out-group members while remaining cognizant of the fact that the link itself depends on their ability to contribute their distinct expertise to the others.

Frame Collaboration As the Solution to Group Needs

The natural impulse for groups and their members is to satisfy their needs for identity, efficacy, and security by becoming inwardly focused, by using group territory to meet these needs, and by engaging in territorial behaviors to protect their ongoing ability to continue using the territory for those purposes. Consequently, they ignore or fail to recognize opportunities to satisfy their needs through interaction with other groups.

Leaders can turn this around and satisfy a group's need to construct and express group identity by labeling collaborative attitudes and behaviors as a valued characteristic, and by defining engagement (or lack thereof) in collaborative information exchange as the means by which a group establishes its standing on the "eagerness to collaborate" characteristic. Raising the profile of eagerness to collaborate as a dimension of identity allows groups to refer to each other not only in terms of their territory proper, but also in terms of their approach to sharing and exploring territory. In this way, leaders create new opportunities for groups to enrich their identities by attending to and adjusting the intensity and manner of their efforts to interact with other organizational groups.

With the increasing popularity of cross-functional teams, it seems that it should be especially easy to sell collaboration to group members as a way of developing new competencies and enhancing their sense of efficacy. However, because people are often drawn into collaboration along functional or disciplinary lines, group members may instead feel that they have been chosen to primarily "represent" and advocate for their group's ideas and approaches in the interaction. Even when leaders emphasize the desire for different groups to collaborate in order to contribute their conjoint insights to the organization, the message directs group attention to demonstrations of its efficacy rather than to opportunities to improve it. We therefore suggest that leaders endorse collaboration in the organization not only as an opportunity to contribute to other groups and the organization, but also as a vital opportunity to draw upon the resources and perspectives of other groups to enable otherwise inaccessible growth and achievement.

Leaders can also address the group need for security in the organizational environment by shaping group members' understandings of information exchange and collaboration. One might start with the likelihood that a group's inward territorial focus will highlight the security risks that cross-boundary collaborations entail: vulnerability, loss of total control, and predictability of the group's activities. We recommend that leaders turn this concern on its head, focusing people's attention on the fact that these same features of collaboration also offer groups an awareness of, influence over, and ability to comfortably adjust to each other's intentions, so that each group can avoid being blindsided by out-group activities down the line. By thus highlighting the prospect of substantial losses, leaders can capitalize on the group's need for survival and increase the willingness of groups and their members to accept the security risks posed by information exchange and collaboration.[25]

Enable and Encourage Effective Negotiation Behaviors

We believe that organization members fail to maximize value in their cross-divisional negotiations because of a lack of negotiation training and insufficient encouragement to use value-creating techniques. Without help, organization members are not likely to disconfirm for themselves the myth of the fixed pie, nor to recognize and remedy their natural inattention to others' interests. It is therefore no surprise that negotiation training is now considered a standard element of the curriculum in leading business schools worldwide. Leading organizations cannot afford to fall behind in promoting this core competency; by placing untrained employees in roles that involve interfacing across divisions, organizations expose themselves to unnecessary risk and forfeit tremendous opportunities to create value.

The second aspect of helping organization members negotiate effectively across divisional boundaries is to establish strong, explicit norms that encourage the ongoing exercise of value-creating techniques—collaborative information gathering and disclosure. When executives who participate in the aforementioned El-Tek simulation are asked, "How would the CEO of El-Tek want the two division heads to negotiate?" they almost universally know the answer: the CEO would want the two division heads to put their data together, create the biggest pie for the organization as a whole, and then negotiate to determine who claims what share of that maximized value.

What we learn from that simulation and this discussion is this: although hiding relevant information during cross-division negotiations unnecessarily burns value, people do it all the time. Optimal outcomes therefore demand that a leader instill and reinforce norms that promote a collaborative approach to value creation in negotiation, encouraging information sharing and explicitly discouraging information hoarding. Of course, competitive tactics are appropriate for divisions seeking to divide the pie after its total value has been maximized, but collaborative norms better serve the value-creation process.

Conclusion

We argue that no matter how a multidivisional organization is designed, it needs to find effective ways to spontaneously and responsively coordinate information and activity across its units. This chapter discusses how optimal patterns of such collaboration can be depressed by three key barriers: favoritism toward one's in-group; territorial behavior by or on behalf of organizational groups; and flawed, value-destroying approaches to cross-divisional negotiations.

In addition, we discuss three strategies for overcoming these barriers. First, by linking specific group goals to the broader goals of the organization, leaders can balance the motivational benefits of divisional-level goals with the cooperative benefits of shared organizational-level goals. Second, by framing collaboration as an opportunity for groups to enhance and secure their places in the organization, leaders can inspire organization members to more eagerly explore other divisions' territories. Finally, we discuss strategies to enable and encourage effective negotiation. These entail training workers in value-creating approaches to negotiation and developing strong norms that support collaborative information gathering and disclosure.

As societies, industries, and markets become more dynamic and complex, decentralized organizations will continue to increase their need for effective, dynamic collaboration across divisional lines. It is our hope that this chapter helps clarify some of the key barriers to this kind of boundary-crossing, while at the same time offering useful solutions to overcoming them.

Notes

1. *9/11 Commission Report: Final Report of the National Commission on Terrorist Attacks Upon the United States* (Washington, DC: U.S. Government Printing Office, 2004).

2. James D. Thompson, *Organizations in Action* (New York: McGraw Hill, 1967); John K. Galbraith, *Designing Complex Organizations* (Reading, MA: Addison-Wesley, 1973).

3. Paul R. Lawrence and Jay William Lorsch, *Organization and Environment: Managing Differentiation and Integration*, rev. ed. (Boston: Harvard Business School Press, 1986).

4. Henri Tajfel and John C. Turner, "The Social Identity Theory of Intergroup Behavior," in *Psychology of Intergroup Relations*, ed. S. Worchel and L. W. Austin (Chicago: Nelson-Hall, 1986).

5. Ibid.

6. Robert A. LeVine and Donald T. Campbell, *Ethnocentrism: Theories of Conflict, Ethnic Attitudes, and Group Behavior* (New York: John Wiley, 1972).

7. Muzafer Sherif et al., *Intergroup Conflict and Cooperation: The Robbers Cave Experiment* (Norman, OK: University Book Exchange, 1961).

8. Lawrence Wright, *The Looming Tower: Al-Qaeda's Road to 9/11* (London: Allen Lane, 2006).

9. Michael Billig and Henri Tajfel, "Social Categorization and Similarity in Intergroup Behaviour," *European Journal of Social Psychology* 3, no. 1 (1973): 229–252.

10. Marilynn B. Brewer and Madelyn Silver, "Ingroup Bias as a Function of Task Characteristics," *European Journal of Social Psychology* 8, no. 3 (1978): 393–400.

11. Ernest Beaglehole, *Property: A Study in Social Psychology* (New York: Macmillan, 1932); Gurcharan Das, "Local Memoirs of a Global Manager," *Harvard Business Review*, March–April 1993, 38–47; and Michael G. Pratt and Jane E. Dutton, "Owning Up or Opting Out: The Role of Emotions and Identities in Issue Ownership," in *Emotions in the Workplace: Research, Theory, and Practice*, ed. Neal M. Ashkanasy, Charmine E. Härtel, and Wilfred J. Zerbe (Westport, CT: Quorum Books/Greenwood, 2000).

12. Jon L. Pierce, Tatiana Kostova, and Kurt T. Dirks, "The State of Psychological Ownership: Integrating and Extending a Century of Research," *Review of General Psychology* 7, no. 1 (2003): 84–107; and Jon L. Pierce, Tatiana Kostova, and Kurt T. Dirks, "Toward a Theory of Psychological Ownership in Organizations," *Academy of Management Review* 26, no. 2 (2001): 298–310.

13. For other territorial behaviors at the individual level, see Graham Brown, Thomas B. Lawrence, and Sandra L. Robinson, "Territoriality in Organizations," *Academy of Management Review* 30, no. 3 (2005): 577–594.

14. Albert Bandura, *Self-Efficacy: The Exercise of Control* (New York: W. H. Freeman, 1997).

15. Max H. Bazerman and Jeanne M. Brett, *El-Tek Simulation* (Evanston, IL: Dispute Resolution Research Center, Northwestern University, 1988).

16. Howard Raiffa, John Richardson, and David Metcalfe, *Negotiation Analysis: The Science and Art of Collaborative Decision Making* (Cambridge, MA: Harvard University Press, 2003).

17. Max H. Bazerman, "Negotiator Judgment: A Critical Look at the Rationality Assumption," *American Behavioral Scientist* 27, no. 2 (1983): 211–228.

18. Max H. Bazerman and Katie Shonk, "The Decision Perspective to Negotiation," in *Handbook of Dispute Resolution*, ed. M. Moffitt and R. Bordone (San Francisco: Jossey-Bass, 2005).

19. We define *negotiation* as a situation in which two parties are jointly making a decision and do not have identical preferences.

20. *9/11 Commission Report*.

21. Muzafer Sherif, "Superordinate Goals in the Reduction of Intergroup Conflict," *American Journal of Sociology* 63, no. 4 (1958): 349–356; Samuel L. Gaertner and John F. Dovidio, *Reducing Intergroup Bias: The Common Ingroup Identity Model* (Philadelphia: Psychology Press, 2000); Samuel L. Gaertner et al., "How Does Cooperation Reduce Intergroup Bias?" *Journal of Personality and Social Psychology* 59, no. 4 (1990) 692–704; and Samuel L. Gaertner et al., "Reducing Intergroup Bias: The Benefits of Recategorization," *Journal of Personality and Social Psychology* 57, no. 2 (1989): 239–249.

22. Sherif, "Superordinate Goals in the Reduction of Intergroup Conflict."

23. Gaertner and Dovidio, *Reducing Intergroup Bias*; Gaertner et al., "How Does Cooperation Reduce Intergroup Bias?"

24. Gaertner et al., "Reducing Intergroup Bias: The Benefits of Recategorization."

25. Daniel Kahneman and Amos Tversky, "Prospect Theory: An Analysis of Decision under Risk," *Econometrica* 47, no. 2 (1979): 263–291.

10

Operating Across Boundaries

Leading Adaptive Change

Ronald Heifetz

Center for Public Leadership, Harvard Kennedy School

H<small>UMAN BEINGS</small> have long known how to create productive inter-group relationships. Hunters and gatherers knew how to trade, marry across bands, and collaborate seasonally on hunting herds for food. After beginning to settle into agricultural communities ten to fourteen thousand years ago, people created large social systems with multiple, internal group boundaries, applying their early know-how to more-complex arrangements. We drew upon shared history, tradition, and language as we created more-intricate and defined norms of interchange and developed ramified authority structures in which those who were given authority identified and generated complementary goals for their groups and super-ordinate goals for groups of groups.

As we know from studies of traditional societies like the !Kung, cultural norms routinize the knowledge and behaviors needed in normal times to coordinate both in-group and intergroup interactions. In times of challenge, however, those with authority must be able to step in and coordinate problem solving on problems for which the usual norms of social operation do not quite suffice. Someone or some subgroup of authorities, often elders and specialists, must dip into a deeper reservoir of knowledge and make decisions to resolve conflicts both within their community and between communities. The variety of instruments to promote productive intergroup exchange must be learned and practiced by authorities within each group whose trust from their own group is based, in part, on their competence in managing routine, and yet critically productive, transactions across group boundaries.[1]

Successful intergroup relationships are ubiquitous. One can simply walk down the street to any set of neighborhood shops and listen to a store owner describe the many arrangements with vendors and suppliers that sustain a business. Indeed, perhaps no commercial entity functions without successful daily intergroup transactions. In a sense, any organization's current authority structures, expertise, processes, and cultural norms can be seen as adaptations to a past set of challenges that demanded innovation in managing complex intergroup activity. Having enabled the organization to thrive, these once-creative adaptations became routine. People learned, by and large, what they were supposed to do.[2] Those with the greatest adaptability thrived, passing on their lessons to posterity, whereas many organizations and communities failed and perished in the face of new adaptive pressures.[3]

We need to explore intergroup leadership, then, not because we have little successful experience with it but because we face important challenges for which our current repertoire of strategies for managing relationships across group boundaries still does not suffice. Beyond the financial and economic crises of 2008, we live with the daily wastes of social division, prejudice, and war. Less dramatic, but equally wasteful, are the failures to achieve synergy across divisions within an organization or between companies rendered one entity after an acquisition.

This chapter briefly outlines the kind of work required when our organizations and communities face intergroup problems requiring some degree of new organizational or cultural adaptation. We focus on three aspects of adaptive work: the commonality of loss, the politics of inclusion and exclusion, and the task of renegotiating loyalties. But first we briefly explore the metaphor of adaptation itself as it applies to our collective lives.

Adaptability

The term *adaptation* comes from evolutionary biology. As with any metaphor, particularly one as abused as Darwin's theory of natural selection, we need to be cautious with the insights it offers and the ways we use them. In biological systems, adaptive pressures arise outside an individual organism: the ecosystem generates new challenges and opportunities. In cultural systems, however, pressures to change may emerge from external sources (changes in taste, competition, technology, and public policy) or internal sources (shifts in orienting values, organizational priorities, balances of power, and competencies). In either case, an adaptive challenge routinely generates intergroup conflict in which the gap between goals and actual conditions is perceived differently—internally by different groups within a larger organization, or externally between separate groups, organizations, or factions.

These gaps cannot be closed with routine behavior and existing know-how. To meet an adaptive challenge, groups must change some of their own priorities, loyalties, and competencies as they develop a set of responses and relationships that enable them to thrive anew collectively in the face of new external challenges, or to achieve a new internally generated normative conception of what thriving may mean in their environment, or both. For example, external challenges posed by Toyota demanded new intergroup behavior of all sorts among engineering and business units within General Motors. Internal challenges posed by civil rights activists in the United States demanded new intergroup behavior among many groups within U.S. national boundaries.

In biology, evolution *conserves* most of an organism's core processes. More than 98 percent of human and chimpanzee DNA is identical; a less than 2 percent difference accounts for our dramatically increased range of function. Similarly in cultures, adaptive leadership is only in part about change: successful change is likely to build on the past. Rarely does success seem to be the result of a zero-based, ahistorical, start-over approach, except perhaps as a deliberate exercise in strategic rethinking. Most radical revolutions fail, and those that succeed have more, rather than less, in common with their heritage. The American Revolution, for example, created a political system with deep roots in British and European political philosophy, experience, and culture. New, thriving businesses such as Google have much more in common with their antecedents than less, both technologically and organizationally.

Yet we cannot lose sight of the fact that in biology, as in culture, new adaptations *generate loss, and for human beings, a host of emotions associated with those losses*; not many people like to be displaced, rearranged, or reregulated.

One group's innovation can make the people in another group feel incompetent, betrayed, or irrelevant. New adaptations can threaten and disturb individual identity, anchored in past and current group loyalties. As students of leadership and change have long explored, adaptive pressures often generate a defensive reaction as people in groups try to ameliorate the disruptions and pain associated with their losses.[4] The practice of leadership therefore requires first the diagnostic ability to recognize these losses and identify predictable defensive patterns at both group and intergroup systemic levels. Second, it requires the know-how to counteract these defenses in order to keep people engaged and facing the challenge within and across group boundaries, accepting losses on behalf of collective necessity and gains, and developing new integrative capacity.

The Old Testament offers an archetypal example of how new challenges and aspirations threaten group identity. Leading the Israelites out of Egypt, Moses knew where to go: follow trade routes (which we now know had been in use for more than thirty thousand years) across the Sinai. Moses arrived at the Promised Land within eighteen months of the Exodus, but when he sent scouts to investigate, all of them but Joshua and Caleb reported not only a fruitful land but also cities with people who looked like giants: "We seemed like grasshoppers in our own eyes, and we looked the same to them." The Bible tells us that lacking faith in themselves and in God, they demanded that Moses take them back to Egypt, enslaved but secure.

Moses fell on his face in despair. He had discovered the hard way that the problem was located in people's hearts and minds, beyond any expert solution he or divine power could provide. With the support of God and a small faction that included Joshua, Caleb, and Aaron, Moses prepared himself for the long haul. Identity, anchored in slave–master intergroup relationships, had to evolve into a new identity anchored in new institutional and spiritual relationships among the Israelites themselves. Moses spent nearly thirty-nine more years leading people on a journey toward a faithful and self-governing society, and even then the job was not finished.[5]

Adaptive challenges stress the organism. If the species is lucky, it will have variant individuals in its population who are capable of surviving (albeit under stress) in the more-challenging environment, buying time for further variations to emerge and consolidate more-robust adaptations. Joshua and Caleb can be seen as the variant, adaptive individuals among the group of scouts sent into Canaan.

One task of leadership, therefore, is to identify the sources of *positive deviance* in the population, sources of more-adaptive innovation already emerging in some groups in the culture, from which to build new capacity.[6] But building on and consolidating these adaptive variants takes time, because people in different groups must learn, across boundaries, how to take advantage of them. Thus, the practice of leadership involves orchestrating conflict and discovery across group boundaries, regulating the disequilibrium those differences generate in the organization, and holding the parties through a sustained period of stress. During this period they sift out what is precious from what is expendable within their own groups, and they identify and run new experiments in variation to determine which innovations will work collectively.

The Commonality of Loss

What inhibits our ability to respond to adaptive challenges in a timely fashion with innovation and courage? Sometimes, of course, the challenge is beyond our capacity. Vesuvius erupts, and we simply cannot do anything about it, hard as we might try. But sometimes, even though we might have it within our collective capacity to respond successfully, we squander the opportunity. For these cases, we suggest that the common factor generating adaptive failure is resistance to loss.

Losses come in many forms among individuals, organizations, and societies, from direct losses of goods such as wealth, status, authority, influence, security, and health, to indirect losses such as competence and loyal affiliation. In our experience, the common aphorism that people resist change is more wrong than right. People do not resist change per se; they resist loss. People usually embrace change when they anticipate a clear net benefit. Rarely does anyone return a winning lottery ticket. People resist change when change involves the possibility of giving up something they hold dear.

We find two common pathways in the patterns by which people resist losses and risk adaptive failure: diversion of attention and displacement of responsibility. These take a wide variety of forms in organizations and politics, including using decoys and distracting issues, tackling only the aspects of the problem that fit a group's competence, jumping to solutions without adequate diagnosis, misusing consultants, blaming authority, scapegoating, personalizing the issues, launching ad hominem attacks, and externalizing the enemy.

These protective patterns may restore intragroup stability and *feel* less stressful than facing the changes that adaptation would require. However, they also enable groups to avoid engaging with one another in the often-disruptive process of sifting through their cultural DNA in order to decide what to keep and what to leave behind.[7] They end up trading off the long term on behalf of the short term. Many people who worked for GM and Ford perceived risks in their companies' strategic commitment to producing big cars with large fuel appetites and hefty emissions. They could see the skyrocketing demand for oil in vibrant new economies in Asia and growing urgency about climate change. But they could not engage their colleagues, senior management, unions, and workers sufficiently to mobilize a timely change in the cost basis and kinds of cars GM and Ford produced.

Sometimes such defensive behaviors are deliberate and provide strategic protection against the threat of change, but sometimes they are unplanned, poorly monitored, or unconscious reactions. Reality testing—the effort to grasp the problem fully—is an early victim of the reaction to social and personal disequilibrium associated with adaptation. People may initially assess and address problems realistically. But if that assessment does not pay early dividends, moving into a protective posture may take precedence over enduring the prolonged uncertainty associated with weighing divergent views, running costly experiments, and facing the need to refashion loyalties and develop new competencies. For example, the failure of Xerox to exploit the breakthrough technologies developed at its own Palo Alto Research Center—technology then seized upon by Apple and others—has become legendary only because it dramatizes a common phenomenon.

With sustained distress, people often produce misdiagnoses: a society may scapegoat a faction because of a dominant perception that it is indeed responsible for the problem, or worse. A classic study of thirty-five dictatorships showed that all of them emerged in societies facing crisis.[8] The Great Depression of the 1930s generated such deep yearnings for quick and simple solutions in many countries around the world that groups in them lost the capacity to operate across boundaries to critically and open-mindedly reality-test different strategies for restoring their own local and national economies. A reversion to narrower identity groups took hold. Charismatic demagoguery, repression, scapegoating, and externalizing the enemy were all in play, leading to the catastrophes of World War II.

The Politics of Inclusion: Defining the Groups in Play

Adaptive work consists of the learning required either to resolve internal contradictions in people's values and strategic priorities or to diminish the gap between these priorities and the realities people face. This work entails spurring groups to clarify what matters most, in what balance, with what trade-offs. What will it mean for us to thrive? And who is "us," anyway? Where do we set the boundaries of the system? In the case of a local industry that pollutes a river, people want clean water, but they also want jobs. In the long run, given the spread of environmental values, an industrial polluter will deeply harm its reputation or even fail if it neglects the health of its host community. Conversely, a community may lose its economic base if it overlooks the needs of its industry. Do we bound the system at the level of the business organization, or the local community it inhabits?

Determining which parties and issues to include in cross-boundary consultation is a strategic decision. Leadership requires asking the critical question, Who should play a part in the deliberations, and in what sequence? Including too many parties can overload people's capacity to learn and to accommodate one another. However, social systems that fail to be inclusive may devise an incomplete solution or a solution to the wrong problem. At a minimum, those who lead must keep track of missing perspectives. Not only can lack of information undermine the quality of collective work among the included groups, but also excluded parties may sabotage the process of sustainable change.

Deciding who should play a part in the deliberations is not a given, but is itself a critical strategic question. Strategy begins with asking, Who needs to learn what in order for the group to make progress on this challenge? How can one build a holding environment and strengthen the bonds that join the stakeholders together as a community of interests so that they withstand the divisive forces of problem solving? Is a concern so critical that it threatens the community's survival? Does a party represent a constituency that must accept change if the larger community is to make progress? Does the party's perspective generate so much distress that including it would disrupt the work of building any kind of coalition within the functioning cross-boundary working group? If the party is important in the medium or long term but not in the short term, one might initially exclude it from a working group.

This is one of the pains of leadership. People must sometimes be excluded and the issues they represent put aside, regardless of their validity. Consider the issue of slavery when the U.S. Constitution was being drafted during the Federal Convention of 1787. During that summer, many divisive issues had to be resolved by framers representing very different perspectives on the nature of government and the balance between liberty and order, local and national control, and the division and sharing of powers. To prevent fragmentation into North and South, the framers made a deliberate decision to avoid a strong stand on the institution of slavery—but they did not reach that decision until after some effort. In August 1787, they tried to tackle slavery, but James Madison quickly sensed that if they persisted in doing so, they would unravel the whole tapestry of union and lose the opportunity to form a more coherent federal government than that provided by the Articles of Confederation.[9]

This decision, however brutal in its effects, made sense even to some who abhorred slavery. "A more perfect union" mattered more, and some seventy-five years later when slavery was finally abolished, the union tested by war was strong enough to survive. But the experience of the Civil War also illustrates the extraordinary danger of leaving a tough issue on the back burner for too long. Although the issue may go away, it may also explode into a future crisis.

Running that risk may be necessary. But when adaptive capacity increases as the community successfully addresses its initial set of problems, it is prudent to reintroduce the neglected issues. Perhaps had politicians done so more vigorously and effectively in the first decades of this nation, and before cotton became central to the South's economy and social and cultural life, the Civil War could have been averted. Indeed, momentarily in 1790, during the first Congress, the North faced the need to share the pains of change by sharing the capital losses of Southern plantation owners, but the losses seemed inconceivably high at the time. The North refused to pay the costs of eliminating slavery, then only to pay far greater costs in the losses of the Civil War itself in treasure, life, and the nation's long-term political health.

Leadership is at once the grand art of engaging the polity in its work, tolerating high levels of intergroup conflict and holding people's attention and responsibility within and across groups to issues in a timely fashion. It is also the personal art of staying alive to fight another day. In both senses leadership is a distinctly political activity. Although the benefits and costs of exclusion and inclusion fluctuate, a bias toward the inclusion of issues and parties gives those who lead more options for diagnosis and action. Developing the network of intergroup relationships also creates resources and builds resilience for future crises.

Refashioning Loyalties Across Boundaries

Working groups that come together to address an adaptive problem nearly always consist of representatives of factions communicating across boundaries. Like a legislative group, working groups are likely to mirror the complexity of the larger system.

To forge such a group of groups, those who lead must understand the relationships among the factions and the pressures from each representative's constituents. Each faction has its own grammar for analyzing a situation in ways that make sense to its members. Shaped by tradition, power relationships, and interests, this internal language of problem solving is used largely unconsciously, but members of the faction know intuitively when it is misused. In leading multiparty groups, leaders therefore need to sense the separate languages and identify the loyalties that anchor how each group makes sense of its current situation. Every first-rate diplomat and negotiator has an ear for groups' styles of discourse and subtexts of interest.

More difficult is the need to convince participants to refashion elements of their in-group loyalties as they work across boundaries to forge a coalition as a working group that produces a proposed adaptive solution. In leading such a process, leaders in essence seek to form a new coalition with these people, where the coalition entity—the working group—has a purpose that redirects the narrower purposes of the factions. If leaders succeed, then the working group will achieve a new self-perceived boundary of identity and cohesion of self-interest. New loyalties emerge among representatives working across boundaries, a process that often takes many months of confidential meetings. We call this phase I of adaptive work. New loyalties anchor a new collective identity.

However, the most difficult challenge often lies ahead, in phase II, when the members of the working group must go back to their constituents to promote the new adaptive arrangements. It is at this point that many negotiations and adaptive intergroup processes falter. After a working group succeeds in coming up with integrative ideas, each "representative" member must lead her own constituents in incorporating and refining the results of the group process, or else the deal unravels. Confronting what negotiation theorists call the *constituency problem*, the working group coalition can be pulled apart when members face accusations from their constituents that they have sold out.[10] Claiming they have been betrayed, constituents demand a return to previous postures.

To succeed in phase II, representatives must consult with each other on how best to communicate new shared understandings to their organizations, and together they must develop a problem-solving infrastructure that helps build each faction's capacity to adapt to change. A coordinated strategy across factional boundaries—with many opportunities for midcourse corrections by working-group members as they encounter resistance, and new information, within their own factions—greatly increases the odds that constituents will accept and implement the proposed solutions achieved in phase I of problem-solving negotiation.

Yet collaborative leadership consultations between working-group members on implementation strategy and tactics may be the most neglected phase of multiparty negotiations, and a common source of breakdown. Leading the process requires constructing relationships that hold these factional representatives together despite the accusations of betrayal that will pull them apart.

For example, Israeli and Palestinian negotiators spent many hours and days in Oslo in 1993 refashioning deep personal loyalties to achieve common ground. It is probably fair to say, however, that they did not sufficiently prepare themselves to engage their own people in a parallel process of adaptive compromise and innovation. They did not have a flexible and adaptive joint strategy with which to make repeated midcourse corrections in their efforts to reshape the entrenched perspectives of their own peoples. Accused of disloyalty, they were overwhelmed by the backlash within each of their communities. They began to damage their newly formed alliances, and they allowed the progress they had made to be derailed by extremists.

Experiencing and being accused of disloyalty generate extraordinary dissonance, because negotiators risk rupturing the primary relationships that anchor their identity and power. Sometimes, their constituents would rather die or kill than face the emotional pain of experiencing ruptured ties, accusations of betrayal from their peers, and the imagined dismay of their ancestors, and they hold their politicians responsible to preserve these loyalties rather than challenge them. Refashioning loyalties lies at the heart of adaptive work, and it explains why it is so dangerous and difficult. Rabin and Sadat were assassinated by their own people. Egyptian president Muhammad Hosni Mubarak warned Arafat after the Camp David negotiations in the summer of 2000 that any proposal that asked refugees to give up a return to their ancestral homes would lead to Arafat's assassination, too.

To orchestrate multiparty conflict, one must create a containing vessel, a holding environment of structures and processes to sustain each representative in a heated set of interactions. This may take months or years, because the process of enrichment among the leading negotiators also means a loosening of some of the habits of thought and loyalties that each brings to the process from being at home with his own kind. But constituent pressures are usually more powerful than these new bonds of understanding and collaboration. Tested, then, with various kinds of loyalty tests, and confronted with dangers that can include the risk of death, expulsion, or loss of influence and authority within one's own faction, working-group members are usually inclined to regress, cleanse themselves of the contaminating influences, reject the learning that came from engaging with other groups, and default to their individual cultural narrative once again.

Thinking politically, then, one would view any cross-boundary working group as a kind of legislature in which one is dealing, not simply with individuals, but with people who, regardless of their personal preferences, serve in representative roles and depend on the good will of their constituents for formal and informal authority (job, credibility, affiliation). Constituents' capacity to absorb changes that involve a mix of potential benefits and losses does far more to determine the representative's latitude for variability and innovation than the personal preferences of the representative.

Therefore, in managing multiparty conflict, leading negotiators need to create a political map that identifies the perceptions of benefit and loss in each constituent group. A factional analysis is critical to strategic planning, because implementation ultimately requires adjustments of the hearts and minds in the periphery, and without such an analysis, those leading a process often become blindsided when presenting their innovative plan as they encounter constituencies who have not been through the same kind of process the representatives themselves went through to formulate the plan and its priorities. Benefits and losses need to be assessed, not simply in the usual tangible terms of property negotiation but also in terms of the loyalties that need to be renegotiated both in current professional relationships and in the hearts of constituents in relationship to their friends, families, and ancestors. Moreover, real losses include the additional challenges to identity associated with changes in responsibility and competence.

Let's examine these more closely to comprehend the power of these ties and their potential to generate adaptive failure. In the case of Israeli settlers and Palestinian refugees, the task of refashioning loyalties within each faction, which continues to block factions from reaching any peace agreement, has been central and profound. Many Jewish settlers grew up being told by their grandparents, "You are the miracle generation. For the first time in one hundred generations, you can return to live on the same sacred ground as our ancestors. You can fulfill the dream to return our people to the land God gave us three thousand years ago." At the very same time, many people living in refugee camps were told by their grandfathers on their deathbeds, "Here is the key to our home. Guard this key, and return our family to our land." Growing up in squalor, they were sustained by stories of their homes amid groves of olive trees.

A peace settlement will quite likely require each faction to give up part of these dreams. The settlers and refugees will have to say in their hearts and among themselves, "We have failed, at least in part, to fulfill the legacy of our ancestors." Israeli settlers will have to move off of those stones. Palestinian refugees will have to mourn and memorialize their keys. Experiencing disloyalty and being accused of failure and betrayal generate extraordinary dissonance, because they risk the rupture of primary relationships that anchor identity. The internal personal negotiation, and the intrafactional negotiation, bring with them the pain of feeling that one has betrayed the people whose love and dreams one carries, individually and collectively.

Loyalties are internalized "object relations," and therefore the refashioning of loyalties changes one's individual and relational identity. A successful effort to refashion loyalties enables one to become sufficiently secure and at peace in one's relational identity that one can say in one's heart, "Ancestor, I can fulfill much of your dream, but I wrestle with realities that you did not foresee. I have to give up some of your dream to help our family thrive in the complexities of today's world."

Few tasks in life, perhaps, are more difficult and more violently resisted than facing the emotional pain of ruptured ties and accusations of betrayal. Refashioning loyalties is at the heart of the adaptive work that must happen at the personal and in-group level if new solutions are to emerge at the intergroup level.

Conclusion

Human communities have always had to acquire new adaptive capacity. With each new wrinkle of complexity, often generated by new technologies, people have had to invent and discover new ways to transact life and business across group boundaries. New ways to create bonds of affiliation and trust that could withstand the divisive emotions generated by difficult negotiations must have evolved over millennia. So it should not surprise us that in the face of our extraordinarily changing and globalizing technologies, practices, and aspirations, we continue to face challenges that outstrip our current repertoire.

In drawing on the metaphor of biological adaptation, I have suggested that progress has three basic elements: identifying which cultural DNA to conserve, which to lose, and which innovative DNA would enable the organization or society to thrive in new and challenging environments. I describe this as a largely conservative process in light of the small proportion of the total volume of DNA that changes even with radical leaps in capacity, such as from ape to human.

Applied to cultures, politics, and individual lives, however, we can see that even what appears from a distance to be a minor loss may constitute a significant disloyalty and potential rupture of key relationships that anchor our relational identities. In retrospect, we might see the continuity with heritage and past, but in the present, the pains of change have an immediacy that makes it easy for people to lose perspective of the value of compromise and innovation. Intergroup leadership, then, begins with respect for these direct and indirect losses so that partners across boundaries can engage in phase II of their work, developing and refining in operation a strategy with appropriately conserving rhetoric so that people can imagine bringing the best of their history into the future.

The adaptive work itself is done in both in-group and intergroup spaces. In a sense, the challenge for any party often arises externally through pressure from other groups. If work is to move forward, some set of allies across boundaries from each group must step forward and generate in-group tensions, importing the challenge and now rendering it internal. Thus, human rights activists have often looked for allies *within* opposing factions to generate internal dissonance and thus dynamism toward change.[11] Of course, the loyalties within any group are usually stronger than those between groups, and therefore the likelihood that loyalties will be renegotiated increases when people are placed in tensions of loyalty with those they trust within their own group. It may, for example, be easier for a doctor who is sympathetic to alternative therapies to persuade more-conservative doctors to try an alternative therapy than it would be for the alternative practitioner to do so. In a sense, then, the politics of intergroup leadership is the intimate art of collaborating across boundaries with allies who can lead in-group change.

Notes

1. See Ronald A. Heifetz, *Leadership Without Easy Answers* (Cambridge: Belknap/Harvard University Press, 1994), chapter 3.

2. See Philip Selznick, *Leadership in Administration: A Sociological Interpretation* (New York: Harper and Row, 1957).

3. See, for example, the case of Easter Island, in Heifetz, *Leadership Without Easy Answers*; Selznick, *Leadership in Administration*, chapter 2; or Jared Diamond, *Collapse: How Societies Choose to Fail or Succeed* (New York: Viking Penguin, 2005).

4. See, for example, the works of Chris Argyris; also Ronald A. Heifetz and Marty Linsky, *Leadership on the Line: Staying Alive Through the Dangers of Leading* (Boston: Harvard Business School Press, 2002).

5. The Bible, Numbers 13–14; Aaron Wildavsky, *The Nursing Father: Moses as a Political Leader* (Tuscaloosa: University of Alabama Press, 1984).

6. M. Sternin, J. Sternin, and D. Marsh, "Scaling Up a Poverty Alleviation and Nutrition Program in Vietnam," in *Scaling Up, Scaling Down: Capacities for Overcoming Malnutrition in Developing Countries*, ed. T. Marchione (Amsterdam: Gordon and Breach, 1999).

7. For analyses of both the adaptive and the self-defeating aspects of defensive behavior at the individual level, see Anna Freud, *The Ego and the Mechanisms of Defense*, rev. ed. (New York: International Universities Press, 1966); and George E. Vaillant, *The Wisdom of the Ego* (Cambridge, MA: Harvard University Press, 1993), chapter 1. At the group and organizational levels, see Wilfred R. Bion, *Experiences in Groups* (New York: Basic, 1961); Chris Argyris, *Strategy, Change, and Defensive Routines* (Boston: Pitman, 1985); Larry Hirschhorn, *The Workplace Within: Psychodynamics of Organizational Life* (Cambridge, MA: MIT Press, 1988); Chris Argyris, *Overcoming Organizational Defenses: Facilitating Organizational Learning* (Boston: Allyn and Bacon, 1990); and Heifetz and Linsky, *Leadership on the Line*.

8. J. O. Hertzler, "Crises and Dictatorships," *American Sociological Review* 5 (1940): 157–169.

9. At most, the framers gave Congress the power to outlaw the importation of slaves after 1808. They had initially chosen the year 1800, but that date was set back. In any case, the constitutional clause meant little. By the time of the federal convention, Virginia and Maryland had already stopped importation of slaves, because the birth of U.S.-born slaves proved sufficient for their economic aims. See James Madison, *Debates in the Federal Convention of 1787*, vol. 2 (Buffalo, NY: Prometheus, 1987), sessions of August 21, 22, and 25, 1787, pp. 442–447, 467–469.

10. William Ury, personal communication, September 1993.

11. See Ellen Chesler, *Woman of Valor: Margaret Sanger and the Birth Control Movement in America* (New York: Simon and Schuster, 1992); and Ronald A. Heifetz, *Leadership Without Easy Answers*, chapter 8.

PART III

Cases in Context

11

Leadership for Enhancing Coexistence

Promoting Social Cohesion Among
Groups in Pluralistic Societies

Alan B. Slifka

Co-chairman, Halcyon Asset Management, LLC

A CCORDING TO the World Health Organization, someone dies in a war every one hundred seconds. Some 310,000 people died in wars in 2000 alone. In all, 191 million people—half of them civilians—perished as a result of warfare in the twentieth century. Enhancing social cohesion and coexistence between populations of difference is one of the most important challenges of our time. We must develop the knowledge and skills we need to live together more peacefully.

Although it is critical to improve relationships between countries, a growing number of conflicts begin within countries before spilling over their borders. This has been true in the Balkans, the Middle East, and Africa. For example, the Lebanese civil war of 1975–1990 quickly drew in Syria, Israel, and the Palestine Liberation Organization. Similarly, the first and second Congo wars in the 1990s eventually became some of the deadliest international conflicts in history, directly involving eight African nations. As in any relationship, intergroup conflict inevitably escalates without prompt corrective action.

143

Former U. S. president Bill Clinton has stated that a primary responsibility of every government is to take continual steps to ensure that the country is not splintering into factions that resolve their unmet needs by escalating conflict. Ricardo Lagos, former president of Chile and now president of the Club of Madrid, an independent organization of sixty-six former heads of state that provides advice to leaders working for democracy, puts this point succinctly: "Without social cohesion, a nation is lost." However, often governments seem unaware of their responsibility to build and maintain social cohesion and of the critical need to create institutions charged with preventing and diffusing conflict. What is more, few people realize what can be accomplished by governments that do develop the capacity to ease tensions.

Social cohesion can be defined as a society's ability to recognize that all its citizens have equal rights while acknowledging, respecting, and valuing their differences. The ability of citizens of various ethnic and religious backgrounds to live in a shared society (i.e., coexist) while respecting each other's uniqueness and differences is central to prosperity. Much as a healthy environment has become a universal goal and an expression of social responsibility, the ability of people to feel at home in their communities and nations needs to become a global social value and an urgent social priority.

Developing a culture of coexistence requires a critical mass of intergroup leaders who share a vision of a society that works cooperatively and constructively in a world of difference. A shared future between diverse groups can be attained only if these leaders nurture and model that vision, fanning it from a few embers into a flickering flame. Such leaders must understand the forces working against coexistence and must know how to overcome them by tapping the knowledge and solutions developed by leaders promoting cohesion in formerly conflicted societies and by people working in the fields of coexistence policy, practice, and studies.

Most important, coexistence leaders must have the courage, conviction, and political will to overcome the forces of skepticism and separation. The unwillingness of Jews and Arabs within Israel to confront such forces reveals the costs of separation, whereas the courage of leaders throughout Northern Ireland in fostering coexistence between Catholics and Protestants attests to the promise and benefits of social cohesion. Thus, this chapter draws examples of barriers to coexistence largely from the current situation of conflict between Jews and Arabs in Israel. The chapter then uses the model of Northern Ireland to discuss what leadership at the governmental level can do, as well as what individual leaders can do to promote coexistence.

Barriers to Coexistence

Each divided society is unique in its people, history, culture, and religious context. Nonetheless, six core problems and principles are common to all divided societies.

Painful Memories: Religious, Ethnic, Cultural, and Regional Conflicts

For years, members of tribes, clans, and other communities recall instances of disrespect for their intimate relationships and alliances, and these memories become subject to inaccuracies introduced during retold narratives. Lack of knowledge of "the other" grows with time and unfavorable experiences, allowing suspicions to solidify. Thus, even after hundreds of years of latent peace, jealousies may erupt into riots and even war, seemingly from nowhere. Historical animosity, mistrust, and fear tend to blind polarized communities to the enormous costs of separation and to the benefits of mutual respect and cooperation.

Trauma, Resistance to Change, and Addiction to the Status Quo

Historical enemies with entrenched points of view are quick to believe that cooperation is impossible and that the other will never become a reliable partner. Thus they are reluctant to undertake the enormous effort required to resolve their differences. Not only do lingering suspicions and deep-seated animosities create an inhospitable climate, but also the number and volume of naysayers create a nearly impenetrable barrier to positive change.

The situation resembles one that is familiar to many marriage counselors, who ask an unhappy couple, "Well, do you want to separate?" Each spouse wants to be independent and avoid a disapproving, unappreciative spouse. What is more, the obstacles to staying together appear insuperable. Yet separation is not a feasible option: the economic costs are too high, the emotional and security risks too great, and the dislocations to home and hearth too painful to consider. The benefits of staying together are immediate and attractive, if only both parties could be treated with a little more respect and consideration. However, instead of deciding to build a shared life together despite the difficulties, the couple focuses on all the reasons that each has been mistreated and abused, and why staying together is simply not a viable alternative. They prefer to live in continued misery rather than seek a practical solution.

Differing Backgrounds, Experiences, and Conditioning

Psychologist Reuven Gal, a leader in the field of coexistence, lists three fundamental obstacles to progress:

- Lack of basic knowledge of the other and the other's needs

- Long-standing fundamental differences in cultural values

- Differences in how communities feel, act, and react in varying circumstances

Anthropologists have long studied groups having deep-seated cultural differences. For example, in the Middle East, tribal and clan differences and hostility toward strangers, as well as deep-seated aversions based on long-standing religious, cultural, and historical differences, are major barriers to peaceful coexistence.

These differences, and the lack of acceptance of the other, may be exacerbated by differences in living standards and by the unwillingness of a majority to give a poorer minority any hope of gaining equality of opportunity. After a few generations, chronic mistreatment of the aggrieved minority leads to despair and a belief that only civil war or forced government overthrow can improve existing conditions.

The lack of awareness of a minority's needs becomes more oppressive with time, and the minority reacts by blaming the majority's insensitivity on flawed cultural values. Insensitivity, cruelty, revolt, and hatred surface on both sides. The need for a shared society becomes ever more evident, but the ability and willingness to create one seem like a hopeless dream.

Minorities' Desire for Inclusion Without Loss of Cultural and Religious Identities

How can minorities feel comfortable retaining their identities while also enjoying the benefits of shared lives and shared interests?

For example, Arabs living in Israel take great pride in maintaining their identity, culture, and "national" affiliation as Palestinians, considering themselves Palestinian Arabs residing in Israel rather than as Israelis.

Most do not readily serve with the Israeli Defense Forces nor participate in Israeli institutional life. The recent establishment of a Civil Work Force, which Arabs can join in lieu of serving in the Israeli Defense Forces, attempts to make citizenship a shared obligation. However, the reluctance of Arabs to join this institution highlights the difficulties of developing an integrated society.

A recent poll conducted by the Abraham Fund Initiatives showed that whereas 84 percent of Jewish citizens feel at home in Israel, only 34 percent of Arabs do. The strains among Arabs of feeling like outsiders within their own country have become intense. Yet polls also indicate that few Arabs want to leave Israel, because they are very attached to their homes, land, gardens, and place of birth, and because their freedom is the most extensive and their standard of living by far the highest in the Palestinian world. Thus Arabs feel disconnection and strong ties with other Arab communities in the region while also feeling important, although perhaps more distant, ties to Israel. The result is ambiguity and frustration at not feeling at home.

Discrimination and Inequality of Opportunity

Despite the dangerously low level of satisfaction among Arabs, the Jewish majority continues to be insufficiently responsive to Arabs' unmet needs (citing security concerns and the lack of Arab interest in participating fully in Israeli affairs). The result is a growing level of dissatisfaction among Arabs with their present condition, along with a growing tendency to blame their Israeli neighbors.

For example, Arabs in Israel say they suffer from extreme discrimination, national oppression, land confiscation, unequal resources, and threats of transfer. They also often state that their country (Israel) is at war with their people (Palestinians), and they point out that many of their relatives live in Jordan, Lebanon, and other nearby Arab countries. Yet established political leaders do not talk enough about these problems nor do enough to address them.

In 2002, an 800-page report by the Orr Commission, initiated by Chief Justice Theodore Orr in the wake of Arab riots of 2000, recommended numerous changes in government policies regarding Arab citizens of Israel, and a year later the Lapid Commission also suggested specific policies and programs to remedy exclusion and discrimination. Although the Israeli government received many favorable comments on

these reports, however, it largely ignored both the reports and their recommendations.

Until Arabs see progress, they will continue to feel unequal, unwanted,
and unhappy. Indeed, as the Arab minority becomes more outspoken
about its concerns and needs, the Arab and Jewish communities are showing growing signs of separation rather than integration. The Arabs want
more control over their educational system, something that could exacerbate cultural differences, although polls indicate that they are actually
seeking equal opportunity in many significant areas of civil life. Moreover,
whereas the Arabs also want Israel to be "a state of its citizens," Jewish citizens strongly prefer a democratic Jewish state. The Arabs also want to
feel that their needs are recognized and respected and to experience a
sense of true belonging.

The main obstacle to such an outcome, according to Amit Sa'ar, an officer in the Israel Defense Forces with an MA in coexistence studies, is a
lack of will: "The weaknesses of Israel's policymaking toward the Arab minority are first and foremost a result of multilayered lack of will to address
the issue seriously. The lack of will exists in the Jewish public, in the Israel
administrative and bureaucracy, and in Israel policymaking circles."[1]

Yitzhak Rabin was the last prime minister to publicly state that equality between Israel's Jewish and Arab citizens was important. Several prime
ministers have since made preelection promises, but meaningful dialogue
between Jewish and Arabic citizens has failed to occur in the face of major
crisis such as the Intifada, as well as domestic political hot potatoes. The
practical problems of living in a war zone have served as an excuse to ignore internal conflict.

Lack of an Entity Charged with Responsibility
for Promoting Social Cohesion

In Israel, both the minority and the majority lack an official, representative body dedicated to establishing social cohesion that can effectively
promote coexistence.

On the Jewish side, no commission, ministry, or ad hoc group—permanent or interim—has been charged with furthering a mutually beneficial
shared future. The prime minister's office and a ministerial committee
have usually handled the "Arab issue"; the occasional appointment of a
minister for Arab or minority affairs has seemed largely ceremonial, because this minister has not had a budget. And because the prime minister

always has a full schedule and a full plate, the vital need to strengthen Jewish–Arab relations and promote policies to support them has always fallen victim to the crisis of the day or week. The essential question is whether better leadership and a greater willingness to deal with the difficult challenges of majority–minority relations, despite the pressures of daily life in Israel arising from significant security concerns, would produce more progress.

The Arab community, on the other hand, is led by the National Committee for the Heads of the Arab Local Authorities in Israel, popularly known as the Arab Follow-up Committee. Composed largely of Arab mayors as well as intellectuals and other community leaders, this committee is respected and powerful, although not popularly elected. A recent vision statement authored by members of this group makes it clear that Arab citizens feel the effects of discrimination, do not feel strongly and exclusively a part of the Jewish state, and desire more exclusively Arab institutions, as well as veto power over major political decisions. However, none of four documents recently issued by various Arab groups mentions the need for or desirability of cooperation between the two communities, nor does it offer a vision of a shared future. Because neither group appears to be inclined to actively promote coexistence, there is a significant need for intergroup leaders to step in and actively establish the social cohesion necessary to create a shared future.

When one considers the success of countries such as Canada, New Zealand, Mauritius, the United States, Cyprus, Indonesia, and Northern Ireland in bringing together formerly splintered communities—and the likelihood that a more integrated, cohesive Israeli economy might grow by as much as ten billion shekels, according to some estimates—one wonders why Arab and Jewish leaders alike are not more willing to consider a shared future. Employment in the Arab communities could only rise, along with the standard of living throughout Israel. If both parties resolved to replace fear with forward motion and actively agreed to explore how best to build a shared society and achieve the maximum economic, social, and security benefits, they could break through endless empty debate and instead produce tangible solutions.

Unfortunately, Israel has never developed a culture of cohesion, and even now its leaders are not promoting it. Social cohesion is a value and implies a responsibility to be social, connected, cooperative, and caring. Most important, it indicates a willingness to work toward coexistence despite differences. Still, the fact that a culture of coexistence and cohesion does not yet exist is not a permanent barrier: the true barrier is an absence of leadership in both communities that agrees on the necessity of creating such a culture.

Leadership: What Government Can Do

Governments, in particular, must take active steps to promote equality, diversity, inclusion, and coexistence among people living within their borders. The efforts of Northern Ireland to further peaceful coexistence and social cohesion between Catholics and Protestants provide an excellent model. The cessation of conflict between those communities is a notable achievement; even though the two groups appear to have a great deal in common, the roots of that conflict go back hundreds of years. England's occupation of Northern Ireland was one significant barrier to coexistence, with the taking of land an important issue. A series of wars and other violence and death also created significant fissures. Finally, the Catholic community has been much poorer and underdeveloped, inflaming hatred of oppression, inequality, and intolerance for generations.

Despite the deep roots of the struggle and a host of divisive activities on both sides, in 1985 the government's Standing Advisory Commission on Human Rights—recognizing that economic and military approaches to ending the conflict had been ineffective—commissioned Mari Fitzduff and Hugh Frazer to report on opportunities to promote coexistence and social cohesion. Their report recommended creating a unit at the heart of government to address community relations, as well as an independent unit outside government to foster social cohesion. The governmental unit, established in 1987, represented an important beginning. Today its mandate encompasses equality and equity, community relations, evaluation and research, linguistic diversity, and social inclusion.

The nongovernmental Community Relations Council, created in January 1990 with a staff of seven people, has since expanded to twenty-five, and its initial budget of $2 million has grown to $12.6 million, funded by the British government and the European Union. The government also offers funding to local district councils, which have endorsed the goals of the social cohesion process.

Meanwhile, researchers surveyed thousands of people to produce a full understanding of the barriers to social cohesion. For example, investigators at INCORE—a leading organization working on coexistence based at the University of Ulster—asked respondents to choose an objective for the country's community-relations policy from among three options.

- Accept trends toward a divided society and attempt to stabilize relationships within and between the two main communities.

- Encourage a more shared and integrated society while also promoting respect for cultural diversity and identity.

- There should not be a community-relations policy.

The results of the INCORE survey, published in November 2004, were surprising. Despite strongly held opinions soaked in generations of blood and conflict, 82 percent of respondents wanted to strengthen respect for individual identity and cultural diversity while also encouraging a more integrated society. Only 15 percent wanted to maintain the divided society, and 2 percent saw no need to continue to work toward establishing a community-relations policy.

Citizen activists and community groups also developed an enormous amount of information over ten years aimed at the general public as well as specific subgroups, including politicians, religious communities, and the business community, on the benefits of a shared future and the dangers of continuing the "troubles."

Many Catholics, Protestants, and leaders in the Northern Ireland government resisted these steps. However, the British secretary of state, England's main representative in Northern Ireland, ensured that the country's civil service supported these efforts, and key leaders inside and outside government also offered significant endorsement and encouragement.

Sizable funds provided by third parties—including the European Union, which aimed to ensure regional stability by jump-starting efforts to create a shared future between Catholics and Protestants—were invaluable in paying for the studies, private meetings, and electronic and written materials that helped the country move from being a place of conflict to developing a vision for a shared future. Indeed, without funding from outside sources, a process that aims to promote social cohesion over many years will often flounder.

Paul Murphy, Northern Ireland's secretary of state, wrote a forward for *A Shared Future* that outlines the government's commitment to coexistence as a core policy.

The Government's vision for the future of Northern Ireland is for a peaceful, inclusive, prosperous, stable, and fair society firmly founded on the achievement of reconciliation, tolerance, and mutual trust and the protection and vindication of human rights for all. It will be founded on partnership, equality and mutual respect as a basis of good relationships. The essence of reconciliation is about moving away from relationships that are built on mistrust, in deference to relationships rooted in mutual recognition and trust. Where relationships have been shaped by threat and fear over a long period we must make changes. We must make those changes through policy and how to address that threat and fear. In my view the absence of trust will set back both economic and social development; we will fail to realize the talents of our more diverse society. The fundamental principles and aims of this document will begin to underpin how we all, Government, political representatives, local authorities, civic society, can work together to bring about a shared future for all of us in Northern Ireland.[2]

The government's first Triennial Action Plan, announced in 2005 as part of this effort, outlines the actions myriad agencies—including those overseeing housing, education, culture, commerce, and health and safety—will take to promote social cohesion. The action plan also presents the indicators the government will use to track progress on peaceful coexistence, including the attitudes of citizens toward each other.

Overall, Northern Ireland's experience shows the need for leadership not only on the part of the government but also on the part of coexistence scholars, nongovernmental organizations, and private citizens to provide the moral support, research, and personnel required to make the notion of a shared future a national goal.

Leadership: What Individual Leaders Can Do

Leaders who attempt to communicate with the other raise fears within their own group of betrayal, danger, and loss of group identity and mark the leaders as shortsighted, foolish, impractical, and even traitorous. However, unless a few people devote themselves to sustaining progress on coexistence, political forces and extremist elements can conspire, through internal circumstances and external events, to delay action. Such delays in an atmosphere of mistrust reinforce negativity and suspicion as well as doubt that any solutions can be found.

Pressures on political leaders who encourage peaceful coexistence and threats to their legitimacy are particularly acute in regions where conflicts have simmered over hundreds or even thousands of years. Individuals promoting coexistence under such difficult circumstances must have an unusual amount of inner strength, conviction, and courage.

The willingness of some leaders to take difficult, unpopular positions ultimately determines whether significant social change occurs. Indeed, successful efforts to create a new vision and win widespread buy in among the rank and file—who usually lack the foresight to imagine or believe in large-scale social change—often require one strong leader at the top. A highly regarded individual who continuously promotes an agenda of social change can slowly move a population to accept prior enemies as partners in a shared future.

Nelson Mandela, Bishop Desmond Tutu, Eleanor Roosevelt, Martin Luther King, Jr., and Mahatma Gandhi exemplify the fortitude, conviction, patience, and steadfastness required to heal deep rifts and foster social change. Others who have led social-cohesion efforts include Nobel Peace Prize winners Shirin Ebadi (Iran), Daw Aung San Suu Kyi (Burma), and Rigoberta Menchú, as well as Ellen Johnson-Sirleaf, Liberia's president and African's first elected female president.

Without the work of such leaders, coupled with the active support of other influential leaders and institutions throughout society, it is impossible to mobilize enough people to regard an alternative vision as viable and desirable and create a sea change. Unfortunately, few people have the courage to talk about the need for change despite the popularity of such a position.

An allegory sheds light on the importance of leadership. When the Israelites left Egypt, they encountered the Red Sea—a seemingly insurmountable obstacle. Not only were deep, dangerous waters ahead of them, but also the Egyptian Army was pursuing them. People were immobilized by fear and uncertainty until one person, Nachshon, jumped into the waters. Somehow the great sea parted, and everyone was able to cross to the other side. One person made a decisive move, others followed, and all avoided disaster.

In many conflicts, historical animosities foreshadow only more futility and disaster and endless pain, suffering, and death. The courage to try a new approach—the willingness to lead across groups—can shift situations that appear to be insolvable.

Improving Leadership for Coexistence

Scholars attending a conference organized by Coexistence International, an initiative that promotes coexistence, at Brandeis University in June 2006 recommended a number of critical actions.

- Recognize and identify community diversity within state borders.

- Acknowledge diversity as a reality that positively contributes to the country's economic and moral development.

- Ratify and implement relevant international declarations and covenants concerning respect for differences, tolerance, and peace.

- Work with national and local government agencies, civil and social organizations, and community leaders to identify key barriers to coexistence and develop policies to address them.

- Create institutions to implement and monitor these policies, in tandem with civil and social groups.

- Codify policies into laws, where appropriate.

- Keep the public informed of the benefits of the policies, and include the public in the process of creating and implementing them.

- Engage with all identity groups on a regular basis to ensure that they feel included in government policies and programs.

I would like to add the overarching need to put a responsible person or people in charge of promoting inclusion and equality. That individual must have the respect of other leaders, must be located at an address known to the public, and must have a staff and a budget commensurate with the task of creating policies and programs. Similar positions have been created for other large-scale issues. For example, some forty years ago, the environmental movement emerged from relative obscurity to unite a number of disciplines, including forestry, water and waste management, animal husbandry, air quality, and climate. By the time of the Earth Summit in 1992, most countries had appointed a minister of the environment to head an agency charged with protecting natural resources.

The government's role is to ensure that all people within a nation's borders feel safe, have equality of opportunity, and do not worry because they are different. Every government that accepts that role should establish a Ministry of Equality and Social Cohesion, charged with guaranteeing every inhabitant of the country the right to live with others in a respectful, secure environment. Such a ministry, and its leader, would help government "get it" and would encourage every other agency to be mindful of the need to encourage human potential and cooperative living. Such a ministry can also encourage schools to teach the subject of coexistence—how to better live with others—and require it for matriculation.

To overcome inertia in torn societies, leaders must emphasize that hatred, mistrust, and separation exact measurable economic costs, whereas social cohesion can bring concrete economic and social benefits. Regions that are virtually at war usually suffer economically, because business leaders seldom invest in such regions, given the attendant disruptions to labor and supplies. Local economies in regions in conflict also decline, because people are reluctant to deal with merchants associated with the other. For example, in Israel, Arab and Jewish interests are widely interspersed in the Galilee, in the Negev, and in mixed towns such as Acre, Haifa, Tel Aviv, Nazareth, Beer Sheva, Jerusalem, Lod, and Ramle. As in other countries having civil unrest, when riots among Arab citizens broke out in October 2000, commerce between Arab and Jewish communities fell off sharply.

And yet, as events in South Africa and Northern Ireland attest, conflicts based on deeply rooted pain and anguish can be eased and even reversed. Such progress requires years of seemingly unproductive dialogue. Actions must eventually replace words, as only proven deeds can replace mistrust, and change must be incremental. Most important, each side must slowly begin to see more of its needs met, as real and visible benefits solidify and accelerate the healing process. A lessening of conflict often spurs economic growth, for example, as business leaders begin to invest in former conflict zones.

The greatest barrier to social cohesion is the lack of understanding of, and confidence in, its benefits. Thus, one core task of leaders promoting social cohesion is to convey the costs to a society that is always on the brink of unrest and to describe the benefits that accrue to one that promotes coexistence and social harmony.

Conclusion

Governmental agencies and nongovernmental organizations can perform the important work of facilitating coexistence even in relatively benign regions. For example, in the United States, coexistence challenges arising from immigration pressures have been gaining prominence and urgency. States in the Southeast and Southwest, as well as those regions as a whole, could benefit from examining social tensions and needs through a coexistence lens and from creating agencies charged with facilitating social cohesion. By institutionalizing policies and responses designed to foster cohesion, these states and regions could inhibit growing social pressures that will only worsen if subject to long-term neglect.

Ultimately, social cohesion is the product of a coexistence-literate society that understands its benefits, as well as the costs when social cohesion fails. It requires broad acceptance of a vision of a shared future as essential to maximizing the society's productivity. This acceptance can occur only with the active support of hundreds of economic, social, business, and civic institutions, and also the support of government leaders who are willing to make coexistence and greater cohesion a priority and advocate for and institute policies and programs that promote those fundamental values.

Experience in a number of regions shows that, given the political will and reductions in inequality, efforts to encourage social cohesion can lead to a shared society despite long-standing obstacles. Societies will either coexist or self-destruct. Fortunately, given the right leadership, coexistence is eminently achievable.

Notes

1. Amit Sa'ar, personal communication.
2. Office of the First Minister and Deputy First Minister, *A Shared Future: Policy and Strategic Framework for Good Relations in Northern Ireland*, March 21, 2005, http://www .asharedfutureni.gov.uk.

12

Bringing Groups Together

The Politics of Africa and Elsewhere

Robert I. Rotberg

Harvard Kennedy School

WHEN EXPERIENCED African political figures came together for the first time in 2003 explicitly to strengthen leadership on their continent, they did so in an atmosphere of convulsive crisis. The Congo, the Sudan, and Zimbabwe (not to mention Liberia and Sierra Leone) were each suffering from massive and prolonged leadership failures. What could be done? Could the quality of leadership in Africa be strengthened? Could the glaring deficits in intergroup leadership across the sub-Saharan African region be remedied somehow? Could responsible leadership as a skill set be taught? Could those skills be transferred from the countries in Africa that had demonstrated a mastery of leadership for good to those other African countries where leadership was woefully lacking? Or were there decisive structural issues, institutional deficits, income impediments, or cultural obstacles that would continue to inhibit the strengthening of African political leadership?

Possibly, too, the "bringing groups together" concept was foreign to Africa. Could leadership be functioning primarily as a zero-sum exercise in a variety of countries short of social capital and reciprocity of trust, and long on adversarial competition for limited advantage and scarce real goods? Most African presidents and prime ministers, and most politicians, were excluders and not includers. Nelson Mandela had become the great inclusionist, but he was a rare leader in Africa. Others, such as Congo/ Zaire's Mobutu Sese Seko, Kenya's Jomo Kenyatta and Daniel arap Moi, Uganda's Idi Amin, Ghana's Kwame Nkrumah, Sierre Leone's Siaka Stevens, and Zimbabwe's Robert Mugabe were skillful in the arts of division and conquest. They systematically pitted one ethnic group against another, or Africans against Asians, or Africans against whites—all, Milosevic style—for political advantage.

The Botswanan and Mauritian Models

Whether or not the concept of bringing people together for the common good is or is not foreign to African traditional political practice, Botswana and Mauritius have long practiced that art. Their respective founding leaders—Sir Seretse Khama and Sir Seewoosagur Ramgoolam—were determined to be inclusionary and thus to be nation builders at a time in the evolution of modern Africa when single-party (and one-man) rule, Afro-socialism, and brute dominance rather than power sharing were all the rage.

Khama in some ways had the easier task, because 80 percent of his nation's people spoke Setswana, the national language. But seven distinct ethnic groups still comprised that linguistic congeries, and non-Tswana groups were well educated and active in business and the civil service. Elsewhere, those minority groups would have been pushed aside. But not in Botswana, where Khama, like Mandela later, made sure that everyone (even ex-colonial whites) who contributed to the development of the new nation (independent in 1966) could prosper from its growth and his contributions. (Botswana was then dirt poor; only after 1975 did the discovery and exploitation of gem diamonds produce great wealth.)

Khama, because of his rational charisma as the paramount chief of the largest grouping among the Tswana speakers, because of his experience overseas and his education at the University of Oxford, and because of personal attributes, rejected the notion that he should pervert democracy (as many of his fellow leaders elsewhere in Africa were doing in the 1960s) and rule autocratically.[1] He also came to power with an inner plan—a vision—to which he hewed despite his nascent nation's deep poverty, despite the physical and other deficits left behind by the departing British rulers, and despite his country's profound lack of trained human and technical capacity. Khama never believed in shortcuts. He never believed in scapegoating other groups. His vision was a vision for all inhabitants of his desertlike domain, not only for a select few fat cats or for his own Bamang-wato tribesmen or kinfolk.

Mauritius became independent from Britain at about the same time as Botswana—in 1968. But the situation in that offshore island nation (a found-ing member of the Southern African Development Community) was much more trying. In colonial times, Mauritius had been plagued by vicious race riots.[2] Everyone assumed that tension between the various ethnic groups of the island would periodically continue to erupt into violence, especially if the first government of the island behaved as so many other new African and Asian governments behaved to their peoples: by favoring the majority (as in Sri Lanka) or by discriminating assertively against one or more minori-ties (as in Sri Lanka, Indonesia, and a host of mainland African countries).[3]

Mauritius, a sometime Dutch and French colonial possession but in British hands since 1795, at independence boasted a 52 percent Indo-Mauritian majority. Most Indo-Mauritians were descended from immigrants who had come to Mauritius from India in the nineteenth and early twen-tieth centuries. Nearly 30 percent were of Creole and Franco-Mauritian heritage, including descendants of slaves carried to Mauritius from the African mainland. About 17 percent were Muslims, also from India, and about 3 percent were Chinese. Very few were British, despite the island having been ruled by Britain in the nineteenth and twentieth centuries.

Mauritius was a truly plural society. The immigrants from India had come from the subcontinent to Mauritius to cut sugarcane, the export crop that at independence produced 95 percent of the island's foreign-exchange earnings. The French and a few English speakers owned sugar estates or were in commerce or government. Many merchants were Chinese or In-dian. The ruling political class under the British had been French, English, and Creole speaking. Indeed, at independence Creole (spoken by Indo-Mauritians and Franco-Mauritians alike) was the dominant tongue, but Mauritians also understood or spoke French and English, the languages of commerce and of government, respectively. Hindi was spoken only by 32 percent of the population, Urdu by 17 percent, and French by 8 percent.[4]

Mauritius was a veritable mixed bag in terms of peoples, languages (ten), and religions (fifteen). An agricultural monoculture, Mauritius was ripe for economic stagnation (sugar prices fluctuated madly on the world market and were sometimes very low) and intercommunal strife. Ram-goolam understood his and his nation's stark choices. He could rule as the country's first prime minister with a heavy hand and the electoral support of the Hindu majority. Or he could reach out to others on the island and develop a strategy capable of benefiting all. After analyzing and weighing his available options, he openly rejected the leadership choices that had been made very differently in Sri Lanka, deciding that the only way forward for the island, and the only way forward for his own people (despite their majority), was to create a truly plural democracy.[5] If he demonstrated inclusiveness, if he reached out to all groups (Hindu and Muslim alike, and Asian and non-Asian), and if he presided over a tolerant and even-handed government, then—and only then—could racial tensions recede and everyone on the island prosper.[6]

Like Khama, Ramgoolam exemplified the critical variable of visionary and committed leadership in difficult times. In the same years, Lee Kuan Yew was fashioning an entirely new Singapore with some of the same clear-headed thinking as shown by Khama and Ramgoolam, albeit with a greater emphasis on stability over democracy. But all three, especially Khama and Ramgoolam, understood that a robust plural society would succeed only if it rested on sure economic foundations.

Khama very early rejected the ostentatiousness of his mainland African fellow presidents. His country was poor, so he managed it chastely and made the most of what were then limited resources. When diamonds were found, Botswana had the institutions and procedures created by Khama that enabled the country to benefit from its resource bonanza and avoid the perils of Dutch disease.[7]

Ramgoolam understood two truisms usually ignored by leaders of new nations: that political harmony depended (as it did in Singapore) on the lifting of all boats and all peoples on a tide of common prosperity, and that a sugar economy could never produce that prosperity, particularly because it was based on keeping a class of citizens indefinitely as serflike cane cutters. Ramgoolam (and his advisers) brought export processing zones to Mauritius, thereby transforming the nation's cane cutters into textile factory workers and fashioners of fabric. Mauritius, which grew no cotton, soon became a major exporter of textiles, importing the raw materials and transforming them into cloth, thanks to foreign investment and favorable tax and other advantages, including a strong rule of law.[8] Later, after textiles, Mauritius became a wool fabric and garment manufacturer, and later still, an assembler of electronic and other technologically sophisticated goods. Jobs were created, and sugarcane fields were paved over. Where there were once donkey carts and lumbering old trucks piled high with cane, there are now massive commuter traffic jams and a vibrant middle class.

Other, Aberrant Models

In these cases, but not in the Congo, in Kenya, or in Sukarno's Indonesia, leaders chose to bring groups together and thus to become nation builders. Constructing a nation on the basis only of majority ethnic domination is impossible, and a recipe for conflict and civil war. Nevertheless, in all directions from landlocked Botswana or Indian Ocean-bound Mauritius in the 1960s and 1970s, presidents and prime ministers of young nations were emphasizing chauvinistic ethnic division, and, by providing economic and employment opportunities or preferences only to their own kin, or kin of their kin, they in many cases undermined the presumed legitimacy of the new states (and their own regimes). Conflict often followed, prosperity rarely.

Instructively, Guyana—also a sugar-growing ex-British plural colony with an immigrant Indian cane-cutting majority and an Afro-Caribbean minority—never enjoyed responsible leadership. More in the pattern of Sri Lanka, the dominant class in Guyana tried to keep power for itself, later losing it and suffering many decades under an authoritarian rule by representatives of the large minority. To this day, lacking positive intergroup leadership during its early days of independence, Guyana remains an emergent nation plagued by cross-communal strife, serious crime, overdependence on sugar, and declining standards of living. Guyana might have been another Mauritius, but it lacked visionary leaders and easily defaulted to the usual zero-sum calculation of many racially and culturally combative countries.[9]

Discrimination in Africa and elsewhere in the postcolonial developing world took many forms: the provision of roads and electric power in some areas over other areas; the location of new facilities in the leader's own area and not equitably across the nation; or the privileging of one or two ethnic groups for governmental positions over others. All were ways of discouraging out-groups from believing that they could enjoy the fruits of an emergent nation. That state failure and civil war followed in many African cases should thus come without surprise. The Central African Empire/Republic, the Congo, Liberia, Sierra Leone, and the Sudan are all obvious cases. Similarly, discrimination against Aceh, Sulawesi, the

Malukus, or Papua for many years led to conflict in Indonesia, as it now does in southern Thailand.

Ethnicity and Political Culture

The former African heads of state, former heads of government, and current executives and cabinet ministers who came together in 2003 well understood—after roughly forty years of independence in most of Africa—how most leaders in Africa had abused their positions, hindered nation building, and failed to learn the lessons of Khama and Ramgoolam. There was remarkable unanimity among the group that coalesced in 2003. Collectively, they said that prevalent forms and styles of leadership had served sub-Saharan Africa and Africans poorly. There had been elections almost everywhere, but most were meaningless and rigged. There were resources and resource-derived wealth, but large portions had been appropriated by a few hands and siphoned off into Swiss banks. There was little to show for foreign aid, too, much of it having served to improve the lifestyles of ruling classes more dramatically than the fortunes of entire nations. Democracy and rule of law were rare commodities. There had been too many coups, too much military and autocratic rule, too much despotism, and too much rampant corruption.[10]

The diagnostic unity in 2003 was surprising, because African leaders for the most part had been and are loath to criticize their fellow rulers in public or even in private. Moreover, it was politically incorrect to suggest that poor performance in Africa—an absence of economic growth, a lack of judicial independence, infrastructural deterioration, increased peculation, and a focus on clan or lineage in preference to the people as a whole—should be ascribed to bad, narcissistic leadership.[11] Yet when three former presidents, a serving vice-president, two former prime ministers, a serving foreign minister, several former finance and justice ministers, and numerous other ministers from a dozen sub-Saharan African countries met in 2003, there was no disagreement about the nature or dimensions of the problem. Everyone quickly agreed that the problem was real and severely consequential. (Admittedly, the leaders gathered in 2003 were hardly selected randomly. They were all known for their integrity in office and out, and for their commitment—a rare characteristic then—to positive intergroup leadership.)

In the African context, bringing groups together is still—and often—interpreted as compelling out-groups to conform to national norms deter-

mined by a majority or a plurality ethnic constellation. There is an awareness of, but not always a respect for, differences. Plurality of outcomes and
paths to nationalism are still suspect in many countries, although Mauritius, Botswana, and Zambia have embraced a multiethnic approach to all
aspects of governance and economic advance.

Accepting pluralism is a distinct leadership choice. Because most sub-
Saharan African leaders claw their way up to power through the military
or the other available national institutions, by definition they become rep-
resentatives of interest groups—the north versus the south in Nigeria, the
Kikuyu against rival Luo in Kenya, southern Malawi against northern
Malawi, and so on. Only South Africa was a nation before indigenous independence (in 1994), but in today's South Africa it is easy to discern growing
tension between the more populous Zulu and the once ruling Xhosa.
There were countervailing pressures on all-powerful recent president Thabo
Mbeki either to act for the commonweal or to cement the privileges and
dominance of Xhosa speakers against Zulu speakers and all others—
whether Pedi or Venda speaking. (South Africa recognizes eleven official
languages.)

Each nation has a distinct political culture—a bundle of values organizing the way in which politics is conducted and the rules by which power
is distributed. In many contemporary African countries there is a formal
expectation of democratic governance, often honored in the breach, but
little predisposition for anything approximating true deliberative democracy outside Botswana, Mauritius, South Africa, Ghana, and Tanzania.
Nor is there any awareness within the prevailing political cultures in those
places that nations cannot be constructed or kept together without a determined emphasis on intergroup harmony, absent any forced assimilation. Only in a few countries, in other words, are leaders aware of the need
to bring together antagonistic groups for the greater good of the proto-
nation. Instead, the default prescription is almost always coercive. Unlike
the Indian model, the predominant African model is centralized, even in
South Africa.

Where, rarely, the local political cultures now assume the need for
evenhandedness and the fair treatment of differences and different ethnic
groups, those forward-looking political cultures have been influenced by,
if not socialized by, the exhortations and examples of particular leaders.
That was certainly the case in Botswana, where Khama passed on a particular baton to his chosen successor, Sir Ketumile Masire, and Masire in
turn passed it on to Festus Mogae, Botswana's president until early 2008.

Mauritius, since Ramgoolam's time, has regularly alternated governments and ideological persuasions at the ballot box, but all based on a political culture of tolerance and democracy that was crafted by Ramgoolam during his deft first term as prime minister. Pluralism, for him and his government, was a positive good, and not an impediment to national advance. As a result, Mauritius has benefited from a succession of leaders, each of whom has promoted and respected ethnic, linguistic, and religious groups working together for common national goals.

Bad and Good Leadership

These kinds of attitudes and approaches were not common among African leaders in the early twenty-first century. But when the experienced African heads of state and heads of government came together in 2003, with further meetings well into 2004, they decided that it was important, indeed critical for the future of Africa, that they attempt to set African leadership on a more inclusive course, emphasizing intergroup values—although no one used the word *intergroup*.

Masire was among the senior members of the conclave. Before his and their eyes was the malign example of President Robert Mugabe of Zimbabwe. Even by 2003, he had single-handedly destroyed a once prosperous country with what were once the best human capacity resources per capita in all of Africa and the most fully balanced economy on the continent, and the situation under his leadership in the years since then has only grown worse.

When Mugabe pushed the country downhill after 1998 for reasons of personal aggrandizement, he did so by unraveling the social compact that had held disparate ethnic and racial groups together. He privileged his own people regarding control of the usual spoils of office and also distributed to them exclusively the spoils of unbounded corruption. When he falsified elections and turned, snarling, on political opponents and ethnic out-groups, he rapidly began undermining the value system that had long held the nation and its groups together in pursuit of common goals. He broke the back of the formerly independent judicial system, destroyed the accountability provided by a private daily newspaper (all television and radio outlets are owned by the state, as well as the only daily newspaper still published), employed violent means to intimidate political opponents, and bankrupted the state while lining his own and his cronies' pockets.

The leaders assembled in 2003 were determined to nurture more future Mandelas and Khamas and fewer Mugabes. Obviously to them, Mugabism was bad for Africa as well as being catastrophic for Zimbabweans. But members of the leadership group were also motivated by a compelling view that leadership mattered—that good leadership was more decisive in poor, fragile countries than in rich, stable ones. They knew that human agency bred either war and impoverishment or peace and prosperity. They did not have to be convinced individually or as a group that leadership qualities had determined Africa's economic and political decline since the 1960s. Only through strengthening leadership could Africans make life better and more productive for their peoples.

A Code of Leadership

Over the course of periodic meetings that stretched well into 2004, the leaders decided to establish themselves as the African Leadership Council. They crafted a mission statement, a remarkable Code of African Leadership, and an action plan dedicated to building leadership capacity in Africa, implicitly for the strengthening of intergroup leadership. Ruling for the good of all was obvious to the members of the council. Not only was governing in that manner for them the essence of good leadership, but doing so also reduced conflict and enhanced the likelihood of prosperity. A narrower concept of leadership was recognized by the members of the council as commonly used but counterproductive for Africa and Africans.

The first sentence of the council's mission statement states, "Good leaders globally guide nation-states to perform effectively for their citizens." It also states that "good leaders . . . provide their citizens with a sense of belonging to a national enterprise of which everyone can be proud. They knit together rather than unravel their nations and seek to be remembered for how they have bettered the real lives of the governed rather than the fortunes of the few." Later the document suggests that bad and dangerous leaders "tear down the social and economic fabric of their countries . . . Despotic rulers . . . oppress their own fellow nationals."[12]

The Code of African Leadership expresses a clear, if implicit, commitment to the principles of intergroup leadership that arise from the individual and collective realization that Africa's critical need is to overcome the many compelling forces that divide Africa and Africans. Except for Botswana, Mauritius, and South Africa, there are now no fully fledged

sub-Saharan nations, only states or proto-nations. Many are still embry-
onic. Leaders can build new nations, as in the first two cases, from diverse
groups gathered within the mostly artificial postcolonial borders of the new
Africa. But they must build consciously and avoid succumbing to the many
pressures that might predispose a leader and his regime to privilege some
linguistic or ethnic groups over others. To rule evenhandedly is hard and
unexpected in Africa, but the Code of African Leadership and the demonstrated tendencies of the members of the African Leadership Council indicate that experienced and wise leaders understand that no other approach
can bring and hold nations together.

The Code of African Leadership contains twenty-three commandments. The first suggests that leaders in Africa exist to serve their peoples
and nations and not themselves. Leaders, the code says, should "offer
a coherent vision of individual growth and national advancement with
justice and dignity for all." This implies that most leaders do not attempt
to create justice and dignity for their subjects. Other commandments
demand that African leaders encourage "broad participation" of individuals and groups, "including all minorities and majorities"; respect human
rights, strengthen rules of law, enshrine freedom of expression, and promote policies that foster the well-being of all of their citizens—and
much more.

The council specifically offers to advise international organizations,
individual countries, donor agencies, and individual African leaders on
how best to improve leadership quality. The group stands ready to assist
civil societies in countries undergoing serious leadership crises (but few
have called). The council, as a body of African leaders of esteem chaired
by Masire, has also been proactive, urging greedy national leaders to adhere to constitutional term limits. The council has also attacked corrupt
practices. It wants to be a collective conscience for Africa, if fellow African
leaders will allow it to do so.

Training New Leaders

The council believes realistically that it will have more impact if it builds
capacity for leadership among the next generation and future generations
of African political leaders. To that end, it wants to instill the arts of good
leadership and good governance in young elected politicians who are destined to become leaders. It wants those young persons to follow the

Khama, Ramgoolam, Mandela track and not default to the Mobutu and Mugabe track.

The council's idea is to bring together selected young elected political leaders yearly to be trained in the arts of leadership, especially intergroup-focused leadership. Political parties, embassies, and international organizations would nominate worthy up-and-coming political leaders. The council would select them after interviews and would then attempt to build capacity by progressing through a series of carefully crafted seminars.

The council has created an elaborate curriculum to fulfill its mission. One section focuses on ethnic and other intercommunal differences and on how those differences could be addressed to build nations harmoniously and to avoid the creation of conflict. There is a section on governance, too, which emphasizes how governments should perform positively for national advancement and group cohesion.

Nearly all political leaders learn how to operate, and lead, by observing and then emulating (or discarding) the traits and methods of leadership of their predecessors. As they advance politically, they naturally note how their forbears won elections, dealt with constituents, forged coalitions, overcame opposition, and articulated their leadership visions in public. In many cases, they too often observed their predecessors running rough-shod over opponents, enriching themselves and their cronies, ignoring the public will, and speaking with a forked or mendacious tongue. In other words, many African leaders today receive as much negative as positive re-inforcement. They observe leaders failing in their intergroup missions but being acclaimed and given national and international reinforcement. There have been too few examples of external positive reinforcement for responsible, nation-building leadership.

A yearly capacity-building exercise for cohorts of young leaders carried out for as long as a decade would have to address these questions of reinforcement by exposing young elected political leaders to positive national outcomes that derive from clear leadership decisions or sets of decisions—profiles in courage, for the most part. Since in every conceivable case those kinds of decisions favored the bringing together of peoples and eschewed ethnic, linguistic, or religious fractionalization, they are ones that proto-leaders need to learn. They also need to understand why and how ethically appropriate and morally courageous leadership actions produce more, rather than less, legitimacy and create stronger legacies for leaders.

Contrasting the consequences of bad, self-referential, and corrupt leadership with the accomplishments of inclusive, uniting, nation-building leadership should be instructive and offers a useful and aspirational challenge for ambitious young leaders. With reasonable goals to strive for and positive models to emulate, the future political leaders of Africa would—at the very least—be socialized along with their instructional cohort to value and work toward responsible leadership.

Conclusion

Intergroup leadership represents a choice. Current leaders, fixed in their positions at the top of a political pole and already subject to abundant negative reinforcement, face too many disincentives to alter their styles and behavior. But the next generation—the deputy ministers and promising parliamentarians—need not be schooled only in the old ways. They can learn how to bring groups together and how to gain the benefits of such intergroup success. They can learn how advantageous it is to uplift rather than prey upon their peoples. They can learn how to unite them. By looking at successful and lamentable Asian and European as well as a few African examples, they can learn how best to accomplish such endeavors, for the home country's benefit as well as their own.

Ambitious young politicians are only occasionally instinctive intergroup facilitators. Even Mandela, a consummate as well as an intuitive inclusionist in his postprison years, was hardly a politician who focused on bringing groups together during his earlier days as a robust, combative freedom fighter.[13] It was during his long years in prison, and as he grew in stature as the leader of the large number of apartheid opponents incarcerated with him, that Mandela became appreciative of intergroup issues. His growing understanding of the Robben Island prison wardens as persons also influenced his post-incarceration approach to other South Africans and his emphasis on uniting and not dividing.

The virtues of an intergroup emphasis for political leaders are obvious, especially in less-than-fully-integrated emergent plural societies where contrary values are common and it is easy and expedient to win votes by declaring racial, color, linguistic, ethnic, or religious exclusion more desirable or more fundamental to a group's future within a nation. There are innumerable ways to play those exclusionary cards, especially in countries with parliamentary and proportional representational methods of voting.

Triumphing in politics by embracing the reverse is harder and rarer. But developing countries where intergroup leadership has been practiced, and where nation building has taken place, are the countries with higher-than-average incomes, stability, good levels of participation, and excellent governance.

Notes

1. For Khama, see Thomas Tlou, Neil Parsons, and Willie Henderson, *Seretse Khama, 1921–80* (Braamfontein, South Africa: Macmillan, 1995). See also Patrick Mlutsi, "Botswana's Democratic Institutions: Their Strengths and Prospects," in *Botswana in the 21st Century*, ed. Sue Brothers, Janet Hermans, and Doreen Nteta (Gaborone, Botswana: Botswana Society Publications, 1994), 21–38.

2. For Mauritius, see Deborah Brautigam, "Institutions, Economic Reform, and Democratic Consolidation in Mauritius," *Comparative Politics* 30 (1997): 45–62; Brautigam, "Mauritius: Rethinking the Miracle," *Current History* 48 (1999): 228–232; and William E. S. Miles, "The Mauritius Enigma," *Journal of Democracy* 10 (1999): 91–104.

3. For Sri Lanka, see Neil De Votta, *Blowback: Linguistic Nationalism, Institutional Decay, and Ethnic Conflict in Sri Lanka* (Stanford, CA: Stanford University Press, 2004), 42–165.

4. Claude Cziffra, "Microcosmic Mauritius," http://www.iias.nl/iiasn/iiasn4/iswasia/microcos.txt.

5. For Sri Lanka, see Robert I. Rotberg, "Sri Lanka's Civil War: From Mayhem Toward Diplomatic Resolution," in *Creating Peace in Sri Lanka: Civil War and Reconciliation*, ed. Robert I. Rotberg (Washington, DC: Brookings Institution Press, 1999), 4–7.

6. For Ramgoolam, see Anand Mulloo, *Father of the Nation: The Story of Mauritius, 1900–2000* (Port Louis, 2000).

7. See John D. Holm, "Curbing Corruption Through Democratic Accountability: Lessons from Botswana," in *Corruption and Development in Africa: Lessons from Country Case-Studies*, ed. Kempe Ronald Hope and Bornwell C. Chikulo (New York: Palgrave MacMillan, 2000), 288–304.

8. See Susan Rose-Ackerman, "Establishing the Rule of Law," in *When States Fail: Causes and Consequences*, ed. Robert I. Rotberg (Princeton, NJ: Princeton University Press, 2004), 182–221.

9. For Guyana, see Abdul Karim Bangura, "Georgetown Shuffle: Ethnic Politics of Afro-Guyanese, Amerindians, and Indo-Guyanese in Postcolonial Guyana," in *Perspectives on Contemporary Ethnic Conflict: Primal Violence or the Politics of Conviction?* ed. Santosh Saha (Lanham, MD: Lexington Books, 2006), 197–224.

10. Robert I. Rotberg, "Strengthening African Leadership," *Foreign Affairs* 83 (2006): 14–18; Rotberg, "The Roots of Africa's Leadership Deficit," *Compass* 1 (2003): 28–32.

11. See Barbara Kellerman, *Bad Leadership: What Is It? How It Happens, Why It Matters* (Boston: Harvard Business School Press, 2004), 3–48; Seth L. Rosenthal and Todd L. Pittinsky, "Narcissistic Leadership," in *Leadership Quarterly* 17 (2006): 617–633.

12. For the full text, see Robert I. Rotberg, *Governance and Leadership in Africa* (Philadelphia: Mason Crest Publisher, 2007), 26–27.

13. See Tom Lodge, *Mandela: A Critical Life* (New York: Oxford University Press, 2006), 17–42.

13

The Context for Intergroup Leadership

Women's Groups in Saudi Arabia

May Al-Dabbagh

Dubai School of Government
Harvard Kennedy School

INTERGROUP LEADERSHIP, an emerging area in leadership studies, can benefit from a more thorough understanding of the role of contextual factors in the intergroup dynamic. Although the leadership literature has given disproportionate attention to the role of the leader, and more recently to the role of the follower, less work has been conducted on the context of leadership.[1] The social psychology literature has provided valuable lessons about the important role of context in intergroup relations and especially about the ways in which the self can be defined in terms of its membership in different groups.[2] However, much of the work building on these original notions of social identity has oversimplified the conceptualization of the role of context.[3] A more nuanced conceptualization of the intergroup dynamic would give more weight to individual factors in the context of structural or contextual factors, using both individual and social variables in theory and research.[4]

Using the nascent women's movement in Saudi Arabia as a case study, this chapter examines how context, as represented by economic, political, and social factors, is an important dimension in understanding intergroup leadership. Because the context of the women's movement in Saudi Arabia includes more than two interacting groups, where identity is embedded in emotionally meaningful contexts and where there are multiple ways for the self to be construed, it provides a powerful example of the role of context in intergroup leadership.

This chapter shows how women's groups in Saudi Arabia are making use of a change in context to connect to one another in an unprecedented manner. Three pathways are proposed for the influence of context on intergroup leadership. First, context affects the fundamental formation of groups, because context shapes identity (i.e., identity formation). Second, context shapes opportunities for collective action within subgroups in society (i.e., collective action). Third, changes in context can create opportunities and incentives for cooperation across groups (i.e., intergroup leadership). More importantly, these three pathways are interdependent. Changes in one can mean changes in the other two, and vice versa.

To lay the groundwork for a discussion of how these three pathways shape intergroup leadership, I provide a conceptual framework that combines theories from the social-movements literature and the socioanthropological literature on gender in the Middle East, followed by a brief description of the women's groups interviewed for this study and an overview of the economic and sociopolitical context in which Saudi Arabian women's groups operate. The remainder of the chapter is divided into three main sections that illustrate the pathways by which context affects intergroup leadership: context shapes identity formation, context shapes opportunities for collective action, and changes in context create incentives for intergroup leadership. The chapter concludes by considering the implications of the Saudi case for the role of context in intergroup leadership more generally.

Conceptual Framework, Method, and Setting

In the social-movements literature, political-process theorists have emphasized the role of structural factors in the emergence and expansion of social movements. In particular, three concepts relevant to both intragroup and intergroup leadership are identified: political opportunity, mobilizing resources, and cultural framing.[5] *Political opportunities* are aspects of the political environment that can act as incentives for individuals (or groups) to behave collectively by influencing their expectations for success or failure. *Mobilizing resources* involves the social networks and formal organizations that group leaders create and use when they perceive a political opening. *Cultural framing* refers to the shared meanings that people bring to their situation.[6] The political-process framework helps identify the ways in which politically opportune contextual changes have created incentives for leaders of women's groups in Saudi Arabia to engage in a new intergroup dynamic; they mobilize resources for intragroup collective action in new ways and engage in efforts to reshape social identity through cultural framing processes.

The socioanthropological work on gender in the Middle East both complements and complicates a political-process reading of the relationship between the state and the women's movement.[7] More specifically, this body of work highlights how the state's ideology is implicated in identity formation and collective action. In the case of Saudi Arabia, the gender ideology promoted in the political culture idealizes women's domesticity, elevates sex segregation, and is intimately tied to the ideologies that legitimate the monarchy.[8] Through the construction of an ideology of "ideal womanhood" (I only use quotes when I directly quote someone, not to draw attention to a term), women become the symbol of national identity; their appearance, behavior, and role in society at large symbolize the leadership's commitment to protecting its "tribal family" from Western influences and challenges to patriarchal control during times of social change.[9]

The ideology of ideal womanhood can be, and has been, manipulated to secure both progressive and restrictive policies by the state.[10] It is precisely this malleability that can inform the cultural framing processes for the women's groups as they negotiate their differing positions in the web of state authorities and agencies, all of which shape and maintain the ideology of ideal womanhood. Thus, differing strategies of engagement with various actors, both within and outside Saudi Arabia, have implications for intragroup cohesiveness and intergroup leadership.

While political-process theory serves to identify pathways between context change and intra- and intergroup dynamics, the gender and identity literature can explain why social identity is relevant to both intra- and intergroup dynamics. By using both perspectives together to examine the case of Saudi women's groups, we gain a useful framework for analyzing the pathways that connect changes in context with identity formation, collective action, and intergroup leadership.

In-depth interviews with twenty leaders of women's groups in Saudi Arabia provided the primary data for this chapter, from official or institutionalized groups such as members of chambers of commerce to fluid networks of activists and writers who connect in unofficial groupings to collectively lobby for certain issues through their writing. All of the interviewees have orchestrated collective efforts for a more equitable role for women in public life through writing, organizing, or protesting. However, they differ in their backgrounds. Some were educated in Saudi Arabia, whereas others studied abroad. They occupy different ideological points along the feminist "spectrum" and describe themselves as liberal, modernist, Islamist feminist, or conservative. They are from different regions in Saudi Arabia and have varying perspectives on how to define an agenda for social change. Thus, these interviewees were an ideal sample for establishing intra- and intergroup leadership patterns among Saudi women's groups.

The current political, economic, and social context for the nascent women's movement in Saudi Arabia has its roots in developments since the establishment of the politico-religious alliance that unified the regions of the Arabian Peninsula in 1932. Beginning at that time, relatively cosmopolitan communities experienced an active attempt to replace their identities, based on ostensibly "unorthodox practices," with a new identity that served the nation-state.[11] Women were the main losers in this process, because their shared community and space for collective sisterhood outside the home were built on these heterodox practices.[12] Because women's experience of community through ritual was reconfigured with no alternative provided—the mosque was a predominantly male space— the simple social segregation of women from men was transformed into a situation wherein women found themselves alienated from each other.[13]

Economic factors had a profound impact on women's identity and on the creation of disincentives for collective action as well. The oil boom of the 1970s funded an impressive development process that provided women with unprecedented educational and employment opportunities.[14] However, these development policies, combined with the politico-religious factors specific to nation building, led to the institutionalization and enshrinement in law of what were previously social conventions or localized traditions.[15] Modernization had a mixed effect on women's lives: it afforded them new spaces for collective engagement, but it also bound them to restrictions set by the gender ideology of the state, which claimed religious and cultural authenticity.

The post-9/11 era in Saudi Arabia witnessed a drastic reformulation of national identity—and a new understanding of the role of Saudi Arabian women. Externally, the rhetoric of U.S. foreign policy toward authoritarian regimes turned threatening, especially in the wake of military expansion leading to the occupation of Iraq.[16] Saudi men and women found themselves in the middle of a new discourse on the war on terror, one that was hostile to their government, religion, and culture.[17] Internally, terrorist attacks in Saudi Arabia worked to delegitimize Wahhabi ideology and called into question the exact nature of the politico-religious alliance.[18] These circumstances led to an evolution in the Saudi intellectual field that resulted in alliances between historically ideologically opposed groups, including liberals, secularists, Sunnis, and Shiites, who were united in their criticism of the prevalent orthodox ideology.[19]

Saudi Arabian women found themselves in a peculiar position vis-à-vis these contextual changes. The U.S. government made the promotion of women's rights central to its campaign to democratize the Arab world—a campaign that highlighted the position of Saudi women at the center of a discourse on modernity and cultural authenticity and as symbols of national identity. Furthermore, a change occurred in the state's official position on women. In the same way that the Saudi media included previously marginalized intellectual and confessional voices, national newspapers began printing pictures of Saudi Arabian women, long censored in the media; Saudi television programs featured interviews with successful businesswomen; and official delegations to foreign countries, such as King Abdullah's first visit to China, included women.

Three events stand out as cases of reform that show the complex ways in which women were both included and excluded from the reform process: King Abdullah's "National Dialogue" in 2003, the municipal elections in 2003, and the Chamber of Commerce elections in 2004.[20] Whether or not these reforms were genuine, comprehensive, and consistent, they tell us much about the ways in which women's groups were engaging with emerging concerns about national unity (in the face of internal terrorism) and national identity (in the face of perceived Western hostility).

The National Dialogue: Under King Abdullah's auspices, a conference was held in 2003 bringing together for the first time in the history of the country religious leaders of different confessional groups, including previously marginalized ones. The third session of the National

Dialogue, which focused on "Women's Rights and Duties," generated numerous suggestions to expand the role of women in public life, thus challenging, on a national platform, the existing legal and social restrictions.[21] However, because the final recommendations required the consensus of all attendees, the final charter included few of these suggestions.

The municipal elections: The municipal elections, first announced in 2003, covered half the seats of municipal councils nationwide. The Saudi media reported the event as a historic moment in the creation of a participatory political culture. Initially the rules on women's participation were ambiguous, but a subsequent announcement made it clear that women, in fact, were not eligible to participate.[22] Although the elections excluded women, the ambiguity surrounding the initial election announcement left a space for women's groups to act publicly.

Chamber of commerce elections: In 2004, women were allowed to participate in board elections for the chambers of commerce and industry. Jeddah, in the western region of Saudi Arabia, saw the biggest victory as two women were elected to the board. In all other regions no women won, although some were appointed. The significance of this event is that women were allowed to participate in an electoral process for the first time. Moreover, women in different parts of the country shared the experience of being included in, rather than excluded from, a reform initiative.

All three reform initiatives provided women's groups with unprecedented opportunities for engagement. The interviewees for this work discussed them extensively, enabling us to closely examine the interlinked pathways that connect contextual factors with changes in identity, collective action, and intergroup leadership.

Context Shapes Identity Formation

The post-9/11 context in Saudi Arabia gave birth to the first officially sanctioned public questioning of the ideology of ideal womanhood. The National Dialogue brought different parties with diverse opinions to a national platform to discuss "Women's Rights and Duties" and made it possible to revisit the predominant gender ideology as a legitimate subject for debate. Despite the tone of disappointment that characterized many of the interviewees' descriptions of the conference, the experience of participating in it had many unintended positive, indeed subversive, side effects.

The fact that the conference failed to change the terms of the debate on the ideology of ideal womanhood highlighted the need for a clear framing of the issues that could enable a collective voice to emerge. This lesson was not lost on the conference participants. One of the founders of the women's section of the Jeddah Chamber of Commerce and Industry, the Khadija bint Khuwailid Center, spoke excitedly about another conference she helped organize called "The Realities of Women's Participation in National Development." The conference, hosted by the chamber, dedicated most sessions to identifying obstacles to women's economic participation.[23]

However, the real discussion at hand was a reformulation of gender within the new definition of national identity. In this woman's words, "The ugly reality of the forces that were oppressing women unjustly became apparent after the events of 9/11. In our conference we wanted to make clear that no one has a monopoly on religion. As a Muslim woman, I must find my rights myself and not wait for someone to dictate to me what they are." The event resulted in a revisionist interpretation of ideal womanhood that mobilized discursive resources, perceived as authentic and endogenous. These were, in effect, the building blocks for a new language for collective feminist consciousness in Saudi Arabia.

Although Islamic feminism is not a new concept in Saudi Arabia, it is the precise way in which the toolbox of Islam can be used for mobilizing resources for collective action that was lacking.[24] For example, arguments against segregation may not directly oppose the concept but challenge its definition, which is based on the Wahhabi principle of *Sad al athra'* (that all actions that could lead to sin are prohibited).

Furthermore, the sheer symbolism of the event was powerful in the context of segregated public space in Saudi Arabia. The conference, which not only was "'mixed'" but also was organized by women, and which men attended as speakers, was held under the auspices of the king's daughter, Adila, and this meant that it could not be discredited. In a symbolic way, the conference was a belated rebuttal to the arguments raised at the National Dialogue and articulated an alternative view of ideal womanhood, sanctioned by the presence of state authorities including members of the royal family and the legislative and executive branches of government. The speakers' presentations were compiled, distributed on CDs, and made accessible via the Internet as resources for future national debates and for the daily microprocesses of negotiation that businesswomen face. The conference illustrates how the process of identity redefinition afforded by contextual changes is a precursor to, and is intricately connected with, opportunities for collective action.

The National Dialogue illustrates how contextual changes shaping identity can have an effect on intergroup situations as well. The conference capitalized on the fact that women's rights were a legitimate topic for discussion and thus spurred regional competition between women's groups to prove their leadership. In the words of the founder of the Khadija bint Khuwailid Center, "The discussion about women's rights did not end with National Dialogue. We invited speakers from different regions in Saudi Arabia to show that our claims are also felt nationally, and we sponsored students to include the new generation. And now the Chamber of Commerce in Riyadh is doing the same."

Thus leaders of this women's group consciously incorporated regional representation, selectively built alliances with powerful figures, and reconfigured the cultural framing for national gender ideology. This arrangement enabled the creation of a model or prototype to be emulated in other cities, while simultaneously facilitating supportive cooperation between women's groups interregionally. Here, the link between identity and intergroup leadership becomes evident: the contextual factors shaping identity can also create incentives for intergroup leadership.

Context Shapes Opportunities for Collective Action

Historically, the gender ideology of the state has defined a context in which Saudi Arabian women have had little opportunity to publicly act on a matter of collective concern. The most famous example of the futility of women's protest occurred when a group of forty-seven women drove their cars in Riyadh in a peaceful demonstration in 1990. Although they were not breaking any law, their actions were interpreted as a serious threat to the legitimacy of the state's role as a protector of ideal womanhood. In fact, the crisis in legitimacy was caused by popular discontent with the presence of U.S. troops on Saudi soil and dissatisfaction with incomes that had sunk one-third from levels in previous decades due to flawed economic development processes in the post-oil-boom era.[25] The demonstration conveniently deflected attention from deep-rooted tensions in the political and economic arenas.[26] The ban on women driving was legalized, and the protestors were severely punished. This highly publicized incident of collective punishment came to symbolize the futility of protest and the danger involved in collective action.

The new political, economic, and technological realities characterizing Saudi Arabia in the early twenty-first century offered new opportunities for collective action. A leading human rights activist from the central region described her experience as the organizer of a monthly writer's forum comprising one hundred fifty female writers and academics. The group's activities take place on the Internet or in private homes, and it has successfully advocated for issues previously considered too sensitive to debate, such as judicial reform. When an important issue is identified, the activist sends e-mails to writers in her network, encouraging them to write about the issue. Religious arguments and "proofs" are routinely provided to members to bolster their arguments.

This lobbying effort does not dictate to writers what they should say but provides a platform for identifying issues that women face locally or regionally and turns them into issues of national concern. One such issue is the heavily publicized case of the "Qatif girl," a young woman who was gang-raped and yet sentenced to two hundred lashes because she was alone with an unrelated man in a car. The campaign the group organized bombarded local newspapers and magazines with articles calling for a reversal of the verdict. The result of these lobbying efforts, among other internal and external pressures, was a reversal of the verdict and the introduction of a judicial reform process. The electronic networks enabled orchestrated national debates about local incidents that previously would not have received attention at the national level.

Such instances of collective action can also be translated into opportunities for intergroup leadership. For example, a public debate about women's share of the space in the Grand Mosque showed that a human rights activist was able to transcend national boundaries and demand more literal space in public life based on Islamic rights. The debate started when the media leaked the news of a proposal to shift the women's prayer area away from the mosque to keep it separate from the men's area. Before an actual law was passed, the leading activist organized a lobbying campaign in the Saudi newspapers highlighting the un-Islamic nature of limiting women's spaces in the mosque. Her article was picked up by an international organization of Muslim women that formed an online petition featuring more than fifteen hundred signatories. Soon after, an official statement was issued downplaying the seriousness of the proposal and the likelihood of its implementation.

The transnational networks of Islamist feminists had found their way, electronically, to the Saudi scene, and they had reframed an issue, primarily thought of as a Saudi issue, into a Muslim one. This instance of intergroup leadership highlighted how the state's gender ideology can be challenged, not through its reformulation but through highlighting its potentially negative impact on the state's relations with external players. New technologies helped women's groups reach their goal by contextually redefining their identity and infusing it with new meaning.

Changes in Context Create Incentives for Intergroup Leadership

The change in context described in the previous two sections highlights how changes in identity and collective action can facilitate intergroup co-operation. However, intergroup leadership depends upon reconciling the trade-off between fostering in-group cohesiveness and intergroup cooperation.[27] Unless a group can define its parameters for interacting with other groups, a diversity of opinion can threaten the solidarity of its members. The organizer of the writer's forum illustrated this challenge when members of her group spent hours achieving consensus on the nature of their interaction with Western organizations such as embassies and NGOs.[28] Reaching consensus on this issue mattered deeply, because the recent reconfiguration of internal and external political alliances had altered the implications of engaging with Western organizations. Choices made regarding group allies also affected intergroup relations among women's groups in Saudi Arabia. Moreover, the group's focus on achieving consensus challenged the prevailing patriarchal top-down decision-making methods. This transformational leadership dynamic could extend to intergroup situations to formulate an identity grounded in participatory culture, challenging the status quo.[29]

Women's groups in Saudi Arabia also demonstrated intergroup leadership by creating overarching goals that united members of diverse groups in different regions. Driven by the shared experience of potential exclusion from the municipal elections, the leader of a women's group in the central region took the state's ambiguous stance on women's participation as a chance to contact women's groups all over the country and encourage them to nominate their members for election. In her own words, "We needed to have a presence, especially when it wasn't clear whether we were going to be prohibited from joining. We used our network and wrote and lobbied to get women to nominate themselves from different cities. Even women who weren't thinking about running, after we contacted them, it gave them a certain way of thinking about themselves and their role in society; about their responsibility to participate."

These groups transformed a situation of ambiguous and potential exclusion into a chance to publicly announce a shared national goal and demonstrate women's readiness to participate in politics. So even though women were excluded from participation in the municipal elections, the process of contacting potential candidates resulted in the flowering of regional groups that are planning for the next round of elections. Despite the legal restrictions on women's participation in this instance, group leaders emphasized overarching goals and planned for future intergroup engagement. In effect, by reaching out to other groups, a new potential identity was imagined and constructed, making intergroup cooperation more viable in the future.

A final mechanism for intergroup leadership is the creation of identities of difference or dual identities to facilitate intergroup cooperation. In her interview, a participant in the elections of the chambers of commerce in the eastern region almost exclusively referenced the western region. She explained that in the eastern province women were still breaking barriers in the community: "Male members of the chamber shied away from supporting us. They gave us funding, but quietly, because they were worried about how it would make them appear." Conversely, her account of the Jeddah elections attributed the women's victory to the support of the men: "Women have networks which include men and men voted for them."

This source of regional difference can also be a considered a source of strength. After the elections, members of her businesswomen's association decided to rethink the way they were prioritizing: "We can't follow the tactics of Jeddah. Let them do what they do best. We realized that what we need to do is invest collectively. We can start a fund and support candidates financially for future elections. We have other resources, like our connections with businesswomen in the Gulf." This group fostered intergroup cooperation by focusing on difference as a source of strength while maintaining a more-inclusive group identity to avoid conflict or competition between groups. This intergroup leadership strategy returns full circle to creating (or modifying) social identity and consequently fostering intragroup cohesiveness.

Conclusion

The history and context of the nascent women's movement in Saudi Arabia clearly illustrate how shifting political, economic, social, and technological factors combine to form a critical dimension in understanding intergroup leadership. Context is essential to grasping the nature of intergroup leadership among these groups. As we have seen, it affects the fundamental formation of groups, because context shapes identity, shapes opportunities for collective action, and creates incentives for intergroup leadership. These processes occur in an interlinked manner: leadership at an intergroup level can stimulate the construction of a potential or future social identity, and changes in identity can simultaneously drive opportunities for collective action and intergroup leadership.

As Saudi women's groups have responded to these shifts in context, they have developed strategies for intergroup leadership, such as the use of transformational decision-making methods, the creation of superordinate goals, and the construction of dual identities. By employing these tactics, the women's groups have been able to mobilize resources, build alliances, reconstruct group identities, cooperate with one another, and, in some instances, actively challenge the gender ideology of the state.

The case of women's groups in Saudi Arabia also raises important general points about intergroup leadership. When one uses the lens of social psychology to advance research and theory on intergroup leadership, it is helpful to keep in mind that many social psychological theories were originally designed as process theories that require specific content before they can make valid predictions.[30] Therefore, it is imperative not to underestimate the extent to which such processes are affected by the internal validity of the context in which interacting groups exist. In real-life situations intergroup leadership takes place between multiple groups, identity is embedded in emotionally meaningful contexts, and the self can be construed in many ways. Moreover, the context itself is in a constant state of flux, resulting in abundant possibilities for cooperation across groups.[31] Experiences from the field can be complementary to, if not a necessary prerequisite for, conducting experimentally rigorous integrative research.[32]

Finally, the interaction between Saudi women's groups demonstrates how identity constructions are actually "projects" that are not limited to describing groups but are intended to mobilize them.[33] As such, identity construction, by definition, is future oriented and not constrained to current realities. This raises new possibilities for intergroup leadership, such as the potential of a group identity constructed of respect for diversity. Under such circumstances, the trade-off between group cohesiveness and intergroup cooperation may be less of an unsolvable dilemma. The hope is that researchers of intergroup leadership can play a leading role in integrating contextual factors in their theories to bring about new possibilities for an imagined, and better, social world.

Notes

Author's note: I would like to thank Todd Pittinsky, Miles Hewstone, and Owen Andrews for their extremely helpful comments on an earlier version of this chapter.

1. Bruce Avolio, "Promoting More Integrative Strategies for Leadership Theory-Building," *American Psychologist* 62, no. 1 (2007): 25.

2. See, for example, Henri Tajfel's work on social identity and John Turner's work on social categorization. Henri Tajfel, *Differentiation Between Social Groups: Studies in the Social Psychology of Intergroup Relations* (London: Academic Press, 1978); Henri Tajfel and John C. Turner, "The Social Identity Theory of Intergroup Behavior," in *The Psychology of Intergroup Relations*, ed. Steven Worchel and William G. Austin (Chicago: Nelson-Hall, 1986), 7–24; and John C. Turner, "Some Current Issues in Research on Social Identity and Self-Categorization Theories," in *Social Identity: Context, Commitment, Content*, ed. Naomi Ellemers, Russell Spears, and Bertjan Doosje (Oxford: Blackwell, 1999), 6–34.

3. Steven Reicher, "The Context of Social Identity: Domination, Resistance, and Change," *Political Psychology* 25, no. 6 (2004): 922.

4. Tom F. Pettigrew, "Extending the Stereotype Concept," in *Cognitive Processes in Stereotyping and Intergroup Behavior*, ed. David. L. Hamilton (Hillsdale, NJ: Erlbaum, 1981), 303–331.

5. Doug McAdam, John D. McCarthy, and Mayer N. Zald, "Introduction: Opportunities, Mobilizing Structures, and Framing Process—Toward a Synthetic, Comparative Perspective on Social Movements," in *Comparative Perspectives on Social Movements: Political Opportunities, Mobilizing Structures, and Cultural Framings*, ed. Doug McAdam, John D. McCarthy, and Mayer N. Zald (Cambridge, UK: Cambridge University Press, 1996), 1–22.

6. Jeff Goodwin and James M. Jasper, "Caught in a Winding, Snarling Vine: The Structural Bias of Political Process Theory," in *Rethinking Social Movements: Structure, Meaning, and Emotion*, ed. Jeff Goodwin and James M. Jasper (Lanham, MD: Rowman & Littlefield, 2004), 3–31.

7. Ibid. The political-process theory has been criticized for being overly structural and underrepresenting cultural movements and nonindustrial democracies as cases.

8. Eleanor A. Doumato, "Gender, Monarchy, and National Identity in Saudi Arabia," *British Journal of Middle Eastern Studies* 19, no. 1 (1992): 39.

9. The term Doumato coined to refer to the gender ideology of the Saudi state is *the ideology of the ideal Islamic woman*. Ibid., 34.

10. Ibid., 36.

11. Mai Yamani, *Cradle of Islam: The Hijaz and the Quest for an Arabian Identity* (London: I.B. Tauris, 2004).

12. These practices include ritualized religious meditation and recitation (*Sufi zikr*), amulet healing, and visits to shrines and had allowed women to meet outside their homes routinely in collective capacities. Eleanor A. Doumato, *Getting God's Ear: Women, Islam, and Healing in Saudi Arabia and the Gulf* (New York: Columbia University Press, 2000).

13. Ibid., 215. For more details on the denigration of communal rituals that were organized by and served women's needs, see Yamani, *Cradle of Islam*.

14. Muna Almunajjed, *Women in Saudi Arabia Today* (Houndsmills, UK: Macmillan, 1997), 59.

15. These restrictions were seen as compromises to the centralizing state's quest for modernization, which entailed urbanization, mobility, and growth in nuclear households, all of which constituted threats to the preexisting patriarchal extended-family structure. The restrictions on women include the prohibition of traveling without the permission of a male guardian, the institutionalized segregation of the sexes in educational and work institutions, and the prohibition of women's access to university courses and fields of work considered "unsuitable" for the nature of women. Doumato, "Gender, Monarchy, and National Identity in Saudi Arabia," 34.

16. The post-9/11 reforms were also driven by cumulative changes that were primarily internal. For more details see Toby Jones, "Seeking a 'Social Contract' for Saudi Arabia," *Middle East Report* 228 (2003): 44.

17. Andrzej Kapiszewski, "Saudi Arabia: Steps Toward Democratization or Reconfiguration of Authoritarianism?" *Journal of Asian & African Studies* 41, no. 5/6 (2006): 463.

18. *Wahhabism* is a term mostly used by Western scholars to describe the puritanical Salafi religious tradition promoted by Sheikh Mohammad bin Abdul Wahab. For more details on the effect of the terrorist attacks see Jones, "Seeking a 'Social Contract' for Saudi Arabia," 45.

19. The demands for reform by the group of Islamo-liberal reformers included equal rights for all citizens, creation of regional parliaments, freedom of speech and assembly, fair distribution of wealth, and addressing unemployment, among others. See Stéphane Lacroix, "Between Islamists and Liberals: Saudi Arabia's New Islamo-Liberal Reformist Trend," *Middle East Journal* 58, no. 3 (2004): 345.

20. Other reforms include enhancing the size and legislative role of the Consultative Council, allowing journalists and engineers to establish trade associations, and launching five economic cities that are large residential, industrial, and commercial projects expected to create 1.3 million jobs and contribute $150 billion to GDP growth by 2020.

21. More specifically these recommendations included establishing a national machinery for women; expanding women's sections in courts of law; issuing religious prohibitions against domestic violence; widening educational and vocational opportunities for women; and evaluating the current state of public transportation serving women.

22. The initial official statements referred to eligible citizens in the masculine form in Arabic but did not clearly state that women would be excluded as candidates or voters. Subsequently, the official reason given for excluding women was that they could not be identified properly because not all had identity cards. These cards were introduced in 2001 to allow for the identification of women as independent citizens rather than as dependents on their male guardian's cards. Paradoxically, to qualify for an identity card, one must obtain the permission of one's male guardian in the first place.

23. The sessions included a detailed critique of the labor laws affecting women, the presentation of religious arguments supporting recent legal reforms affecting women's businesses, and an evaluation of implementation mechanisms.

24. For more information on the history of Islamic feminism in Saudi Arabia, see Mai Yamani, "Some Observations on Women in Saudi Arabia," in *Feminism and Islam: Legal and Literary Perspectives*, ed. Mai Yamani (Reading, UK: Ithaca Press, 1996), 279.

25. Eleanor A. Doumato, "Women and the Stability of Saudi Arabia," *Middle East Report* 171 (1991): 34–37.

26. Ibid., 37.

27. For a full description of the trade-off, see Todd Pittinsky and Stephanie Simon, "Intergroup Leadership," *The Leadership Quarterly* 18, no. 6 (2007): 586–605.

28. The members listed the pros and cons of cooperating with Western agencies and discussed the differences between accepting financial support and accepting other types of support (such as training programs) and differences between participating in conferences funded by the State Department versus those organized by NGOs.

29. Bernard. M. Bass, *Leadership and Performance Beyond Expectations* (New York: Free Press, 1985).

30. Examples of process theories include social identity and self-categorization theories. Turner, "Research on Social Identity and Self-Categorization Theories," 34.

31. Reicher succinctly described the relationship between identity and context in a state of flux: "Whom we categorize as ingroup and outgroup, whom we see as ally or enemy, and the bases upon which we treat those so categorized are all in constant motion." Reicher, "The Context of Social Identity: Domination, Resistance, and Change," 924.

32. There are several experimental social psychology research programs that triangulate different methods and combine field and laboratory settings. See, for example, Miles Hewstone, "Three Lessons from Social Psychology: Multiple Levels of Analysis, Methodological Pluralism and Statistical Sophistication," in *The Message of Social Psychology: Perspectives on Mind in Society*, ed. Craig McGarty and S. Alexander Haslam (Oxford: Blackwell, 1997), 166–182.

33. Reicher, "The Context of Social Identity: Domination, Resistance, and Change," 938.

14

From Bolted-on
to Built-in

*Diversity Management and Intergroup Leadership
in U.S. Corporations*

Candi Castleberry-Singleton

Center for Inclusion in Health Care
University of Pittsburgh Medical Center

ULTIVATING AND managing a diverse workforce—and succeeding
with a great diversity of customers—are imperatives for corporations, both in the United States and around the world. In this sense, every corporation manages issues that are deeply connected with intergroup relations and lines of difference every day. Corporations must manage the diversity that employees bring into the workplace—and ensure that the workplace is diverse and inclusive in the first place by shaping a corporate identity and culture that is inclusive and welcoming for a great diversity of employees. Corporations must also frame activities such as customer relations, marketing and sales, and brand management in ways that create opportunity among many diverse groups having specific expectations and needs for the products and services they prefer.

Within the United States, diversity management has its roots in affirmative action regulations and social expectations, which have driven companies to adopt policies and practices that seek to increase diversity by including U.S. workers drawn from the various domestic communities.

Diversity management has also become important to corporations because the nation's demographic profile is changing[1] and, with it, the composition of the labor force—and consumer markets.[2]

At the global level, business leaders clearly see that their companies need globally diverse staff to compete, and they are changing the way they do business to become more diverse. To lower costs, expand sales, and achieve quarterly and year-over-year growth for Wall Street, companies have moved manufacturing and production to low-cost locations around the world and are expanding product sales. As they do so, they have learned how to hire and retain skilled local managers and executives wherever they operate.

Yet even though U.S. companies doing business worldwide are investing serious effort in building and managing diverse global staff, progress on diversity within U.S. companies has stagnated. Ironically, activities that companies gladly pursue to grow business outside the United States, such as modifying sales approaches for new markets, adopting new behaviors and styles to manage local talent, and respecting cultural differences, face resistance in the United States. Moreover, as U.S. companies doing business worldwide manage diversity in their international operations, most are doing so without increasing overall diversity resources in their organizations. An increased focus on global diversity seems to mean reduced resources for diversity management in the United States.

The contrast between the apparent effectiveness of U.S. companies' global diversity efforts and the stagnation of their domestic initiatives raises a number of questions. Why are U.S. diversity initiatives stalled? What can companies do to create new momentum for domestic diversity efforts? Are there lessons to be learned from the global experience with corporate diversity—managing differences in a business enterprise across national boundaries—that can help diversity management within the United States? And what do these findings about problems in domestic programs and success on the global front teach us about the challenges of intergroup leadership—leading across lines of difference, or leading in a world of diversity? Because the U.S. economy and demographics are changing rapidly and the globalization of business will only increase, the answers to these questions are vital to companies' future success.

U.S. Diversity Management: Background

On March 6, 1961, President John F. Kennedy issued Executive Order 10925, "Establishing the President's Committee on Equal Employment

Opportunity," the first federal directive on affirmative action. Since then, some progress has been made in creating opportunities in the workforce and in increasing the presence, importance, and compensation of women and minorities in U.S. corporations. But the regulations that have largely driven the increase in workforce diversity also may have become the biggest obstacle to continued progress.

Affirmative action legislation was designed to eliminate employment discrimination so that underrepresented groups could gain entry into the job market. Employers, in essence, were being compelled by the government to be fair toward minorities in their hiring and employment practices. From this reality—employers being compelled to hire people from groups they do not themselves belong to and that they have been systematically overlooking in their employment practices—come both the promise and the challenge of diversity management.

The 1961 executive order, followed by the Civil Rights Act of 1964, another executive order, and the Equal Employment Opportunity Act of 1972, set up the affirmative action system as we know it, creating the underlying structure on which diversity management rests. Kennedy's order stipulated that government contractors "will not discriminate against any employee or applicant for employment because of race, creed, color, or national origin."[3] The order went on to require that contractors "take *affirmative action* [emphasis mine] to ensure that applicants are employed, and that employees are treated during employment, without regard to their race, creed, color, or national origin. Such action shall include, but not be limited to, the following: employment, upgrading, demotion or transfer; recruitment or recruitment advertising; layoff or termination; rates of pay or other forms of compensation; and selection for training, including apprenticeship. The contractor agrees to post in conspicuous places, available to employees and applicants for employment, notices to be provided by the contracting officer setting forth the provisions of this nondiscrimination clause."

Thus, this order, which laid the foundations for broader legislation covering all employers, made affirmative action a required effort for the employer, an effort that reaches into every major aspect of the relationship between employer and employee, from hiring to promotion to termination.

Other enduring elements of affirmative action programs were also foreshadowed in Kennedy's executive order. By encouraging "the furtherance of an educational program by employer, labor, civic, educational, religious, and other nongovernmental groups in order to eliminate or reduce the basic causes of discrimination in employment on the ground of race, creed, color, or national origin," the order launched the training—or cultural change—element of diversity management. By granting the government the authority to review employers' records to ascertain compliance with affirmative action goals, the order foreshadowed the role of the Equal Employment Opportunity Commission as an investigator of compliance. By setting up a grievance process, the order again anticipated one of the EEOC's core responsibilities: investigating and resolving claims that employers have discriminated against employees or potential employees on the basis of race, creed, color, national origin, religious belief, or gender.

As these regulations took hold in the 1970s, affirmative action managers in U.S. corporations—with no real guidance or direction from the government—put together affirmative action programs that included a wide range of human resource policies and practices related to recruiting, hiring, evaluating, promoting, and firing employees. They launched training programs for managers and line employees to encourage fairness in the workplace and facilitate a collaborative, cohesive work environment. And they created systems for documenting their compliance and responding to grievances.

As affirmative action programs matured, their focus broadened. Over time, diversity work expanded to include the development and management of diversity recruitment activities, diversity training, diversity branding campaigns, diversity sponsorships and philanthropy, and supplier diversity. Diversity practitioners also took on the responsibility to manage various employee groups that were intended to provide networking opportunities as well as a platform for voicing their concerns. In recent years gender, disability gay, lesbian, bisexual, and transgender (GLBT), religion, and issues regarding four generations in the workplace became a part of diversity's purview.

Barriers to Progress

Although U.S. corporations' affirmative action efforts have yielded decent results for women and women minorities over the years, they have gone forward in an atmosphere of implicit (and sometimes explicit) opposition and resistance. Opposition has clearly been expressed at the national level through a series of important court cases and state referendums that have greatly limited the reach of affirmative action over time. Inside U.S. corporations, however, the process has been more subtle. We will look at three issues that characterize how affirmative action works against itself within companies and hinders effective intergroup relations: change fatigue, expansion of the mission, and regulatory constraints.

Change Fatigue

The problem of change fatigue arises from the long engagement companies have had with affirmative action and diversity management—an engagement of more than three decades—and the ever-changing training approaches, terminologies, and objectives that managers have been expected to absorb and promote. Consider the issue from the perspective of a manager who has been with a company since the late 1970s. He received training in affirmative action early in his career, when the focus of corporate affirmative action programs was on hiring and retaining women and minorities in greater numbers and promoting tolerance and collaboration. Over time, this manager would have witnessed some progress on these fronts, but he would also observe and absorb unspoken attitudes about the limits of affirmative action and would see for himself the measurable but limited impact and lack of sustainable impact of affirmative action on hiring, retention, and promotion of women and minorities.

Mission Expansion

The expansion of the affirmative action mission has in some ways contributed to stagnating progress on diversity and has resulted in politically correct conversations on the topic. Although no one could question the rightness of corporations avowing fair and equal treatment for all, including people with disabilities, older employees, gay and lesbian employees, and even white males, the broadened focus also siphons energy from the original mission of bringing in, and advancing, more minorities and women.

Think again of the middle manager, now middle-aged, attending a new round of diversity training. He knows, from having lived through the years since affirmative action began, that the original mission is still far from completed. And now the trainer is saying, "At our company, we are all diverse. We all come from unique backgrounds, face unique challenges, and bring unique strengths into the workplace. To bring out the best in all of us, our company embraces diversity of thought." A seasoned executive can be forgiven for wondering whether these words commit the company to an aggressive policy of total diversity or serve to dilute urgency and focus when it comes to making measurable progress with specific groups, such as women, working fathers, minorities, and the disabled. In many companies, the expanded diversity mission is not accompanied by an expansion of diversity resources or staff, and that makes progress on the core of diversity even more challenging.

Regulatory Constraints

Finally, progress at the core of diversity—the hiring, retention, and advancement of minorities into the higher levels of management—is hindered by some of the structural requirements of affirmative action, referred to as compliance. The regulatory system is based on documentation and reporting. This means that any company documentation and practices that touch on the hiring, compensation, retention, and advancement of minorities can be called for and scrutinized during Office of Federal Contract Compliance Programs (OFCCP) audits or investigating EEOC claims of unfair treatment. As a result, those in a position to advance the careers of minority staff have learned to be exceedingly careful about what they say and put on paper about minority employees. This has a chilling effect on open communication about employees and about organizational issues. It also limits what those in a position to affect their careers say or do, creating a kind of feedback vacuum around these employees, who often don't get the full spectrum of authentic mentorship, sponsorship, feedback, and information they need to manage their careers or their performance.

It must be said that the regulatory system has helped address issues of fairness and discrimination in the workplace, but companies have focused more on the regulatory requirements than root cause. The focus on compliance rather than understanding the barriers to inclusion can clearly be seen in the enduring problem that companies have retaining promising diverse employees and is at the root of the difficulty of devising truly effective organizational change supported by leadership.

On a broader scale, company leaders are reluctant to deeply research why diversity within their firms is stagnant or to understand the lack of inclusion within the firm's culture because, at least in part, doing so would create a large body of documentation about the problem that could be used against the company in a discrimination complaint. Companies as well as the government have an ample supply of statistics about affirmative action and diversity management, but there is little documented information or communication about the specific cultural and other issues that may be hindering diversity progress within companies.

Overall, when we consider domestic efforts to manage diversity and make the workforce—and, in particular, higher levels of management—more diverse, we find companies investing minimal resources to meet the requirements of the law and advance a range of initiatives to produce a diverse workforce and create a cohesive atmosphere. Women and minorities are only slowly improving their representation in higher levels of management, we haven't created a culture of inclusion in the workplace, and conversations about either topic have become politically correct.

The Global Perspective

As companies expand globally, they also encounter the challenge of diversity—of managing an enterprise in which people from different groups work together and that provides products and services to a diversity of customers. But even though domestic diversity initiatives seem stalled, diversity management on the global level moves rapidly forward. Companies are quick to tackle the challenges of bringing together operational staff drawn from the populations of countries where they are manufacturing or marketing products, and senior management from the United States invests enormous effort in learning about the cultures of the countries where new operations are growing.

For example, McDonald's changed its core product line to enter a market of 900 million potential diners in India. The Hindu aversion to harming animals makes most Indians largely vegetarian in their eating habits. To succeed in India, McDonald's created a menu of vegetable- and bean-based burgerlike patties.[4] Disney's two Asian theme parks—Tokyo Disneyland and Hong Kong Disneyland—did not follow Disney's long-standing model of total ownership. Tokyo Disneyland is owned by Oriental Land Company, which pays royalties to Disney, and Hong Kong Disneyland is a joint venture between Disney and a Hong Kong government entity.[5]

These examples point to the depth of engagement these companies have with mastering differences, changing traditional business practices, and acquiring cross-cultural competence in order to do business. To successfully do business in the United Kingdom, Germany, China, India, or more recently the Czech Republic, companies are willing to invest years in getting to know people and processes. The same companies, ironically, have yet to master the cultural competencies for dealing with U.S. minorities, women, people with disabilities, or GLBT employees and customers.

The reason for this may be the difference between doing something because you are told to, and doing it because you want to. Virtually no leader of a U.S. company opposes having a diverse workforce or a cohesive, supportive work environment for a diverse group of employees. Nonetheless, affirmative action at the core of domestic diversity management generates organizational resistance. This resistance in turn is tied to a certainty that the tasks associated with managing diversity are bolted on around the edges of the company's core strategy and objectives, rather than integrally bound up with the heart and soul of strategy and objectives. These bolted-on requirements are seen by managers as costs to be managed and minimized rather than as investments that can lead to bottom-line rewards. Conversely, acquiring cultural competencies that enable global expansion is directly tied to strategy and goals. These strategic investments are perceived as essential for increasing the company's value and as a must-do for success in global markets.

Finally, it must be observed that even though we can safely compare the driving forces behind companies' domestic and global diversity management efforts, the two spheres differ enormously in one important way: how diversity is conceptualized in the United States versus in other regions of the world. In other words, countries where U.S. firms are expanding operations do not have the same expectations for—or have legislation that compels—workforce diversity as in the United States. Abroad, U.S. companies may be managing a workforce that, in sum, is diverse and global, but this does not mean that local workforces in each business location are diverse. The biggest challenges, although some are very unique by country, tend to be the inclusion of women in the workforce and leadership and the inclusion of local executives in senior leadership positions.

Cultural competency requires U.S. companies to understand, to adjust behaviors to respect cultural norms, and to be sensitive to the cultural complexity of doing business in each country where they operate. Managing diversity in these countries, companies are more willing to make the adjustments required to maintain viability in non-U.S. locations than they are with reaching out for the bottom-line value of nurturing and sustaining a domestic diverse workforce. Nonetheless, they are focused on the fundamental issue of engaging with difference, across group boundaries outside of the United States.

Advancing Diversity Management from Bolted-on to Integrated Inclusion

Leadership strategies that create momentum for diversity management in the United States and support the growth of cohesive, productive relations among all employees must do three things: integrate, relate, and communicate. In other words, these strategies must integrate diversity efforts into core business practices—a practice I call *integrated inclusion*—as well as build relationships among people of diverse backgrounds and create open communication with all employees.

Integrate

From the standpoint of intergroup leadership, creating an inclusive corporation is a unique challenge. Several chapters in this book discuss how one key to building connections between groups is to have an overarching purpose—an ingredient that every corporation can (or should be able to) supply. When employees join a corporation, they make a commitment to that overarching purpose and add elements of that superordinate identity to their social identity.

Nonetheless, humans being humans, social identity processes in corporations are subtle and powerful. Employees may identify more with their division, their function, or their team than with the company as a whole. They often see their own group and function as unique, and possibly superior, within the company. They perceive and act upon cues and clues about what kinds of people—with what types of group identity—do well. These dynamics clearly play out at an organization's senior levels. If, in organizations that claim a commitment to a diverse workforce, the senior level and the revenue-generating business unit leadership positions are held mostly by white males, employees may conclude that the company manages diversity by sprinkling diverse employees and women in functions such as human resources and marketing, but not at the company's center of power.

Given the pressures and demands of the workplace, any activity or function or goal that is seen as nonessential or marginal—and that has the potential to tag those who take it on as apart from the core mission and

path for the success of the company—will be undervalued. This is one reason that a company that seeks to be truly inclusive must manage diversity as
a core business goal, one that is essential to the company's success. When
that is the case, people will find ways to solve the challenges of diversity.
Just as important, they will watch for and respond to the social identity
cues that show that inclusion is a core task, and not a peripheral one. That
message must come from the company's leaders and must be backed up by
commitments and resources that lend conviction to their words. Simply
put, only when leaders make the case that diversity equals increased value
to owners, employees, and customers can diversity become a part of the
company's identity and a core strand of its strategy and objectives. If it is
important to corporate leaders, it will be important to employees.

When leaders promote diversity in this way, diversity management becomes aligned with tasks that are common to the whole company and all
groups within it. For example, integrated diversity management moves
what is now called diversity recruitment and diversity collaterals (a stand-
alone activity, led by diversity officers) into shared accountability through
mainstream recruitment and marketing, in partnership with human resources and marketing executives.

In a typical diversity management strategy, mainstream business unit
and corporate function efforts—such as talent acquisition, employee and
community partnerships, and marketing and communications—are supplemented by diversity efforts, such as diversity recruiting and diversity
training. I have called the latter "bolt-on" diversity because these efforts
are budgeted separately under human resources, driven by diversity employees, and experienced by general employees as something other than
mainstream (see figure 14-1). Bolt-on diversity is not sufficient for convinc-
ing employees that inclusion is an essential part of the company's success.

Integrated inclusion differs from diversity management in at least
three key ways. First, it teaches corporate leaders to be more inclusive in
day-to-day practices. Second, integrated inclusion makes every employee,
as opposed to diversity employees and a few corporate leaders, responsible
for achieving the organization's goals and a culture of inclusion. Progress
does not depend on the actions of specific diversity employees, and companies are never forced back to square one when key diversity employees
separate from the company. Third, mainstream resources supplement "diversity" resources, such as budget and headcount, but without real additional expense (see figure 14-2.)

FIGURE 14-1

Bolt-on diversity keeps diversity efforts at the corporate margins.

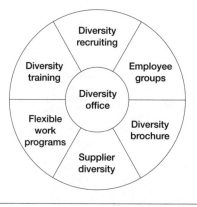

The efforts shown on the top half of the model are typically led by human resources, and the efforts in the bottom half are typically led by managers in business units and corporate functions. But integrated inclusion gets its life from being at the center of a company's efforts, sharing company resources with the company as a whole rather than receiving a separate budget for managing diversity from the corporate margin. When leaders outside the office of diversity share organizational accountability for implementing inclusive practices in each area of the model, diversity efforts become part of the company's DNA. This is how diversity becomes sustainable and how any given diversity effort can transcend the tenure of any given diversity employee.

Shared accountability requires integrated measurement of diversity and inclusion to help companies determine whether their day-to-day operations are becoming more inclusive. In an integrated approach, each business unit, human resources, customer service, or consumer marketing tracks *all* demographics, including Caucasian data, in a holistic way, so that it becomes second nature in all business activities to perceive the demographic balance and impact of operations. This approach differs greatly from one that provides statistics about minority workforce trends. In this case we are shifting the emphasis from only diversity workforce reporting, where only a few review the data, to mainstream demographic trends of all operational reporting to include demographics in consumer

FIGURE 14-2

The integrated inclusion model provides a path to integrated inclusion.

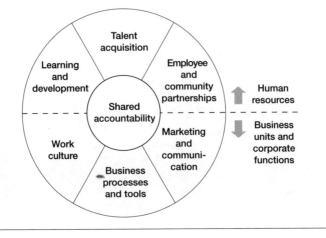

trends, advertising spend, customer satisfaction, and other areas. The transition from diversity requires moving from program management to organization change management, something that often takes longer but can yield sustainable results and reward.

Moving toward integrated inclusion helps companies go with the grain of human responses to diversity and group difference issues. An *American Sociological Review* article on corporate affirmative action diversity policies suggests that stand-alone, mandatory diversity training can actually activate, rather than reduce, bias.[6] In contrast, in a study conducted by the University of Illinois, Sun Microsystems leaders and employees found that embedding cross-cultural skills, or cultural acumen, into existing leadership competencies is a more effective approach to enhancing the positive adoption of cross-cultural skills.[7] In other words, leaders and employees recognized the need for cultural acumen but suggested that true cultural acumen should be reflected in each of the business acumen competencies rather than as one or two bolt-on competencies.

Relate

We must also acknowledge the significant role that social networks play in the work network; they cross the lines of employment. Most companies have employee referral programs, and more than 25 percent of employees are hired through these formal programs. Employees refer people from their social networks. At the executive level, these networks (which tend to be business-social networks or work-based relationships) have a powerful influence on whom executives hire. For example, when a new executive comes in at a senior level, he or she tends to bring team members in from previous positions.

The fact that people call upon their social networks to find employees is not, in itself, a problem. But when people's networks are not diverse, the referral system, whether social or virtual (i.e., LinkedIn or Facebook), tends to reinforce a lack of diversity.

Never in history has it been more important to build relationships that transcend differences and to possess cultural acumen, both within the workplace and in the company's outreach to potential employees, customers, and other stakeholders. Cultural acumen can be learned. But it is in many ways a social art as much as a set of professional skills, and, as such, it requires an outlook that is personal and social as well as professional and career oriented. In other words, there needs to be a connection between the way people interact across lines of difference when they are not at work and when they are at work. If you are not in the habit of making friends with people from different groups away from the job, how likely are you to befriend coworkers and build good relationships across lines of difference on the job?

Companies cannot, of course, mandate that employees make friends across lines of difference, nor can they engineer employees' personal lives to shape their friendships. What, then, can companies do to encourage the kinds of unscripted, personal contact that builds cultural acumen and confidence about people from different groups?

Talent scout programs are one example of a corporate program that creates an opportunity for informal relationship building. In this approach to building relationships with diverse populations, the company leadership, the staffing organization, and the leaders of the inclusion effort build and maintain a database of diverse candidates (including white males) for job openings before they occur. To make this approach work, the company's corporate leaders proactively source talent during events they normally attend, such as industry trade shows, sponsorship events, and professional conferences. Because these events are not related to diversity recruitment, they don't feel like yet another diversity program. This proactive approach

introduces candidates to leaders before a job opening and thus bypasses
the problem of companies being unable to find diverse talent for hiring
opportunities.

This approach has three obvious advantages. First, corporate leaders
expand their networks by engaging potential employment candidates in
environments in which they are comfortable. Second, engaging those
prospects does not require leaders to add events or travel to their existing
schedules. Third, leaders can get a feel for living, breathing, diverse candidates (rather than only reading their résumés) without being under time
pressure to fill a position. The talent database is sponsored by corporate
leaders, managed by staffing, and overseen by human resources in succession planning and talent review processes—another example of how diversity efforts can be built in, as opposed to bolted on.

Communicate

If organizations are to build transcendent relationships they must first foster a culture that combats employee cynicism; employees must believe
that they can speak freely about workplace and marketplace issues and that
their company will receive their input in good faith, as opposed to punish-
ing them for their honesty.

In an ideal world, changing the U.S. regulatory structure for affirmative action would help U.S. companies foster open communication about
diversity and therefore identify and resolve diversity issues. Currently, regulations have a chilling effect on open communication and feedback between managers and employees, because company documentation about
the status of diversity initiatives can be used to support a plaintiff's case in a
discrimination or reverse discrimination lawsuit. This has caused organizations to become cautious about gathering information required to address
root cause issues within the organization. However, it is very unlikely that
regulatory practices will change any time soon. Even so, companies can
learn from employee engagement surveys, focus groups, and exit interviews that provide information on employee perceptions on a multiplicity
of topics, including business processes, work environment, employee development, leadership behaviors, diversity management, and cultural
competency, if employees don't fear retaliation and believe that their concerns will be addressed, regardless on which side of diversity they sit.

Monster.com's Top Companies for Diversity Survey is an example of
an external opportunity for employees to share truly anonymous perspec-

tives of employers' efforts to support diversity and inclusion: "The survey measures the perceptions of a company's employees regarding the employer's performance on specific diversity factors across three broad categories: organizational commitment to diversity, fairness in compensation and culture of inclusion; results are then compared against an established national benchmark for analysis." Those three areas of focus were determined by a nationally representative sample of employees enabling employers to understand how current and future employees are gauging corporate commitment to diversity."[8]

Companies need leaders who lend conviction to their words, who do the hard thing when it is easier to do the popular thing. For example, during the Linkage Summit on Leading Diversity in April 2007, Douglas R. Conant, president and chief executive officer of Campbell Soup Company, shared Campbell's diversity and inclusion strategy, exuding his personal conviction "that diversity management at the company was ultimately his job" [and not solely that of the chief diversity officer]: "Diversity and inclusion are important to our business, to the people who buy our products and to our customers and suppliers. Creating a diverse and inclusive culture is a key component of our strategy to build a strong, engaged workforce."[9] His personal support of the initiative has been critical in driving it forward in the company.

Conclusion

Integrated inclusion is one of the largest change management initiatives that an organization will pursue because of its strong roots in affirmative action and people's individual experiences with diversity both in and outside the workplace. Even with rapidly changing national demographics and the growth of minority buying power, organizations still demand a business case for inclusion initiatives nearly fifty years after the first affirmative action legislation was enacted. This slow pace of change is a testament to the complexity of the issue and the reluctance people feel to change patterns of behavior rooted in personal and social identity.

As emerging research suggests, the key to progress is to identify and leave behind practices such as bolt-on diversity training and hiring—which increase tension—and do more with those, such as relationship building and truly integrated inclusion management, that enhance liking and a commitment to change. Companies would do well to study the emerging literature in areas such as positive psychology in organizational contexts and intergroup liking. New insights into these areas are emerging that will have real relevance for corporate inclusion efforts. Cultivated cross-cultural relationships can be the difference between maintaining the status quo and maximizing changing workforce demographics and emerging market opportunities. History has shown that diversity for its own sake has not led to inclusion. Inclusion, however, can lead to diversity.

Notes

1. U.S. Department of Commerce, Minority Business Development Agency, "The Emerging Marketplace," September 1999. See: http://www.mbda.gov/documents/mbdacolor.pdf.

2. The Selig Center projected that the nation's total buying power would rise from $4.3 trillion in 1990 to $7.2 trillion in 2000, to $10 trillion in 2007, and to $13 trillion in 2012. In 2007, the combined buying power of African American, Asians, and Native Americans would be $1.4 trillion—nearly triple its 1990 level of $452 billion—which amounts to a gain of $909 billion or 201 percent. In 2007, African Americans would account for 62 percent of combined spending, or $845 billion. Over this eighteen-year period, the percentage gains in minority buying power varied considerably by race, from a gain of 294 percent for Asians to 190 percent for American Indians to 166 percent for blacks. All of these target markets would grow much faster than the white market, where buying power would increase by 124 percent. See: http://www.selig.uga.edu/forecast/GBEC/GBEC0703Q.pdf.

3. http://www.eeoc.gov/abouteeoc/35th/thelaw/eo-10925.html.

4. Lucy Craft, "Where's the Beef: Meatless McDonald's Burgers in India," *CBS News*, April 2, 2007. See: http://www.cbsnews.com/stories/2007/04/02/asia_letter/main2640540.shtml.

5. James Sterngold, "Tokyo's Magic Kingdom Outshines Its Role Model," *New York Times*, March 7, 1994; and Keith Bradsher, "A Trial Run Finds Hong Kong Disneyland Much Too Popular for Its Modest Size," *New York Times*, September 8, 2005.

6. Alexandra Kalev, Frank Dobbin, and Erin Kelly, "Best Practices or Best Guesses? Assessing the Efficacy of Corporate Affirmative Action and Diversity Policies," *American Sociological Review* 71 (August 2006): 589–617, http://www.empoweringleadership.org/Resources/Best_Practices_or_Best_Guesses.pdf.

7. The author has knowledge of the study from her personal experience while working at Sun Microsystems.

8. Summary provided by Steve Pemberton, Chief Diversity Officer & Vice-President, Diversity & Inclusion, Monster, Inc.; and "Monster Launches Top Companies for Diversity—an Employee-Based Model for Diversity Benchmarking," *Business Wire*, June 27, 2007, http://www.businesswire.com/portal/site/google/index.jsp?ndmViewId=news_view&newsId=20070627005131&newsLang=en.

9. "Campbell Appoints Rosalyn Taylor O'Neale Chief Diversity and Inclusion Officer," *MarketWatch*, November 10, 2008, http://www.marketwatch.com/news/story/campbell-appoints-rosalyn-taylor-oneale/story.aspx?guid={530377CE-DC6A-43E5-B95E-D487A65CA54C}.

15

Reaching Across the Aisle

Innovations for Cross-Party Collaboration

Mark Gerzon

Mediators Foundation
East West Institute

> *All of us are here for a common purpose, to make the United States*
> *a better place. There is and must be room for all our voices*
> *to be heard to achieve our common purpose.*

—U.S. Representative Peter Welch (D-VT), January 5, 2007

A T A 2007 RETREAT for U.S. Senate chiefs of staff designed to pro-mote greater cross-party collaboration and dialogue between the members, the chief of staff of a well-respected Republican pulled one of the facilitators aside and whispered in his ear. "If this process gets any traction," he said in a hushed voice, "the party leaders will squash it like a bug."

As the editor of this volume correctly observes, there is often an in-group/out-group leadership trade-off, and nowhere is this clearer than in the Congress of the United States.[1] This chapter addresses this subject and poses several questions, including the following.

- Can partisan leaders work for bipartisan purposes?

- What are the obstacles and rewards for doing so?

- What are the trade-offs between working together across the aisle and working effectively within one's own party?

- Can changes made in off-site laboratories be applied to the real world of Capitol Hill?

- What is the relationship between group leadership and intergroup leadership?

This chapter addresses these questions based on the author's experience as a participant and observer in more than a decade of bipartisan retreats and dialogue training with members of the U.S. House of Representatives and chiefs of staff from both the House and Senate. These experiences provided intimate, off-the-record, personal contact with hundreds of House members and dozens of chiefs of staff. My observations are based on personal testimony from members and their chiefs of staff, and on other primary and secondary sources about the House of Representatives and the Senate.[2]

To understand the challenge that Congress faces as an organization, imagine a corporation divided in half, with roughly 50 percent of the executives on team A, and the remainder on team B. To make matters worse, the team leaders discourage workers from collaborating and encourage them to denigrate the executives on the other team. The corporate culture consists of an avalanche of negative stories and half-truths about their colleagues on the opposing team. All executives in this company must be on one team or the other; virtually no independents are allowed. And every two years, they ask their customers to vote to rehire their own team of executives and fire the other!

If such a divided company existed, it would certainly fail to compete against its competitors. It would be so inefficient that it would ultimately go out of business.

Although it continues to function, the U.S. Congress as an institution may face a similar fate—political irrelevance, if not termination. Although many Republicans and Democrats, as individuals, know how to play the role of bridge builders or mediators, the built-in polarization of the two-party system turns the aisle between the parties into a chasm. This dividing line often makes moderate leaders on both sides of the aisle feel powerless. Privately, members of the House and Senate from both sides complain bitterly that their respective party leaders dominate the proceedings to such an extent that they lose their voice.

Even members of the majority party have felt disenfranchised by the two-party straightjacket. "You don't seem to understand," a highly respected and well-placed Republican representative confided during a break to one of the moderators. "I am powerless!" Although Congress was under Republican control at the time, this senior lawmaker felt so disempowered by the party leadership that he literally felt he could make no difference. Because of this partisan stranglehold on the institution, bipartisan collaboration is in danger of extinction.[3]

Why does it matter, at this point in history, that we free Congress from its straitjacket of two-party polarization? It matters because of the complex global challenges that face our nation. The United States cannot fulfill its destiny in the community of nations if our energies are squandered on knee-jerk, paralyzing internecine warfare.

Five Innovations from Off-Site Meetings

Against this backdrop, the question is not why intergroup leadership is rare in the U.S. Congress. The question is how it can emerge at all. To improve these odds, this chapter highlights five innovations developed in a variety of off-site retreats that were laboratories in which one could experiment with alternative processes:

1. Catalyzing cross-boundary leadership from the inside

2. Creating incentives for coleadership that build trust

3. Adopting ground rules that promote genuine dialogue

4. Fostering systemic rather than partisan thinking

5. Inspiring learning and decreasing stereotyping

We then address whether these innovations, if adapted and incorporated into the workings of the Congress, could enhance the effectiveness of the institution. As we explore each of these in turn, it is useful to bear in mind that these five innovations are mutually reinforcing tools that are best implemented comprehensively rather than piecemeal.

This inquiry shows that, to varying degrees, these creative reforms in the process by which Congress operates would not only increase civility and respect between the parties but would also lead to a more effective, more innovative legislative output.

Unfortunately, fostering cooperation in an artificial setting away from Capitol Hill is not the same as building it in the raw, intense environment of party politics, massive lobbying, media magnification of differences, and other equally divisive factors. For that reason, after describing the new approaches from off-site events I analyze how it might—or might not—be put into practice in the day-to-day workings of Congress.

1. Catalyzing Cross-Boundary Leadership from the Inside

During a particularly vicious partisan exchange on the House floor in mid-1996, Representative David Skaggs (D-CO) turned to one of his respected colleagues across the aisle, Amo Houghton (R-NY), to express his dismay. Houghton agreed that the quality of discourse was appalling, and the two of them invited Representative Tom Sawyer (D-OH) and Representative Ray LaHood (R-IL) into a four-way conversation about the abysmal decline in civility that had turned the House floor into a verbal boxing ring.

The four congressmen enlisted another four, and then the eight of them sought out another eight. The sixteen then wrote a letter inviting their colleagues to join them in requesting an officially authorized bipartisan congressional retreat that would focus on how the two parties could function with less bitterness and hostility and more respect and civility. Despite comments in the press about bringing Miss Manners to Capitol Hill, the founders of the retreat process made clear that their goal was not to make everyone be polite. Rather, it was to prevent the House from becoming fatally fractured and to enable its members to fulfill their duties and responsibilities to the electorate.

Faced with a letter signed by eighty-six members, drawn equally from the two parties, Speaker Newt Gingrich and Minority Leader Dick Gephardt agreed to make the retreat a vital part of the new session of Congress. To manage the event, a planning committee was formed, with five members from each party.[4]

2. Creating Incentives for Coleadership That Build Trust

The committee created by members' request for a bipartisan retreat was unlike any other. It brought ten members together as colleagues and not as representatives of the majority and minority parties. They were coconveners jointly designing a shared event, and not party representatives trying to create advantage for themselves.

These ten members were not only coleaders but also a microcosm of the entire community. The five Democrats and five Republicans were selected because they represented the wide range of backgrounds and attitudes of their fellow party members. For this reason, they were a convening body that could build trust across the aisle.

Exploring the issues of incivility at a retreat involving more than half the members of the House, as well as many of their spouses, involved significant emotional and political risks because of the anger, hurt, and resentment that might surface.[5] Even more challenging, it put members at risk politically. If their patterns of acrimony persisted at the retreat, they might be even more publicly embarrassed than they were by their inappropriate behavior on Capitol Hill.

For this reason, privacy was of the utmost concern. Members wanted no outsiders present at the retreat. The press was to be excluded, members were asked to honor the ground rules of confidentiality, and the retreat would be run without professional facilitators.

As a result, the members themselves became the facilitators, and the ten committee members agreed to be trained in facilitation, inviting fourteen other representatives to join them. This group of twenty-four became the retreat's facilitation team. Each of the twelve pairs of coleaders was responsible for one small-group meeting room with approximately thirty members (and spouses).

3. Adopting Ground Rules That Promote Genuine Dialogue

Given the outbursts of sarcasm, hostility, bitterness, and meanness that erupt on the House and Senate floors, members often conclude that Congress should strive to cultivate institutional rules and personal discipline for maintaining rational debate and keeping emotions out of deliberations. The off-site experiences, however, led many of them to a different conclusion: that it is better to invite emotions to come in through the front door so that they do not sneak in through the back door. What astounded veteran members and staff alike was the quality of personal engagement that they witnessed by the participants through the entire process. At every phase—the six months of planning meetings, the coleaders' facilitation training, the retreat itself, and the follow-up—they observed and commented on the emotional richness of the experience.

At the coleaders' facilitation training, for example, the twenty-four members rehearsed a process they would be facilitating at the retreat. In the process, groups composed of four Democrats and four Republicans responded, in council format (one by one, three minutes each), to the question, "How does the quality of discourse in the House of Representatives affect me personally?"

Given the format, the planners estimated that the councils would last thirty to thirty-five minutes, with twenty-four minutes for responses and five to ten minutes for reflection. Instead, each council was still deep in dialogue after one hour, fiercely resisting staffers' efforts to move on to the next agenda item or attend to regular House business.

Exactly the same intense, unexpectedly prolonged participation occurred at the retreat itself. As one member said when he was encouraged to end his small group in time to attend a dinner, "We have needed an anger workshop for so long. We can't stop now." Through this experience, members of the House recognized the vital and potentially healthy role of emotions in the legislative process.

To accomplish this goal, the retreat adopted a set of ground rules, which the members themselves authored and pledged to enforce. The list was posted in every small-group meeting room and (with one minor infraction on the first retreat, and two on the second) was strictly honored for the duration of the two retreats.

That the ground rules adopted at the retreat—respect, fairness, openness, privacy, commitment—seem quite ordinary and unoriginal is, in fact, the point. As any classroom teacher or assembly line foreman would agree, basic civility is necessary in order to accomplish the work at hand— and to bring emotions, which matter very much in the decision-making process, into deliberations in a manageable way. This is even more true on Capitol Hill than in other workplaces because the pressures are intense and the stakes high.

Ground Rules

Objective: To create a safe environment for open conversation

    1. Respect

- Show consideration, avoid violation, treat with deference

- Demonstrate valuing of people and process as much as outcomes

- No personal attacks

2. Fairness

   - Equal time for speakers

   - Speak briefly; time is limited

3. Listening

   - When others speak, listen—don't prepare your remarks

   - Listen with intent to understand

4. Openness

   - To other points of view

   - To outcome

   - To each person regardless of seniority

5. Privacy

   - Treat sessions as confidential

   - Outside the retreat do not attribute comments to others

   - Speak from your own experience

6. Commitment

   - Be present

   - Communicate if absent

4. Fostering Systemic Rather Than Partisan Thinking

During the small group work at the first retreat in 1996, one of the most moving exercises was the mapping of obstacles to civility in the House. Participants were asked to write down on large Post-it notes what they felt were the most important barriers to improving communication in the House of Representatives. Every member was then asked to find someone from the other side of the aisle who agreed with and would cosign what the member had written. These obstacles to civility, each bearing the initials of at least one Democrat and one Republican, were then posted on the wall in one of the following three categories:

   - Obstacles within the House of Representatives itself

- Obstacles in the overall political system

- Obstacles in the larger American culture

The result of this exercise, which took place in twelve small-group meetings simultaneously, was a comprehensive insider's analysis of the challenges to intergroup leadership, including intensified media intrusion and polarized coverage; prolonged political campaigns; greater financial pressures; and the heightened role of unsupervised and increasingly irresponsible partisan groups. As members and their spouses looked at their maps of obstacles and perceived all the ways in which the current system breeds incivility, they felt increased compassion for their colleagues across the aisle and a greater commitment to change the system.

Ten years later, in October 2007, thirty-eight Senate chiefs of staff—half Republicans and half Democrats—undertook a similar process. This time, however, the participants focused on desired innovations and not obstacles. The result was equally impressive: a list of more than two dozen reforms that at least two chiefs of staff (and sometimes as many as eight) from both parties believed would promote positive intergroup leadership in the U.S. Senate. These ideas for reform showed a shift from "us versus them" (in-group thinking) to "us and them" (intergroup thinking).

5. Inspiring Learning and Decreasing Stereotypes

At the various off-site gatherings, there was no legislative agenda. The only goal was building civility, understanding, dialogue, or learning tools for crossing the aisle more effectively. The common by-product of these activities was that, as cross-party collaboration increased, the amount of stereotyping markedly decreased.

For the twenty-four members who were part of the facilitation team, this process began long before the off-site weekend, in planning meetings and facilitation training during which they discovered that their yearning for a better way of conducting the people's business was shared by their counterparts from the other side of the aisle. To be more precise, both Democratic and Republican members who facilitated learned that, in their commitment to civility and creative cross-party problem solving, some members of the other party cared more about civility than some members of their own party. Among the organizers of the retreats, a fragile yet tangible bond developed that supplemented the horizontal Left–Center–Right political spectrum with a vertical Civility–Incivility spectrum (see figure 15-1).

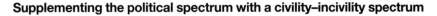

FIGURE 15-1

Supplementing the political spectrum with a civility–incivility spectrum

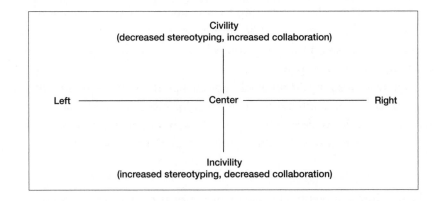

Applying Innovations on Capitol Hill

Can the innovations developed by representatives, senators, and chiefs of staff make the transition from off-site laboratories to on-site political maneuvering and become part of governance? To answer this question, let us reexamine each of the five innovations based on their practical applicability on Capitol Hill.

1. Catalyzing Cross-Boundary Leadership from the Inside

This proves very difficult in the real world of Congress, because there is no forum, no platform, no ongoing basis for developing such leadership. Indeed, as suggested by the chief of staff's comment that opened this chapter, party leadership will almost certainly attempt to limit or contain the effect of reforms such as cross-party groups, events, or initiatives. In addition, Democratic and Republican party leaders will almost certainly discipline members who become too close to the other side.

Historically, the context where members of the House could experiment with positive intergroup leaders was in committee. The committee structure was designed to be a place where small groups from both parties could work together in relative seclusion to build cross-party working relationships in specific legislative areas. But even this relative haven has been invaded by partisanship and centralized control. "I have been on the Agriculture Committee for a heck of a long time," one veteran Democrat said. "Now I wonder why I even show up for committee meetings. There's no real debate, no real policy making anymore. It's all been prearranged in the leader's office."

For cross-boundary leadership to emerge, the off-site innovation of a bipartisan coleader pair could be adopted in each committee. These two members could step in when relations become strained or progress is derailed by venomous debate.

But even this innovation would not change the fundamental reality of committee life: it is inherently structured for hierarchy. Control is in the hands of a unified majority; the minority, even if unified, can only oppose.

That leads us directly to the second potential innovation.

2. Creating Incentives for Coleadership That Build Trust

The omnipresent reality of majority or minority status dominates the culture of Congress. Democrats and Republicans do not work together as peers. From the majority leader and minority leader at the peak of the leadership pyramid to the rank-and-file members of both parties, everyone knows his or her place in the hierarchy.

Thus, the simple innovation at the retreats of developing the position of coleaders has a transformational implication. It suggests that collaboration is not a dirty word but actually a potentially honorable pursuit. Although fully honoring the will of the electorate and the ever-shifting numerical ratio of how the finite seats in the House are distributed, the retreat created an oasis of partnership in a partisan desert.

At one of the series of dialogue retreats for House and Senate chiefs of staff, one participant whispered to a facilitator during a break, "We have been told to oppose all of their amendments. I am told that they have been ordered to oppose all of ours. I really have a problem with that." Then, looking over her shoulder to make sure no one was listening, she added, "I don't think that's leadership!"

Institutionalizing the concept of coleaders would make impossible such knee-jerk, mechanistic, systematic sabotage of creative collaboration. If members were encouraged to find one or more counterparts across the aisle with whom to explore strategic partnerships on specific issues, the House could catalyze creative approaches to policy challenges. The goal would not be to end partisanship but to create a parallel, transpartisan level of engagement in the House that would complement party-based maneuvering.

It is difficult to imagine Democratic or Republican party chiefs creating or supporting such innovations, because doing so would undermine (at least in the short run) their in-group leadership power. However, despite the insularity of Capitol Hill, members of Congress and their staffs do not exist in a vacuum. Even if party leaders intensify disincentives for cross-party collaboration, the voting public, which expects results from both parties and punishes a lack of results at the ballot box, may provide the incentives that representatives need in order to become more collaborative.

3. Adopting Ground Rules That Promote Genuine Dialogue

If the House or Senate wanted to sustain the kind of authentic, emotionally honest, and constructive tone that emerged in off-site laboratories, the culture of the institution would have to more fully embrace two tracks of communication, and not only one. By law as well as by custom, it must provide an advocacy-based forum for pro-versus-con, Democrat-versus-Republican debate. Although the quality of that debate has deteriorated, that form of discourse nevertheless has an avenue for expression.

To work effectively, however, Congress also needs a functioning second track of communication, which we can call *dialogue*—deliberations that allow members to explore competing assumptions, values, and beliefs (see table 15-1).[6]

Debate is excellent for exploring two alternative strategies and for arguing their relative merits. Dialogue is well suited for examining the competing assumptions between the two approaches and for creating new possibilities that may be superior to either of the two existing alternatives. Generally speaking, dialogue should precede debate, and the legislative output is better when both tracks are employed.

Unfortunately, representatives from both parties agree that avenues for dialogue, both formal and informal, have greatly narrowed in recent years. Members spend more time in their districts, leaving little time in Washington for informal dialogue. Party activities and functions are increasingly segregated. "Co-dels" (bipartisan fact-finding delegations on points of concern, both domestic and foreign) have fallen into disrepute. Committees follow party leaders' orders and spend less time in open discussion. The expert witnesses brought in by each party offer slanted partisan perspectives rather than unbiased information.

Lawmakers clearly reflected their assessment of the dialogue-starved Capitol Hill culture in their comments as they left off-site gatherings to

TABLE 15-1

Contrasts between debate and dialogue

Debate	Dialogue
Assuming that there is a right answer, and you have it	Assuming that many people have pieces of the answer
Combative: participants attempting to prove the other side wrong	Collaborative: participants working together toward common understanding
Listening to find flaws and make counterarguments	Listening to understanding and find meaning and agreement
Defending our own assumptions as truth	Revealing assumptions for reevaluation
Framing issues with two polarized sides	Seeing all sides of an issue
Defending one's own views against those of others	Admitting that others' thinking can improve upon one's own
Searching for flaws and weaknesses in others' positions	Searching for strengths and value in others' positions
Creating a winner and loser and discouraging further discussion	Keeping the topic open even after the discussion formally ends
Seeking a conclusion or vote to ratify your position	Discovering new options, not seeking closure

return to work. "Too bad we can't do this on Capitol Hill," was the comment of more than one chief of staff. To make it possible, both parties would have to agree to change the ground rules that operate during specific working sessions. It is clear that they have the power to do so. But whether they have the will is not apparent.

4. Fostering Systemic Rather Than Partisan Thinking

To foster a different kind of thinking requires a different kind of inquiry. Committee hearings are the most natural forum for doing so on Capitol Hill. Unfortunately, hearings have been reduced to well-rehearsed forums in which prefabricated statements are recited by each party to support its own position and discredit the other's. This prevents any systemic analysis from emerging and serves only to further entrench existing views.

Many members and chiefs of staff return from off-site experiences to Capitol Hill excited and energized about implementing innovations such as shifts in committee procedures, new codes of conduct on the House floor, and stricter limits about where reporters congregate in the House. But because party leaders see little benefit in ceding control to third-side entities, the hope that a bipartisan entity will be authorized to implement reforms remains small.[7]

5. Inspiring Learning and Decreasing Stereotypes

As the retreats and other off-site experiences demonstrate, contact alone is not enough to produce positive intergroup leadership. Some members of each party accept and engage in a high degree of combativeness and incivility; others do not. As a rule, party leadership tends to reflect the interests of their less-collaborative, more-partisan followers. This leaves the bridge builders of each party outflanked by their more partisan colleagues. With no structure or leadership to represent their interests, they must either ride unhappily on the partisan bandwagon or be left behind in the no-man's-land of moderation.

New-member orientations are a case in point. Until the mid-1990s, newly elected representatives were invited to orientations designed for members of both parties. Today, each party has its own. From that point on, except for service on committees, Democratic and Republican members never have to sit side by side. They have their own entrances and exits, their own cloakrooms, their own side of the aisle.

A positive innovation, which would require no direct structural changes on Capitol Hill, would be to return to the practice of bipartisan orientation experiences for new members. A cross-party orientation would send an important message to newly elected lawmakers: they are entering the U.S. Congress and being initiated into leading as Americans, and not only as Democrats and Republicans.

For the time being, even though party leaders will continue to discourage fraternizing with the enemy, members should embrace their freedom—and their responsibilities as leaders—and find ways to do so. If they can find enough allies on both sides of the aisle, they will become leaders of a different kind: leaders of the whole.

Conclusion

Research in the area of intergroup relations has established that it is not enough to decrease negative feelings toward "the other." One also must promote positive feelings toward them. Or, in Todd Pittinsky's words, "To transform an overgrown lot into a garden, you not only need to pull weeds. You also need to plant flowers."[8]

On Capitol Hill, intergroup leadership—creative cross-party collaboration on critical legislative challenges—is still the exception and not the rule. During the ten years since the first bipartisan congressional retreat, senators who experimented with running as independents were punished, scores of complex issues were turned into Left–Right litmus tests, and electoral cycles led to even lower levels of voter trust.

On the one hand, it is evident that even an intensely partisan, uncivil, inefficient, and hostile Congress is not fatal to those who work there. The United States will survive even the most depleted kinds of discourse on Capitol Hill. On the other hand, as the years pass without the innovations outlined here being implemented, the danger of long-term corrosion of the congressional process increases. Although there is no absolutely reliable quantitative measure, the institution is losing its stature and is attracting candidates of lower caliber. Congress may act decisively on small matters, but it often fails on significant ones. It is not setting direction for our nation but is instead being whipsawed by media firestorms and blown in different directions by the shifting winds of public opinion.

It is up to us to ensure that the system in which our leaders work is designed for greatness and not pettiness; that it inspires collaboration and not acrimony; and that it lifts them up and does not tear them down. The founders passed on to us an excellent structure for our common home, but only we can make the necessary house repairs.

Notes

1. Todd L. Pittinsky, "Introduction," in *Crossing the Divide: Intergroup Leadership in a World of Difference*, ed. Todd L. Pittinsky (Boston: Harvard Business Press, 2009).

2. From 1995 to 2005, I helped design and facilitate two bipartisan congressional retreats for House members and co-led several retreats for House and Senate chiefs of staff. (Although the dynamics I analyze are also present in the Senate, I focus primarily on the House.) The two retreats for House members in which I was directly involved were held in 1997 and 1999. The four retreats for House and Senate chiefs of staff were held annually, beginning in 2001. I stress particularly the experience of the two retreats for House members but illustrate my main points with supplemental evidence from the chief of staff gatherings in which I participated.

3. It is, unfortunately, a model of domination and subordination. Although every committee has a chairman (of one party) and a cochairman (of the other), they rarely act as partners. The former represents the majority, the latter the minority. The primary loyalty is not to their committee, much less each other, but to their party. In this sense, coleaders are not running the committee collaboratively at all, but instead act more like emissaries from opposing armies.

4. The original eight were Eva Clayton (D-NC), David Drier (R-CA), Tillie Fowler (R-FL), Charles Stenholm (D-TX), Amo Houghton (R-NY), Ray LaHood (R-IL), Tom Sawyer (D-OH), and David Skaggs (R-CO). After the November 1996 election, they added two newly elected members: Jo Ann Emerson (R-MO) and Ruben Hinojosa (D-TX).

5. One of the many difficult issues that the Bipartisan Congressional Retreat Planning Committee (BCRPC) dealt with was whether to include spouses. Eventually, the committee decided to do so on the grounds that it would strengthen the event's overall purpose and also create greater gender balance. As a result, approximately 180 spouses participated in the 1997 retreat.

6. For a more detailed description of the debate–dialogue contrast, see Mark Gerzon, *Leading Through Conflict: How Successful Leaders Transform Differences into Opportunities* (Boston: Harvard Business School Press, 2006), chapter 9.

7. See William Ury, *The Third Side* (first published as *Getting To Peace*) (New York: Viking, 2004).

8. Todd Pittinsky, "Allophilia" (paper presented at the International Leadership Association Annual Conference, Vancouver, Canada, November 2007).

16

Collective Memory and Intergroup Leadership

Israel as a Case Study

Irit Keynan

University of Haifa

COLLECTIVE MEMORY is the recollection of what has been experienced in common by a group, a notion separate from the individual memory.[1] It is the past that is shared, passed on, and even constructed by the group, within the intricate relationship between its historical knowledge and present sociopolitical framework. Collective memory is a powerful force that consolidates in-group cohesion, mostly by strengthening ethnic myths and symbols and thus making a clear distinction between the group and others.[2]

The power of collective memory becomes more accentuated in times of conflict, and the more traumatic the past, the stronger the collective memory's effect on the present, as it brings the past to life at times of threat. This impact can become so powerful that it may render the past indistinguishable from the present. Sometimes societies cannot disentangle themselves from the traumatic past, resulting in both strengthened in-group cohesion and increased conflict with the out-group.[3] As shown by Pittinsky and Simon and by Fitzduff, in-group cohesion is an important

219

mechanism for strong leadership, and, for that reason, leaders may prefer to enhance it at the expense of intergroup relations.[4] They often use collective memory for this purpose either subconsciously or consciously.

This chapter focuses on the way leaders use the power of collective memory in persistent, ongoing conflicts. Collective memory is a factor (although not the only one) that influences the way groups respond to conflicts. It has an immense effect either during security threats connected with acute sociopolitical issues, or through stages of the resolution that involve making compromises. When strategically manipulated by the leader, collective memory can create barriers to advancement toward a peaceful solution and stimulate acts of violence by reminding the group of the possibility of recurrence of past traumas, thus producing emotion-laden symbols promoting the popularity of extremist policies.[5]

Whereas the foregoing scenario depicts the usual use of collective memory by politicians, this chapter argues that alternatives exist. The central goal of this chapter is to demonstrate, using Israel as a case study, that leaders can also harness collective memory to reconcile and assuage conflicts with the out-group, and I investigate the factors playing a role in such use. Although collective memory has been researched from various perspectives, this possibility has not yet been explored.

Collective memory has various layers. Some relate to an overriding traumatic event in the groups' past; others relate to empowering periods of national renewal and strength; and still others can even be shared with the out-group. This chapter shows how by judicious use of the appropriate layers, leaders can employ collective memory to mitigate conflicts. This chapter therefore makes an important contribution by presenting a positive alternative to the familiar negative use of collective memory.

Israel has been chosen as a case study for the following reasons: collective memory plays a central role in Israel's life and culture, and the state is involved in an ongoing persistent conflict—two ingredients that make the use of collective memory both prevalent and crucial.[6] The case of Israel is also a unique example of using collective memory by politicians for radically conflicting agendas. Comparisons of the methods used by the opposing leaders therefore provide important insights into the processes and features needed for the employment of collective memory for reconciliation rather than for sustaining or aggravating conflicts.

The chapter begins with an explanation of the method. Next, the way leaders bring into play collective memory is explored through examples from Israeli history. The third section demonstrates leaders' strategic use of collective memory for exacerbating conflict and emphasizes the impact and use of an extremely traumatic past via a review of Prime Minister Menachem Begin's behavior during the 1982 Lebanon war. The fourth section probes leaders' strategic use of collective memory for reconciliation. It is based on the conduct of Prime Minister Yitzhak Rabin during the peace process with the Palestinians in 1993–1995 and on the activities of grassroots leadership groups of bereaved parents and veterans for reconciliation that followed him. This part identifies the features and principles that guided these leaders' strategies. The chapter ends with conclusion and generalizations.

Method

The primary source for this chapter is a large collection of deliberations and speeches made by leading politicians in the Knesset during the events discussed.[7] These speeches and debates reveal the deepest emotions, fears, and entrenched views of the public from all sides of the political spectrum. All the relevant discussions and speeches were scrutinized; however, two senior leaders at two turning points in the Palestinian–Israeli conflict emerge from the material as central in demonstrating the use of collective memory by leaders: Menachem Begin (Israel's prime minister 1977–1983) and Yitzhak Rabin (Israel's prime minister 1974–1977 and 1992–1995). They both extensively used collective memory as a political tool to gain support for their leadership and for their perception of the options Israel had during the crucial events of their time. This chapter therefore centers on the analysis of their behavior and rhetoric throughout these periods.

Speeches of other members of the Knesset were used to analyze the effect of the leaders' use of collective memory on the public and on other politicians, as well as to understand the difficulties leaders face when trying to change the public's perception of the past and the present and make positive use of collective memory. Leading Israeli newspapers were reviewed as complementary sources, mostly to gauge the public atmosphere and response to the leaders' endeavors.[8]

This chapter is based on examples from only one side of the conflict in order to focus on the use of collective memory by leaders of the same in-group but for opposing purposes, and on the response of this group to their behavior vis-à-vis the out-group.

Leaders' Strategic Use of Collective
Memory Toward Conflict

Groups that have suffered drastic losses share a *chosen trauma*, a phrase coined by Vamik D. Volkan to describe a large group's unconscious choice to add to its identity a past generation's mental representation of a shared event.[9] A chosen trauma is an extreme and dramatic event from which the group has not recovered and that dominates other harsh or even traumatic events in the group's past.

In Jewish history the Holocaust is unquestionably the chosen trauma, marking all aspects of the national psychology. It is considered uncontestable proof of the necessity to establish an independent Jewish state to defend the lives and rights of the Jews.[10] It also confirms the concept of unifying the enemy, namely the belief that the Jewish people still face the same existential danger although the enemy's identity has changed.[11]

Against this background Menachem Begin equated the threat from the Lebanese border in the summer 1982 with the danger of the Holocaust. On June 5, 1982, the prime minister explained to his cabinet why the only option was invading Lebanon: "The alternative to fighting," Begin said, "is Treblinka."[12] Such a comparison left no choice but military action: "Fighting means losses . . . and losses mean mourning and orphans" but "the unacceptable alternative is Auschwitz."[13] These were two of Begin's many remarks in the same vein. He compared the firing of Katyusha rockets into northern Israel to the persecution of the Jews and their children by the Nazis; likened the PLO to the Gestapo; and identified the Nazi decision to kill every Jew it captured with the PLO's actions in the Middle East: "There is a saying in the Middle East nowadays: there is no innocent Jew, all Jews must die."[14]

So dominant was the Holocaust in Begin's consciousness that throughout his career he referred to it as a compass to show Israel the right way.[15] But in June 1982 his speeches exceeded even his own rhetoric. Begin reactivated the chosen trauma of the Jewish people, a practice leaders tend to apply at times of security threats.[16] By bringing the chosen trauma closer to contemporary life, they create a sense of a continual and yet immediate peril hovering over the group, thus greatly intensifying existential fears. Such reactivation is known to be enabled by *time collapse*, a drastic form of the typical blur that collective memory creates in the conscious and unconscious connections between past trauma and contemporary threat.[17]

Begin, himself a Holocaust survivor, was a captive of his own images of the past and at the same time used them to strengthen support for his leadership and decisions. For a while he saw himself as actually fighting Hitler: "I feel like a Prime Minister empowered to command a valiant army facing Berlin, where among innocent civilians Hitler and his henchmen hide in a bunker deep beneath the surface."[18] Begin wrote these words in a formal letter to the U.S. president two months after the renowned Israeli author Amos Oz protested precisely against this time collapse and reminded the prime minister that "Hitler is not hiding in Nabatiya, Sidon, or Beirut. He died and was burned."[19] This was the voice of a minority in the Israeli public that resisted the brutal reactivation of the Holocaust. Oz tried to eliminate the time collapse and expose the manipulative characteristics of Begin's discourse, but to no avail. In light of such metaphors, there is no room for restraint or political solutions. Indeed, the majority of the Jewish Israeli public of all political shades united around the prime minister's decision to respond to the tension with mighty military force.[20]

Collective memory can turn into a double-edged sword. When the consensus on what are perceived as justifiable aims against the out-group is undermined, it becomes a divisive rather than a strengthening factor for in-group cohesion. Ironically, Begin himself fell victim to his own followers' use of collective memory against his decision to evacuate the Sinai desert as part of the peace agreement with Egypt, signed by him a few months before the 1982 Lebanon war. Although the opposition came from a small, extreme minority, it challenged Begin's leadership in a way that shocked him.[21] A few months later, however, he regained full support of his followers, becoming once more the master of collective memory and using it to vindicate going to war across the northern border.

Leaders' Strategic Use of Collective Memory for Reconciliation

Reconciliation aims to create long-term peaceful relationships between groups that have been involved in persistent violent conflicts, complementary to an agreement on sociopolitical issues.[22] But for societies to allow their leaders to commit to any such agreement, a precursory stage is needed. This is a phase that prepares societies for the option of concessions without letting the threatening ghosts of the traumatic past block possible compromise.

Collective memory has a major role in this precursory stage. In light of its powerful influence on sustaining and even exacerbating conflicts as shown in the preceding section, it is next shown how leaders can evoke collective memory for the opposite objective and win support for reconciliation.

Resolving to negotiate with the Palestinians for a peace treaty in 1993, Yitzhak Rabin had to convince the Israeli public that a different view of the former enemy was possible. In addition, he had to counter existential Israeli fears, which were intensified by the overarching presence of the Holocaust in Israeli collective memory.

Rabin used a triple-part strategy: to contain the horrible memories of the Holocaust, to focus on the collective memory of the conflict itself, and to kindle empathy for the suffering of the former enemies, thus creating a layer of collective memory the two societies could share.

In contrast to Begin's interpretation of the Holocaust as irrefutable proof of the never-ending need for segregation and for relying on towering military strength, Rabin adopted the perspective of a self-assured nation that could choose to direct its destiny to a peaceful and safe future and choose to see the Holocaust as a painful memory separate from present events.

Rabin was neither indifferent nor impervious to the national psychology of the Holocaust.[23] He, too, shared the view that Jews were persecuted for being Jews by the Palestinians as by previous enemies.[24] Unlike Begin, however, Rabin was not immersed in the horrifying past and therefore believed that history should not preserve a self-image of a people under siege.[25] This is a prevalent feature in Israeli thinking.[26] As Rabin told the Knesset, "It is up to us to free ourselves from the sense of isolation that has gripped us for nearly half a century."[27]

Most of Rabin's rhetoric in 1993–1995 was focused on the recent layer of the Israeli collective memory: that of national renewal and the conflict with the Palestinians that had been an integral part of Israel's history since its establishment. Unlike the paralyzing memory of the Holocaust, relying on this part of history enabled Rabin to emphasize not only the price of war but also the freedom of choice to end it. In addition, evoking the pain of war as a leading theme in the collective memory allowed him to raise empathy for the same pain of the Palestinians and thus to create a basis for shared aspirations to put an end to grief, and hence to the conflict.

Studies of postwar zones have shown that empathy is important and significant in a process of reconciliation because of its ability to give a familiar and therefore less threatening face to the former enemy.[28] Promoting such feelings toward the Palestinians was extremely hard for someone who fought against them most of his life and did not always demonstrate empathy, especially during the first Intifada (1987–1990). But Rabin was known for his high sensitivity to bereavement and to soldiers' anguish, whoever they were. This sensitivity may have fostered his unique evocation of collective memory, first expressed twenty-five years earlier at the height of his glory as Israel's victorious chief of staff in the 1967 war. In his victory speech, Rabin found it important to raise empathy for the suffering of the enemy alongside feeling the pain of his own soldiers: "The men on the front lines saw with their own eyes not only the glory of victory, but also its cost, their comrades fallen beside them soaked in blood. And I know that the terrible price the enemy paid has also deeply moved many of our men."[29] These were unusually brave words while the country was still mourning its own dead.

Rival groups usually develop separate and contradictory memories of the conflict, and they usually deny the opponent's historical narrative, and that may ignite further conflict.[30] Rabin's attempt to create a shared, empathic layer of collective memory was therefore provocative, and it would change the stereotypic image of the out-group as being nothing but a threat. Rabin continually presented this view of shared pain even when he spoke of the most sacred ethos of Israeli bravery, and even during the fiercest times of the conflict. On the twentieth anniversary of the 1973 war, the most traumatic and heroic war in Israeli history, Rabin avoided the familiar discourse of heroism and self-sacrifice, emphasizing instead the lesson of the limits of military strength and the potential for a political solution, lessons that he believed both Israel and its enemies had learned.[31] Later, in the midst of massive terrorist attacks against Israelis in 1994 and the growing accusations against him as being directly responsible for the deaths of dozens of Israelis and for the deterioration in security since the signing of the Oslo Accords, Rabin continued to speak of the pain and suffering of the Palestinians as equal to those of Israelis. He gave the Knesset details of the hundreds killed and injured on both sides throughout the Intifada years, and he did not hesitate to mention the pain of the Palestinians and their life of hardship under Israeli rule.[32]

As starkly attested to by his assassination in 1995, this strategy could not completely exorcise the horrifying ghosts of the chosen Jewish trauma intensively evoked by Rabin's opponents.[33] The Israeli press of 1994–1995 is replete with statements by politicians aiming to stymie the compromise with the Palestinians and challenge Rabin's leadership. With mounting frequency they portrayed the agreements as leading to a new Holocaust and identified Rabin himself with the Nazi demon. Israel's proposed borders following the Oslo Accords were systematically named "Auschwitz borders," and Rabin was "pushing Israel toward them."[34] Never before in Israel had incitements that brandished the memory of the Holocaust as a destructive weapon been so intense. In the end these incitements created moral justification for the prime minister's assassination.[35]

This development demonstrates the enormous power of collective memory to evoke fear, resentment, and hatred. Leaders having logical arguments are often at a severe disadvantage when competing with such emotive symbols.[36] This is not to mention leaders who try to use collective memory to achieve the opposite goal and mobilize support for leaving the traumatic past behind and working for reconciliation.

But Rabin's legacy did not die with him. The public majority supported the peace process, and territorial compromises were accepted, if with great difficulty. Rabin was assassinated by an extremist, but attempts to stop the peace process by reactivating the Holocaust failed. This suggests not only the great leadership of Prime Minister Rabin but also the viability of his strategy.

Moreover, in recent years Israelis and Palestinians have established groups whose aim is to share the collective memory of pain and bereavement and use it for reconciliation. Parents on both sides who have lost their children in the conflict have set up the Bereaved Families' Forum Supporting Peace, Reconciliation and Tolerance.[37] Palestinian and Israeli veterans have established Combatants for Peace, a movement designed to halt the bloody cycle by raising both societies' awareness of the other side's hopes, fears, and suffering.[38]

Both groups assume a role of intergroup leadership and take it upon themselves to disseminate ideas similar to those of Prime Minister Rabin. However, they take it one step further: they lean on the past traumas that the two sides inflicted on each other as leverage to create a new baseline of the relationship between the rival groups. Moreover, the past traumas are treated by these groups as qualities strong enough to become an additional element of identity held in common with the out-group. Leaning on past traumas helps to build a superordinate identity of the conflict's victims, an overarching identity that is added to the separate and even contradicting identities of either group as Israelis and Palestinians.

Empathy is a major theme in the positive use of collective memory. Shared pain can impart to the other a familiar face, worthy of empathy, thus changing the basic interpersonal attitude patterns between the members of the groups, and subsequently between the two communities.[39] The goal of these two groups is not only to reduce the use of traumatic events to exacerbate the conflict but also to convert it from a narrative of threat and vengeance to a powerful symbol that may lead to reconciliation.

This view resembles Pittinsky's theory of *allophilia*, the creation of positive attitudes toward the other.[40] In Pittinsky's view, the reduction of hatred or the creation of tolerance is not sufficient to prevent the deterioration of intergroup relationships during a crisis. Allophilia should be promoted independently, to reduce hatred, and positive intergroup relations should concurrently be encouraged.

The emergence of the Israeli–Palestinian groups shows that collective memory can be evoked not only by formal political leaders but also by grassroots public leaders, whose positive use of collective memory serves as a leadership tool that can free both societies from enslavement to mutual hostilities.

Conclusion

This chapter shows that although it rarely happens, collective memory can be used for reconciliation and presents the main features of such use.

Collective memory, especially the layer that relates to a traumatic past, is an accessible and powerful resource for strengthening social cohesion and hence leadership. It is especially effective in groups that are involved in persistent conflicts, because the symbols it produces correlate with the atmosphere of fear and hate that these groups experience. Leaders therefore frequently evoke collective memory in a way that contributes to the aggravation of the conflict with the out-group.

However, this study shows that an alternative exists of evoking collective memory for reconciliation. This alternative is much harder and is even likely to set leaders against strong and violent opposition from a public deeply immersed in its traumatic past.

The central feature of the positive use of collective memory takes into account the various layers of collective memory and focuses on the layer of the conflict itself, while keeping the pain of the group's chosen trauma separate from present events. In this layer of the conflict, the price of war paid by the two sides is emphasized as a part that can be shared with the out-group and that allows empathy toward its pain. The shared sorrow can nurture shared aspirations to put an end to wars.

This common layer can facilitate the creation of a daring step: leaning on past traumas as a basis for a shared identity of the conflict's casualties, rather than using them to perpetuate anxiety and segregation. It is a superordinate identity that encompasses the separate identities of the two groups. This process transforms the bloody results of the violence inflicted by the two societies on each other into a new baseline for the relationship between in-group and out-group characterized by empathy and understanding.

The features shown in the Israeli case study indicate how collective memory can be applied for peaceful purposes by intergroup leadership in other conflicts. That this vision of a positive use of collective memory was born despite the overwhelming grip of the Jewish chosen trauma, and in spite of the continuous agony inflicted by both societies on each other, strengthens the confidence in the viability of using collective memory toward peace.

Notes

Author's note: The author thanks Todd Pittinsky and three anonymous reviewers for constructive and helpful suggestions and recommendations, and Yali Hashash for excellent research assistance.

    1. Maurice Halbwachs, *On Collective Memory* (Chicago: University of Chicago Press, 1992).

    2. Barry Schwartz, "The Social Context of Commemoration: A Study in Collective Memory," *Social Forces* 61, no. 2 (1982): 374–402.

    3. Dominick La Capra, *Writing History, Writing Trauma* (Baltimore and London: The Johns Hopkins University Press, 2001), chapter 2.

    4. Todd L. Pittinsky and Stefanie Simon, "Intergroup Leadership," *Leadership Quarterly* 18, no. 6 (2007): 586–605; and Mari Fitzduff, "Ten Things Leaders Ought to Know—and Do—About Conflicts and War," in *Leadership Is Global,* ed. W. Link, T. Corral, and M. Gerzon (Tokyo: Shinnyo-en Foundation, 2007), 87–110.

    5. Stuart J. Kaufman, "Symbolic Politics or Rational Choice? Testing Theories of Extreme Ethnic Violence," *International Security* 30, no. 4 (2006): 45–86.

    6. See Yael Zerubavel, *Recovered Roots, Collective Memory and the Remaking of Israel National Tradition* (Chicago: Chicago University Press, 1995); Anita Shapira, *Land and Power: The Zionist Resort to Force, 1881–1948,* trans. William Templer (New York: Oxford University Press, 1992); Idith Zertal, *Israel's Holocaust and the Politics of Nationhood* (Cambridge, UK: Cambridge University Press, 2005); and Irit Keynan, "Re'i Adama: Patterns of Coping with the Loss of Soldiers in Israel" (Final Thesis, National Defense College, 1996) (Hebrew).

    7. Knesset is the Israeli parliament. All the deliberations and speeches can be found in the Knesset archives and online: http://www.knesset.gov.il.

8. All quotations, from all sources, were translated from Hebrew by the author of this chapter.

9. Vamik D. Volkan, "Large-Group Identity and Chosen Trauma," *Psychoanalysis Downunder* 6 (2005), http://www.psychoanalysis.asn.au/downunder/backissues/6/427/large_group_vv.

10. Irit Keynan, *Holocaust Survivors and the Emissaries from Eretz-Israel: Displaced Persons Camps in Germany 1945–1948* (Tel Aviv: Am Oved, 1996) (Hebrew).

11. Daniel Bar-Tal, *Living with the Conflict: Socio-psychological Analysis of the Jewish Society in Israel* (Jerusalem: Carmel, 2007) (Hebrew); Zertal, *Israel's Holocaust and the Politics of Nationhood.*

12. Cabinet meeting, June 5, 1982, cited by Aryeh Naor, *Government at War: How the Israeli Government Functioned during the Lebanon War (1982)* (Tel Aviv: Yedioth Aharonoth Press, 1986), 47 (Hebrew).

13. Cabinet meeting, June 6, 1982, cited by Ofer Grosbard, *Menachem Begin: Portrait of a Leader* (Tel Aviv: Resling, 2006) (Hebrew), 273.

14. Menachem Begin speaking at the 95th session of 10th Knesset, June 8, 1982, http://www.knesset.gov.il.

15. Yehiam Weitz, "Menachem Begin and the Holocaust" (paper presented at a seminar on Begin's heritage to mark the tenth anniversary of his death, Haifa, Israel, University of Haifa, March 20, 2002) (Hebrew).

16. Volkan, "Large-Group Identity and Chosen Trauma"; Stuart Kaufman, *Modern Hatreds: The Symbolic Politics of Ethnic War* (Ithaca, NY: Cornell University Press, 2001).

17. Volkan, "Large-Group Identity and Chosen Trauma."

18. Letter from Begin to President Ronald Reagan, *Jerusalem Post*, August 4, 1982.

19. Amos Oz, "An Open Letter to the Prime Minister," *Yedioth Aharonoth*, June 22, 1982.

20. See, for example, the editorial column in *Yedioth Aharonoth*, Israel's largest newspaper, on June 6, 1982, which in essence said, "Now there is no opposition . . . now we are all one people in army uniform."

21. Prime Minister Begin speaking at the 65th session of the 10th Knesset, March 2, 1982, http://www.knesset.gov.il.

22. Bar-Tal, *Living with the Conflict.*

23. Yitzhak Rabin speaking to the Knesset to mark fifty years of the Palmach, October 8, 1991, http://www.knesset.gov.il.

24. Yitzhak Rabin speaking at the 129th session of the 13th Knesset, September 21, 1993, http://www.knesset.gov.il.

25. Speech at Sachsenhausen concentration camp, September 16, 1992, http://www.rabincenter.org.il/education/kits/gvulot_9years/marachai-shieur/Pages/default.aspx.

26. Shapira, *Land and Power*; Zertal, *Israel's Holocaust and the Politics of Nationhood.*

27. 129th session of the 13th Knesset, September 21, 1993, http://www.knesset.gov.il.

28. Jody Halpern and Harvey M. Weinstein, "Rehumanizing the Other: Empathy and Reconciliation," *Human Rights Quarterly* 26, no. 3 (2004): 561–583.

29. The full speech can be found on the Knesset Web site: http://www.knesset.gov.il/rabin/heb/Rab_Bio.htm.

30. Robert I. Rotberg, "Building Legitimacy Through Narrative," in *Israeli and Palestinian Narratives of Conflict*, ed. Robert I. Rotberg (Bloomington: Indiana University Press, 2005), vii; Elazar Barkan, "History on the Line, Engaging History: Managing Conflict and Reconciliation," *History Workshop Journal* 59, no. 1 (2005): 229–236.

31. Yitzhak Rabin speaking at the 129th session of the 13th Knesset, September 21, 1993, http://www.knesset.gov.il.

32. 204th session of the 13th Knesset, April 18, 1994, the government's announcement about the security and political situation, Yitzhak Rabin's speech, http://www.knesset.gov.il.

33. Michael Karpin and Ina Friedman, *Murder in the Name of God: The Plot to Kill Yitzhak Rabin* (Tel Aviv: Metropolitan Books, 1999) (Hebrew).

34. Knesset member Rehavam Zeevi, January 1994, cited in *Ha'ir Newspaper*, November 10, 1995.

35. Aryeh Nadler, "Incitement and Assassination," in *Assassination: The Murder of Rabin and Political Assassinations in the Middle East*, ed. Charles S. Liebman (Tel Aviv: Yitzhak Rabin Center for Israel Studies and Am Oved, 1998), 35–48 (Hebrew).

36. Kaufman, "Symbolic Politics or Rational Choice?"

37. On the forum, its aims, and activities, see http://www.theparentscircle.org.

38. On the movement, its aims, and activities, see http://www.combatantsforpeace.org/default.asp?Ing=eng.

39. Halpern and Weinstein, "Rehumanizing the Other."

40. Todd L. Pittinsky, "Allophilia and Intergroup Leadership," in *Building Leadership Bridges 2005: Emergent Models of Global Leadership*, ed. Nancy S. Huber and Mark C. Walker (College Park, MD: International Leadership Association, 2005) 34–49. Pittinsky derives the term from the Greek word meaning "liking, or love of, the other."

17

Interfaith Leadership

Bringing Religious Groups Together

Eboo Patel

Interfaith Youth Core

April Kunze

Interfaith Youth Core

Noah Silverman

Interfaith Youth Core

THE NEED FOR effective leadership that promotes positive inter-group relations is particularly salient when the groups define themselves along religious lines. Human history and contemporary events suggest that conflict between groups divided across religious identities can be particularly violent, owing to the nature of religious motivation.[1] However, recent history also speaks to religious motivation as a vast resource for improving intergroup dynamics and confronting social ills. A question faces humanity in an era of heightened religiosity and frequent and intense contact between people of different backgrounds.[2] Will our age be defined by a clash of civilizations, or will we find ways to live together in peace, to create out of our interactions the beloved community described by Martin Luther King, Jr., in his 1964 Nobel lecture?

This is the great new problem of mankind. We have inherited a big house, a great "world house" in which we have to live together—black and white, Easterners and Westerners, Gentiles and Jews, Catholics and Protestants, Moslem [sic] and Hindu, a family unduly separated in ideas, culture, and interests who, because we can never again live without each other, must learn, somehow, in this one big world, to live with each other.[3]

In this chapter, we explore the role of leadership in determining whether our future will be overcome by those who would divide and destroy on the basis of religious difference or will be constructed by those who will create a balance of mutual respect and cooperation. We begin by categorizing this choice in terms of what we call the *faith line* and then use that dichotomy to articulate a vision and a framework for positive interfaith relations that we dub *pluralism*. Next, we examine the commonalities between our framework of pluralism and different theoretical approaches to intergroup leadership, citing the work of Jessica Stern on the central role that leaders play in movements of religious totalitarianism and the possibility that leaders can also play a crucial role in building religious pluralism. Finally, drawing on our twenty years of combined experience in working to build the interfaith movement through our organization, the Interfaith Youth Core, we identify three competencies that we believe make effective interfaith youth leaders.

The Faith Line: Totalitarians Versus Pluralists

The early twenty-first century has become dominated by news of religious violence from all parts of the world: Orthodox Christians and Muslims in the former Yugoslavia; Jews and Muslims in Israel and the Palestinian Territories; Hindus and Muslims in India and Pakistan; Hindus and Buddhists in Sri Lanka; Christians and Muslims in Nigeria; and the list goes on. In response to this phenomenon, a recent wave of aggressive antireligious sentiment has come to dominate Western newspapers, newscasts, and best-selling books with a story that "religion poisons everything."[4] This combination is particularly dangerous, because it limits how emerging generations understand religious identity, teaching them that their only options are to abandon religious identity or to maintain it and inevitably find themselves in conflict with those who believe differently.

How young people respond to this false choice will have enormous ramifications. For one thing, it is young people who are most often doing the fighting, the killing, and the dying in the religiously linked conflicts around the world. This is explained in part by the fact that the populations of the most religiously volatile areas of the world are stunningly young: some 75 percent of India's more than one billion citizens are not yet twenty-five; 85 percent of the people who live in the Palestinian Territories are younger than thirty-three; and the median age in Iraq is nineteen-and-a-half. Yet it takes additional forces to motivate these young people to forsake youthful concerns for bomb vests. Religious extremists focus their attention narrowly on recruiting young people, because they see a fire there to be stoked and turned into mass murder.[5] These interrelated phenomena put young people at the crossroads of one of the central challenges facing us today.

A century ago, the great African American thinker and writer W. E. B. Du Bois wrote, "The problem of the Twentieth Century is the problem of the color line."[6] Shamefully, the color line is still with us. Yet at the dawning of the twenty-first century, religious identity, also highly salient and highly divisive, has emerged as a new challenge—a new line—that has already shaped and undoubtedly will continue to shape human relations and may dominate the century to come.

We do not believe, however, that the faith line divides people from different religious identities: Jew from Gentile, Muslim from Hindu, Catholic from Protestant, or secular from religious. Rather, the most salient division lies between *religious pluralists*, who actively seek to build bridges of respect and cooperation across differing belief groups, and *religious totalitarians*, who actively seek to destroy those who believe differently.

Religious totalitarians are those who (a) hold that their way of being, believing, and belonging is the only legitimate way on Earth *and* (b) seek only to convert, condemn, coerce, or kill anyone different. Both parts of the definition are equally important—belief and action; one without the other does not constitute a totalitarian. Thus, what characterizes the totalitarianism of Osama bin Laden, Rabbi Meir Kahane, or Eric Rudolph, for example, is not their theology or politics alone, but their willingness to forcibly, and often violently, act against those who do not fit into their worldview.

We derive our conceptual understanding of religious pluralism from the pioneering works of political philosopher Michael Walzer and of

Diana Eck, Harvard scholar and founder of the Pluralism Project. Walzer argues that the challenge of a diverse society is to embrace its differences while maintaining a common life together.[7] Eck states that pluralism goes beyond the mere fact of people from different backgrounds living in close quarters to "energetic engagement with diversity" through "the active seeking of understanding across lines of difference." Such seeking should result not in relativism but in "the encounter of commitments," requiring us to hold "our deepest differences . . . not in isolation, but in relationship to one another."[8]

Following from Eck and Walzer, we understand pluralism as a form of proactive cooperation that affirms the identity of the constituent communities while emphasizing that the well-being of each depends on the health of the whole. We posit that pluralism has three key components:

1. Respect for particular identities (religious and other) of different groups

2. Positive relationships between diverse communities

3. Active partnerships that promote the common good for all groups

This framework of pluralism has much in common with principles from the study of positive intergroup relations. In its simplest form, building pluralism relies on encouraging contact between in-groups and out-groups. Yet, as Pittinsky and Simon point out, "Researchers have long noted that mere contact is not enough to improve group relations."[9] It is critical that the contact be shaped around two superordinate constructs that transcend in-groups and out-groups: goals for the common good (component 3 listed earlier) and respect for identity (component 1).

The well-known 1961 Robbers Cave study by Sherif et al. is one example of how superordinate common good goals can build positive relations between subgroups that have previously experienced tension, leading to a superordinate identity. In this case, the researchers led two groups of boys through activities designed to sow conflict by having the groups compete over scarce resources. The researchers attempted then to reduce the tension through a set of activities to foster the common good, such as collective participation in pulling a vehicle out of a ditch, finding that "conflict was only reduced when the two groups had to achieve a goal that required them to work together (i.e., a superordinate goal). The superordinate goals reduced ingroup/outgroup distinctions and helped group members recategorize their own group identities into a [superordinate] identity."[10]

Although the Robbers Cave study demonstrates the effectiveness of using superordinate common-good goals to improve relations, the model of pluralism we put forth in this chapter seeks not to achieve the total re-categorization—commonly known as assimilation—of subgroup identities (e.g., "Buddhist," "Christian," "Hindu") into the superordinate "pluralist" identity. Pluralism is distinct from assimilation because pluralism requires respect for such subgroup identities (component 1) and is therefore more similar to the mutual intergroup differentiation model identified by Hewstone and Brown and described by Pittinsky and Simon.

> The Mutual Intergroup Differentiation Model [is] a model of positive intergroup relations in which a superordinate identity is promoted alongside the preservation of distinct subgroup identities. [This] model argues that the nested subgroup identities within a superordinate identity should be valued as highly as the superordinate identity in order to promote positive intergroup relations . . . According to the model, recognizing both connection across groups (i.e., superordinate group identity) and difference (i.e., subgroup identities) is the best strategy to engender attitude and behavior change that will generalize to other situations.[11]

Rather than promote an overpowering superordinate "pluralist" identity that may suffocate particular subgroup identities, the model of pluralism we put forth seeks instead to deliberately link particulars of the subgroup's identity to the building of positive relationships and to a commitment to the common good, and thus to the superordinate "pluralist" identity.

Competencies for Effective Interfaith Leadership

Putting this model into action takes leaders having particular competencies. In her seminal study of religious totalitarianism, funded in part by the Center for Public Leadership at Harvard, Jessica Stern emphasizes that leadership is central to building totalitarian movements. At the end of a chapter called "Commanders and Their Cadres" in *Terror in the Name of God*, Stern notes, "Holy wars take off only when there is a large supply of young men who feel humiliated and deprived; when leaders emerge who know how to capitalize on those feelings; and when a segment of society—for whatever reason—is willing to fund them."[12] It does not matter whether the oppression of the young men is real or imagined; "a skilled terrorist leader can strengthen or harness feelings of betrayal and the desire for revenge" either way.[13]

In a personal conversation with one of the authors of this chapter, Stern noted that just as leadership has been central to building powerful movements for religious totalitarianism, effective leadership can also catalyze movements for religious pluralism.[14] We therefore dedicate the remainder of this chapter to discussing the key competencies that a leader must possess to build a movement toward the pluralist side of the faith line.

Ability to Cast a Compelling Vision for Religious Pluralism

As Stern finds, "The same variables (political, religious, social, or all of the above) that seem to have caused one person to become a terrorist might cause another to become a saint."[15] Often, what constitutes the difference is how leaders frame the situation: "The prospect of playing a seemingly heroic role can persuade young men to become ruthless killers in the service of bad ideas, but the bad ideas must be seductively packaged."[16]

A quintessential example of seductively packaged visioning can be seen in a 2001 statement that bin Laden released to Al Jazeera. In it, he tells the story of a boy who discovers that an animal (the United States) is blocking a monk's path (the Muslim world). The boy slaughters the animal, to which the monk responds, "My son, today you are better than me." Bin Laden then comments on the story.

> God Almighty lit up this boy's heart with the light of faith, and he began to make sacrifices for the sake of "There is no god but God." This is a unique and valuable story which the youth of Islam are waiting for their scholars to tell them, which would show the youth that these [the 9/11 hijackers] are the people who have given up everything for the sake of "There is no god but God."[17]

Bin Laden follows this story with another, this one about how the Prophet's uncle, Hamza bin Abd al-Muttalib, killed an unjust man. In this way bin Laden draws a connection and authority from a historical figure during the time of the Prophet that Muslims consider a hero and claims that this man's heroism came from his violence. "He won a great victory," bin Laden says of al-Muttalib. "God Almighty raised him up to the status of lord of the martyrs."[18]

Part of what makes bin Laden's vision so skillful and seductive is his use of narrative. Stanley Hauerwas and other theologians have extensively explored the narrative aspect of religious identity, arguing that narrative is central to individual and communal self-understanding: "Stories are not substitute explanations we can someday hope to supplant with more straightforward accounts. Precisely to the contrary, narratives are necessary to our understanding of those aspects of our existence which admit no further explanation—i.e., God, the world, and the self."[19] According to Dan P. McAdams, a professor of psychology at Northwestern University, "We find that . . . narratives guide behavior in every moment, and frame not only how we see the past but how we see ourselves in the future."[20] This research suggests that the brain is naturally hardwired for narrative construction.

The connection between narrative and identity formation makes it essential to create a narrative of religious violence if one wants to nurture the identity and agenda of a religious militant. In the earlier passage, bin Laden uses both allegorical storytelling and religious narratives to cast a vision of religious violence and convey his point to young Muslims compellingly, essentially telling them, "In order to fully intertwine your story faithfully into the story of Islam, you must engage in violence against those who are unjust and stand in our way." Similarly, creating a narrative of religious pluralism is essential to creating the identity and agenda of a pluralist. Interfaith leaders, therefore, need to be the storytellers of pluralism, framing the current, local situation as one that necessitates the building of pluralism and inspires others to take the lead. We have endeavored to do that in this chapter by framing the issue of the faith line and telling the story of the possibility of religious pluralism.

Literacy in Religious Narratives of Pluralism

An effective leader needs to reach to the heart of each religious community and pull out the narratives that connect that community's story to the vision for pluralism. The leader must know what it is in the tradition of subgroups' identities that allows for their members to equally assume a superordinate identity without minimizing the saliency of either. The greater the extent to which leaders can weave the story of pluralism from the threads of distinct traditions' narratives, the easier it becomes for followers to conceptualize the pluralist identity as a natural outgrowth of their subgroup identity.

This type of religious literacy is an extension of what Stephen Prothero advocates in his 2007 work *Religious Literacy*. Prothero's emphasis is on basic facts and tenets—for example, the names of the major world religions, their sacred texts, key terms, and symbols—and barely addresses the concept of "narrative literacy."[21] Here we emphasize that beyond being literate in the key tenets and general narratives of world traditions, an effective interfaith leader must be eloquent in the specific narratives that illustrate one or more of the components of pluralism.

The best narratives are religious stories, teachings, and practices that speak to the relationships and actions that lead to religious pluralism. Narratives about relationships should point to the importance of relationships with people who are different from each other. For example, a central Qur'anic teaching in Islam is that of Surah 49: "I have made you into different tribes and nations that you may come to know one another." In Judaism, the teaching from Deuteronomy 10:19, "You must befriend the stranger, for you were strangers in the land of Egypt" is primary.

Excellent narratives that speak to action are those that address a value that is shared among most religious traditions and can provide the basis for common action across differing religious groups. For example, the shared value of serving others is articulated distinctly in Buddhism as, "If beings knew, as I know, the fruit of sharing gifts, they would not enjoy their use without sharing them" (Itivuttaka 18); in Christianity as, "I was hungry and you gave me food, I was thirsty and you gave me something to drink . . . Truly I tell you, just as you did it to one of the least of those who are members of my family, you did it to me" (Matthew 25:35–40); and in Hinduism as, "At the beginning, mankind and the obligation of selfless service were created together" (Bhagavad Gita 3:10).

Leaders need to be cautious in using these narratives, however, so as to respect the distinct hermeneutics of each religious community. No interfaith leader can assume religious authority for *all* communities. To do so would be to cross the boundaries of appropriateness, breaching the trust of other religious leaders and violating the principle that pluralism is not a syncretic "new religion" that dominates or subsumes its subgroup identities. The leaders' role is to model this type of literacy in their own tradition and then encourage followers to achieve a similar literacy in their own respective traditions. This requires the leader to be literate enough in other traditions to be able to respond to, for example, a young Jew's story of her family's hospitality by saying, "Doesn't that connect to Judaism's emphasis on welcoming the stranger?"

An example of an excellent narrative, one that intertwines the leader's personal story and the story of her tradition in such a way that it points toward pluralism, comes from Jenan, a Muslim member of the Interfaith Youth Core's staff.

> My family is Muslim. My mom's best friend, Diana, is a devout Catholic. Growing up, Diana and her family were closer to us than our extended family. During visits from Diana, I would drive her to church every Sunday and she would wake me when she would notice that I had missed my alarm for dawn prayer. Our relationship reminds me of the story of Jafar-et-Tayyara, a cousin of the Prophet Muhammad. During the persecution from Mecca, Jafar was given the responsibility of leading a group of Muslims into refuge in the Christian Kingdom of Abyssinia. King Negus discovered the group and asked Jafar to speak of Muhammad. When Jafar conveyed the message of Muhammad and recited the Qur'anic verses about the story of Jesus and Mary, Negus welcomed the Muslim community into his kingdom and encouraged them to practice Islam freely. The Christian community protected their new neighbors, and each community took care of the other while respecting their distinctiveness. Such is the relationship between my family and Diana. While we are all devout in our respective traditions, what brings us together is our own faith journeys, which we have struggled in and experienced side by side. Like Jafar and Negus, the strength of our friendship lies in the values we share.

Not only does Jenan's story relate the personal experience of her family to a story strongly rooted in her tradition, but also it makes the point that Islam has a strong basis for supporting pluralist relationships, as illustrated by the relationship between Jafar and Negus and their respective communities. Having mastered this story, Jenan's responsibility becomes narrating it so that others, upon hearing it, can reflect on whether they too have strong relationships with people who are different from them and whether their religious community has a tradition of pluralism. Jenan can then draw on her knowledge of the person's tradition to help the listener make those connections and proactively be inspired to build pluralism.

Connecting Others to the Narrative of Pluralism Through Concrete Activities

The great rabbi Abraham Joshua Heschel once said, "First we begin in sound and then we must move to deed." Interfaith leaders must be able to create concrete activities through which people can connect their particular identity to the superordinate pluralist identity and goal of the common good. For totalitarian leaders, the concrete activity is violence. For interfaith youth leaders, the activity is interfaith community service and dialogue projects. Not only is service a shared value expressed in all of the world's religious and philosophical traditions—thus providing solid common ground on which to forge mutual appreciation—but also it is something that one can *do*.

Excelling in this competency requires skills in several areas. First, the leader must recruit the right partners and participants for a project. The most effective movement-building projects engage what Malcolm Gladwell calls the "early adopters."[22] These are talented and influential leaders who are first to support a new idea and begin propagating it in their spheres of influence. Their influence should be particularly relevant to mobilizing young people in building religious pluralism; these are often young people themselves, but are also people, such as religious youth advisers, who have particular magnetism with and passion for young people.

Second, the leader designs projects that give participants a strong sense of collective accomplishment and that proactively respect particular religious identities. This follows from the earlier discussion of intergroup leadership theory and religious pluralism as well as best practices in service learning and interfaith work, a full review of which is beyond the purview of this chapter. Such projects have a clearly identifiable and achievable goal that all participants can support with a clear conscience. An example is building a home for a needy family or, if the project is short term, perhaps building a wall of a home. Such a project has a clear goal and will be broadly supported by all participating religious communities. More-controversial projects can be detrimental to building pluralism.

Third, a skilled leader can facilitate dialogue that reinforces the superordinate pluralist identity while protecting the particular subgroup identities. This flows directly from the first two competencies we discussed—casting a vision for religious pluralism and being fluent in the religious narratives of pluralism—but the dialogue should focus on drawing out the pluralist religious narratives from participants' particular beliefs and life experiences. This can be catalyzed by simple story prompts such as, "Tell us about a time when you served others" and, "Is there a story in your religion that inspires you to serve?" This kind of storytelling enables participants to build appreciative relationships with one another while fostering their own pluralist identity.

The final skill for the effective project leader is to identify participants who have leadership potential and to move them toward leadership roles in building pluralism. Every project will attract participants who are capable of making a more substantial commitment to building pluralism. The effective organizer looks out for these participants and asks them to take the next step by becoming a facilitator, helping plan the next project, or telling the story of their participation to others. The opportunities for their leadership are endless. The important piece is that someone recognize their potential and ask them to engage.

Conclusion: Preaching to the Choir

Although the current prevalence and intransigence of global religious violence causes many to conclude that it is a necessary component to human, or at least religious, existence, we contend that this does not have to be the case. Instead, we articulate a vision of religious pluralism that we believe has its roots in religious narratives themselves and relies on sound research in intergroup relations to be successful. We argue that it takes leaders, and specifically interfaith leaders, to build this vision and replace the dominant story of conflict with one of peace and harmony.

One challenge we frequently receive in advocating this work is that we are only preaching to the choir: "Is pluralism only for those who are already inclined toward it and insignificant in changing the hearts of those who are not?" We maintain that through the application of specific competencies, effective interfaith leaders can not only mobilize the audiences that already show up—the proverbial choir—but also increasingly expand the audience.

The preacher–choir analogy actually works well to illustrate those competencies. The first thing a good preacher does is to preach to the choir an inspirational song, a song that articulates a vision of the world as it could be. Second, a preacher makes sure that the choir learns the song— not only hears it but also internalizes it and sings it to others. Third, a good preacher trains all members of the choir to be themselves preachers and sends those choir members out into the world to start their own choirs as choir directors. In other words, the key to our strategy is to convince the existing members of the choir that they are not only participants but also producers. They amplify the sound of the vision, and they expand the audience of the movement.

It is our hope that, through further refinement and application of this strategy, we may yet build and inhabit peacefully the great "world house" that Martin Luther King, Jr., envisioned a half-century ago.

Notes

1. Mark Juergensmeyer, *Terror in the Mind of God: The Global Rise of Religious Violence* (Berkeley: University of California Press, 2001); Samuel P. Huntington, *The Clash of Civilizations and the Remaking of the World Order* (New York: Simon & Schuster, 1996).

2. Gilles Kepel, *The Revenge of God: The Resurgence of Islam, Christianity and Judaism in the Modern World* (University Park: Pennsylvania State University Press, 1994); and Anthony Giddens, *Runaway World: How Globalization Is Reshaping Our Lives* (New York: Routledge, 2003).

3. Martin Luther King, Jr., "Nobel Lecture" (lecture, University of Oslo Auditorium, Oslo, Norway, December 11, 1964), http://nobelprize.org/nobel_prizes/peace/laureates/1964/king-lecture.html.

4. Christopher Hitchens, *God Is Not Great: How Religion Poisons Everything* (New York: Hachette Book Group USA, 2007).

5. Eboo Patel, *Acts of Faith: The Story of an American Muslim, the Struggle for the Soul of a Generation* (Boston: Beacon Press, 2007), 125–150.

6. W. E. B. Du Bois, *The Souls of Black Folk: Essays and Sketches* (Chicago: A. C. McClurg, 1903), vii.

7. Michael Walzer, *What It Means to Be an American: Essays on the American Experience* (New York: Marsilio, 1996).

8. Diana L. Eck, "What Is Pluralism?" 2006, http://www.pluralism.org/pluralism/what_is_pluralism.php.

9. Todd L. Pittinsky and Stefanie Simon, "Intergroup Leadership," *Leadership Quarterly* 18, no. 6 (2007): 586–605.

10. Ibid., 590.

11. Ibid., 592.

12. Jessica Stern, *Terror in the Name of God: Why Religious Militants Kill* (New York: HarperCollins, 2003), 236.

13. Ibid.

14. Jessica Stern, discussion with Eboo Patel, June 14, 2007, New York City.

15. Stern, *Terror in the Name of God*, 283.

16. Ibid., 263–264.

17. Bruce Lawrence, *Messages to the World: The Statements of Osama bin Laden* (London: Verso, 2005), 154.

18. Patel, *Acts of Faith*, 130–131.

19. Stanley Hauerwas, *The Peaceable Kingdom: A Primer in Christian Ethics* (Notre Dame, IN: University of Notre Dame Press, 1983), 26.

20. Quoted in Benedict Carrey, "This Is Your Life (and How You Tell It)," *New York Times*, Health Section, Online Edition, May 22, 2007.

21. Stephen Prothero, *Religious Literacy: What Every American Needs to Know—And Doesn't* (New York: HarperCollins Publishers, 2007), 12.

22. Malcolm Gladwell, *The Tipping Point: How Little Things Can Make a Big Difference* (New York: Back Bay Books, 2002), 197–199.

Index

adaptive change
  basis of adaptive work, 132–133
  benefits and costs of exclusion and
    inclusion, 133–134
  conservation of past experiences and, 129
  constituency problem, 135, 136–137
  critical nature of fractional analysis, 137
  dynamics of a multiparty group and, 135
  intergroup conflict due to differing
    perceptions, 129
  leadership challenge in the face of,
    130–131
  phases of adaptive work, 135–136
  politics of inclusion and, 132–134
  politics of intergroup leadership, 139
  psychological impact of new adaptations,
    129–130
  refashioning of loyalties and, 135, 136,
    137–138
  resistance to loss as a factor in adaptive
    failure, 131–132
  strategic determinations involved in, 133
affinity groups, 95
affirmative action legislation, 188–190,
  192–193, 200
Africa
  consequences of subgroup-based
    leadership, 161–162
  Council's recognition of need for
    leadership, 165–166
  Council's training of new leaders in
    nation building, 166–168
  demonstrated success of intergroup
    leadership, 163–164
  dominate political culture in, 162–163
  Guyana, 161
  inclusionary leadership examples, 158–160

  Khama in Botswana, 158–159, 160
  lack of cultural awareness of benefits of
    intergroup cooperation, 163
  Mugabe in Zimbabwe, 164–165
  Ramgoolam in Mauritius, 159–161, 164
  resistance to accepting pluralism, 163
  unfair treatment of out-group's results,
    164–165
  virtues of intergroup emphasis for
    political leaders, 168–169
African Leadership Council, 165–168
allophilia, xvi, xviii, 227
Arab Follow-up Committee, 149
Arafat, Yasser, 38, 63
assimilation
  vs. biculturalism, 52
  dual identity vs., 11
  and the illusion of group identity
    conflict, 52–53
  pluralism vs., 51, 235

ba, 90
Baker, Dusty, 76, 83
Begin, Menachem, 221. *See also* Israel
Bethune, Gordon, 77
Biko, Steve, 65–66
bin Laden, Osama, 236
Blair, Tony, 63
Botswana, 158–159, 160
boundary nesting tactic, 94–96
boundary reframing tactic, 92–94
boundary-spanning leadership
  challenges for leaders, 88–89
  described, 89
  need for sensitivity to differences, 93
  nesting tactic, 94–96

About the Contributors

MAY AL-DABBAGH is a research fellow at the Dubai School of Government and Harvard Kennedy School. Her research interests include cross-cultural and social/organizational psychology; theory and method in assessing the relationship between the self and context; and cultural and gender differences in leadership, decision making, and job-related outcomes. Al-Dabbagh earned a PhD in psychology from the University of Oxford for her doctoral thesis entitled, "Working Women in Saudi Arabia: A Study of Stress and Well-Being." She earned her BA degree from Harvard University, where she graduated magna cum laude in psychology.

MAX H. BAZERMAN is the Jesse Isidor Straus Professor of Business Administration at the Harvard Business School and is formally affiliated with Harvard Kennedy School, the Psychology Department, the Institute for Quantitative Social Sciences, the Harvard University Center on the Environment, and the Program on Negotiation. He is the author, coauthor, or coeditor of sixteen books and over one hundred eighty research articles and chapters. In 2003, Max received the Everett Mendelsohn Excellence in Mentoring Award from Harvard University's Graduate School of Arts and Sciences and, in 2006, the Life Achievement Award from the Aspen Institute's Business and Society Program.

HEATHER M. CARUSO is a fifth-year PhD candidate in organizational behavior and social psychology at Harvard University. She came to the program inspired by early managerial experience in a multinational start-up, where she became fascinated by the issues people from different backgrounds encounter when attempting to collaborate. In both independent and joint research, she now explores the expression, perception, and negotiation of diverse identities, as well as the critical roles they play in the success of collaborative learning, creativity, and decision making. Her current research focuses on territorial behavior and self-satisfaction as barriers to effective diverse group collaboration.

CANDI CASTLEBERRY-SINGLETON is the chief inclusion and diversity officer (CIDO) at UPMC, a $7 billion integrated global health enterprise. A former CIDO at Motorola and Sun Microsystems, Candi created the Integrated Inclusion Model, a systems integration model that transitions companies from traditional "bolt-on" diversity processes led by human resources, to integrated work processes that shift responsibility for achieving an inclusive culture to every employee. At Xerox Corporation, she led teams in operations and employee development, and acquired extensive experience in sales, product marketing, training, and sales management. Candi received an MBA from Pepperdine University and a bachelor's degree from UC Berkeley.

JOHN F. DOVIDIO is currently a professor of psychology at Yale University. Before that, he was a professor at the University of Connecticut and at Colgate University, where he also served as provost and dean of the faculty. Dovidio has been editor of the *Journal of Personality and Social Psychology—Interpersonal Relations and Group Processes* and of *Personality and Social Psychology Bulletin* and associate editor of *Group Processes and Intergroup Relations*. He is currently coeditor of *Social Issues and Policy Review*. Dovidio's research interests are in stereotyping, prejudice, and discrimination; social power and nonverbal communication; and altruism and helping. He holds an MA and PhD in social psychology from the University of Delaware.

CHRIS ERNST is a research director with the Center for Creative Leadership. His work centers on advancing leadership capacity across globally diverse boundaries. As a researcher, Chris writes and presents frequently on international issues and is author of several books including *Success for the New Global Manager: How to Work Across Distance, Countries and Cultures*. As a practitioner, he has served in expatriate roles in Asia and Europe, leads multicultural teams, and creates and facilitates leadership experiences for client organizations worldwide. Chris holds a PhD in industrial and organizational psychology and currently resides in Singapore.

SAMUEL L. GAERTNER is a professor of psychology at the University of Delaware. His research interests involve intergroup relations with a focus on understanding and reducing prejudice, discrimination, and racism. He has served on the editorial boards of the *Journal of Personality and Social Psychology*, *Personality and Social Psychology Bulletin*, and *Group Processes and Intergroup Relations*. Gaertner's research with John F. Dovidio has been supported by grants from the Office of Naval Research, the National Institutes of Mental Health and, currently, the National Science Foundation. He holds a BA from Brooklyn College and a PhD from the City University of New York: Graduate Center.

MARK GERZON, distinguished fellow at the EastWest Institute and president of Mediators Foundation, is the author of *Leading Through Conflict: How Successful Leaders Transform Differences into Opportunities* (Harvard Business Press). His current projects focus on developing more effective transpartisan leaders in the United States and more effective transnational leadership in the world. He has recently formed a public-private partnership to develop a "Global Leadership Laboratory" that is designing an optimal decision-making environment.

S. ALEXANDER HASLAM is a professor of social and organizational psychology at the University of Exeter. He is former editor of the *European Journal of Social Psychology* and is currently on the editorial board of ten international journals including *Scientific American Mind*. His work with colleagues at Exeter and elsewhere focuses on the study of social identity in social and organizational contexts, illustrated by his most recent book *Psychology in Organizations: The Social Identity Approach* (2nd ed., Sage, 2004). He is a Fellow of the Canadian Institute of Advanced Research and a former recipient of EASP's Kurt Lewin award.

RONALD HEIFETZ, King Hussein bin Talal Senior Lecturer in Public Leadership, Harvard Kennedy School, was the founding director of the Center for Public Leadership. He focuses his research on how to build adaptive capacity in societies, businesses, and nonprofits. His book *Leadership Without Easy Answers* is beyond its thirteenth printing and has been translated into many languages. He coauthored the best-selling book *Leadership on the Line: Staying Alive through the Dangers of Leading* with Marty Linsky. Heifetz consults extensively in the United States and abroad. He is a graduate of Columbia University, Harvard Medical School, and Harvard Kennedy School.

Michael A. Hogg holds a PhD from Bristol and is a professor of social psychology at Claremont Graduate University and an honorary professor at the Universities of Kent and Queensland. He is a Fellow of the Society for the Psychological Study of Social Issues, the Society for Personality and Social Psychology, the Western Psychological Association, and the Academy of the Social Sciences in Australia. His research on group processes, intergroup relations, social identity, and self-conception is closely associated with the development of social identity theory. He has published two hundred sixty scientific books, chapters, and articles on these topics. An associate editor of the *Journal of Experimental Social Psychology*, he is foundation coeditor of *Group Processes and Intergroup Relations*, and senior consultant editor for the Sage Social Psychology Program.

Jolanda Jetten is a professor of social psychology at the University of Queensland. Her research is concerned with group processes and intergroup relations with a particular interest in marginal group membership, deviance within groups, leadership, normative influence and conformity, stigmatized identities, and the relationship between identity change and well-being. This research is supported by grants from the British ESRC, the Australian Research Council, and a University of Queensland Mid-Career Fellowship. She was awarded the Spearman Medal by the British Psychological Association in 2004, and she is currently associate editor of the *British Journal of Social Psychology* and *Social Psychology*.

Rosabeth Moss Kanter holds the Ernest L. Arbuckle Professorship at Harvard Business School, where she specializes in strategy, innovation, and leadership for change. The former editor of *Harvard Business Review* and currently a founding chair of the Harvard University Advanced Leadership Initiative, Kanter received the Academy of Management's Distinguished Career Award for scholarly contributions to management in 2001. She is a consultant to major corporations and author of seventeen books, including her latest, *America the Principled: 6 Opportunities for Becoming a Can-Do Nation Once Again*, and award-winning best-sellers *Confidence, World Class, When Giants Learn to Dance, The Change Masters*, and *Men and Women of the Corporation*.

IRIT KEYNAN, head of the Center for Social Responsibility, Haifa University, is the author of an award-winning book on Holocaust survivors. She teaches social justice at Haifa University. Her research interests include the Holocaust, collective memory, social responsibility, coexistence, and leadership. She has published in professional journals and in the public media in these areas. Keynan serves on several boards of directors of research centers and NGOs. She was the founding director of the Rabin Center for Israel Studies in Tel Aviv, and the director for research and strategic planning at the Jewish Agency. Irit holds a PhD in history from Tel Aviv University.

RODERICK M. KRAMER is the William R. Kimball Professor of Organizational Behavior at the Stanford Business School. The author of more than one hundred scholarly articles, he has published in leading journals such as the *Journal of Personality and Social Psychology*, *The Academy of Management Journal*, and *Harvard Business Review*. He has also coauthored numerous books, including *Negotiation in Social Contexts*, *The Psychology of the Social Self*, *Power and Influence in Organizations*, *The Psychology of Leadership*, *Trust and Distrust Within Organizations*, and, most recently, *Organizational Trust*. Kramer has been a visiting scholar at numerous institutions, including Oxford University, Harvard University, and the Hoover Institution.

MARGARITA KROCHIK is a PhD student in social psychology at New York University and a recipient of the National Science Foundation Graduate Research Fellowship. She received her BA with honors at the University of Virginia, combining coursework in anthropology, sociology, psychology, linguistics, and political science to create her own interdisciplinary major. Her research investigates the dynamics of political ideology within the individual, the interaction dyad, and the group, with an eye toward its downstream effects. She examines both political and nonpolitical outcomes, including voting behavior, resistance to persuasion, support for political institutions and authorities, and the structure of one's mental representations of groups in society. She is particularly interested in identifying the conditions under which shared values and identities can be harnessed to reduce gridlock, transcend ideological divides between partisans, and encourage cooperation between polarized subgroups in society.

APRIL KUNZE is the vice president of programs at the Interfaith Youth Core. Her reflections on interfaith youth work have inspired young people across the world and have appeared in over a dozen publications, including *Review and Expositor, Interreligious Insight, Buzz Magazine, Sourcepoint,* and *Awakening the Spirit, Inspiring the Soul.* Her professional background is in youth leadership, grassroots community building, and organizational development. She is the founder and board chair of The Crib Collective, an organization focused on creating a culture of social entrepreneurship among Chicago youth. A graduate of Carleton College and Public Allies Chicago, Kunze was recently named Public Allies Chicago's Changemaker of the Year.

MARIKA J. LAMOREAUX attended Virginia Tech for her undergraduate degree, Miami University of Ohio for her master's, and the University of Delaware for her PhD, focusing on social psychology. Currently she is a lecturer at Georgia State University. Her primary research interest is in finding ways to reduce intergroup bias through community-based interventions. Her secondary research interest is in understanding psychological cultural differences.

FRANK MOLS is associate lecturer at the School of Political Science and International Studies, University of Queensland, Australia. His areas of interest include: multilevel governance, identity politics, nationalism, regionalism, citizenship, social identity theory, self-categorization theory, and more recently, public policy analysis, modes of governance, and metagovernance. His research is aimed at enhancing our understanding of the more subtle ways in which EU integration transforms the domestic political landscape in EU member-states. More specifically, his research examines how EU integration heightens existing center–periphery tensions in member-states, thereby increasing the scope for local and regional politicians to engage in identity politics.

EBOO PATEL is the founder and executive director of the Interfaith Youth Core. He is the author of *Acts of Faith: The Story of an American Muslim, the Struggle for the Soul of a Generation.* Eboo holds a doctorate in the sociology of religion from Oxford University, where he studied on a Rhodes scholarship. He writes "The Faith Divide," a featured blog on religion for the *Washington Post* and has also written for the *Chicago Tribune*, the *Clinton Journal*, the *Harvard Divinity School Bulletin*, and National Public Radio. He has spoken at the Clinton Global Initiative, the Nobel Peace Prize Forum, and at universities around the world.

TODD L. PITTINSKY explores what lies beyond mere tolerance of the "other." Through the Allophilia Project, he investigates positive intergroup attitudes: the conditions under which they develop and how they shape the ways we think, feel, and behave. His current research focuses on how leaders and leadership affect positive intergroup relations. Pittinsky earned his AB in psychology from Yale and his MA in psychology and PhD in organizational behavior from Harvard. He is an associate professor of public policy at the Harvard Kennedy School and serves as research director of Harvard's Center for Public Leadership.

MICHAEL J. PLATOW is an associate professor in the department of psychology at the Australian National University. He has conducted and published research examining a variety of group and intergroup processes, including leadership and social influence; distributive, procedural, and restorative justice; and in-group favoritism and social identity management. His current research examines the social-psychological processes involved in marginalizing racism. He has published numerous articles in scholarly journals, such as *Psychological Science*, the *Journal of Experimental Social Psychology*, and the *European Journal of Social Psychology*. Michael is an award-winning teacher and has served as president of the Society of Australasian Social Psychologists.

STEPHEN D. REICHER is currently professor and head of the School of Psychology at the University of St. Andrews. He is past editor of the *British Journal of Social Psychology* and a member of the Governing Council of the International Society for Political Psychology. His work centers on the relationship between social identities and collective action. Following from his early work, which analyzed the ways in which collective action is shaped by social identities, he has become increasingly interested in the ways that leaders and activists actively shape social identities in order to mobilize collective action. This work is represented in his book *Self and Nation* (Sage, 2001) with Nick Hopkins.

Todd Rogers is completing his PhD in the joint program in organizational behavior and psychology at Harvard. His research uses a behavioral approach to understanding effective political communication and mobilization. He is currently the executive director of the Analyst Institute in Washington, DC.

Robert I. Rotberg is director, the Program on Intrastate Conflict and Conflict Resolution at Harvard Kennedy School, Harvard University, where he is an adjunct professor of public policy and teaches two courses on leadership. He is also president of the World Peace Foundation. Earlier, he was professor of political science and history at MIT, academic vice president of Tufts University, and president of Lafayette College. He is the author or editor of numerous books on African, Caribbean, and Asian politics and leadership. His most recent books include *When States Fail: Causes and Consequences* (2004) and *Worst of the Worst: Dealing with Repressive and Rogue Nations* (2007).

Noah Silverman serves as content coordinator within the Outreach Education and Training team at the Interfaith Youth Core. Noah graduated Phi Beta Kappa with a BA in religious studies and international relations from Connecticut College, where he wrote his undergraduate thesis on interreligious peace building in Israel and Palestine. He has worked for the World Conference of Religions for Peace at the United Nations, the Interfaith Encounter Association in Jerusalem, and the Council for a Parliament of the World's Religions in Chicago, including staffing the 2004 Parliament of the World's Religions in Barcelona. A Chicago native, Noah grew up attending K.A.M. Isaiah Israel congregation in the South Side neighborhood of Hyde Park.

Alan B. Slifka, the cochairman of Halcyon Asset Management, LLC, is an investment manager and philanthropist. He has served on many corporate and not-for profit boards, including Global TeleSystems Group, the Big Apple Circus, the American Jewish Congress, the Coexistence Initiative, and the Interfaith Center of New York. He is chairman of the Abraham Fund Initiatives, which he cofounded in 1989 as the first and only public not-for-profit organization dedicated to furthering coexistence between Israel's Jewish and Arab citizens through support of programs and projects in Israel. Slifka received his BS at Yale University in 1951, his

MBA at Harvard in 1953, and a doctor of humane letters, *honoris causa*, from Brandeis University in 2003.

Tom R. Tyler is a University Professor at New York University. He teaches in the psychology department and the law school. His research explores the dynamics of authority in groups, organizations, and societies. In particular, he examines the role of judgments about the justice or injustice of group procedures in shaping legitimacy, compliance, and cooperation. He is the author of several books, including *The Social Psychology of Procedural Justice* (1988), *Trust in Organizations* (1996), *Social Justice in Diverse Society* (1997), *Cooperation in Groups* (2000), *Trust in the Law* (2002), and *Why People Obey the Law* (2006).

Jeffrey Yip is a research associate with the Center for Creative Leadership. He is also cofounder and board member with the Halogen Foundation in Singapore. Jeffrey is coauthor of the book *Youth.Sg* and writes broadly on issues related to emerging leadership and leadership development. He has served previously as a consultant to the Singapore government and conducts various leadership workshops for students and educators in the region. Jeffrey's current work is focused on documenting the pathways and practices of business and government leaders in Asia. A Fulbright scholar, Jeffrey has a master's in human development and psychology from Harvard University.